DESCARTES
Selected Philosophical Writings

Based on the new and much acclaimed two-volume Cambridge edition of *The Philosophical Writings of Descartes* by Cottingham, Stoothoff and Murdoch, this anthology of essential texts contains the most important and widely studied of those writings, including the *Discourse* and *Meditations* and substantial extracts from the *Regulae, Optics, Principles, Objectives and Replies, Comments on a Broadsheet,* and *Passions of the Soul.*

In clear, readable, modern English, with a full text and running references to the standard Franco-Latin edition of Descartes, this book is planned as the definitive one-volume reader for all English-speaking students of Descartes.

DESCARTES
Selected Philosophical Writings

translated by

JOHN COTTINGHAM
ROBERT STOOTHOFF

CAMBRIDGE
UNIVERSITY PRESS

CAMBRIDGE UNIVERSITY PRESS
Cambridge, New York, Melbourne, Madrid, Cape Town, Singapore, São Paulo, Delhi

Cambridge University Press
32 Avenue of the Americas, New York, NY 10013-2473, USA

www.cambridge.org
Information on this title: www.cambridge.org/9780521358125

First published 1998
26th printing 2009

Printed in the United States of America

A catalog record for this publication is available from the British Library.

ISBN 978-0-521-35264-2 hardback
ISBN 978-0-521-35812-5 paperback

Contents

General introduction

René Descartes is universally acknowledged as the father of modern Western philosophy. It is to the writings of Descartes, above all others, that we must turn if we wish to understand the great seventeenth-century revolution in which the old scholastic world view slowly lost its grip, and the foundations of modern philosophical and scientific thinking were laid. The range of Descartes' thought was enormous, and his published work includes writings on mathematics, physics, astronomy, meteorology, optics, physiology, psychology, metaphysics and ethics. No one volume can hope to do justice to such an *oeuvre*, but the present selection includes the most famous and widely studied texts, and a good bit more besides. We hope it will be a serviceable and reasonably representative anthology for those who wish to study for themselves one of the most important and fascinating philosophical systems ever produced.

The first work included below (in extracts) is the *Rules for the Direction of our Native Intelligence (Regulae ad directionem ingenii)*. This was the first major piece of philosophy that Descartes composed. It was written in Latin, probably in 1628 or a few years earlier, but was never completed, and was not published during Descartes' lifetime. A Dutch translation appeared in Holland in 1684, and the first Latin edition was published in Amsterdam in 1701. The *Regulae* (to use the title by which the work is generally known) reveals much about Descartes' early project for establishing a universal method for arriving at the truth, and it presents a conception of knowledge which is strongly influenced by mathematical standards of certainty.

The Discourse on the Method, written in French, was the first book that Descartes published; it appeared anonymously in Leiden, Holland, in June 1637. The full title is *Discourse on the Method of rightly conducting one's reason and seeking the truth in the sciences (Discours de la méthode pour bien conduire sa raison, et chercher la vérité dans les sciences)*. By writing in French rather than Latin, Descartes aimed to reach beyond the narrow confines of an academic audience, and the *Discourse* is no scholarly treatise, but a delightfully readable and informal work, containing Descartes' reflections on his early years and education, notes on a 'provisional

moral code' for the conduct of life, and discussion of a number of controversial scientific issues in areas ranging from cosmology to physiology.
Some of this scientific material incorporates the results of an earlier book
on physics, *The World (Le Monde)*, which Descartes had hoped to publish
in the early 1630s, but which he cautiously withdrew on hearing of the
condemnation of Galileo in 1633 (Descartes' book, like Galileo's, strongly
supported the Copernican model of the solar system). But perhaps the
best-known portion of the *Discourse* is Part IV, where Descartes provides
a lucid summary of his metaphysical views, and introduces the famous
pronouncement *Je pense donc je suis* – 'I am thinking, therefore I exist'.

The first edition of the *Discourse* also included three 'specimen essays'
illustrating Descartes' method, namely the *Optics (La Dioptrique)*, the
Meteorology (Les Météores) and the *Geometry (La Géométrie)*. Extracts
from the first of these essays are included in the present selection. Descartes
had begun work on the *Optics* in the late 1620s, and its publication in 1637
aroused considerable scientific interest. The work provides a good
example of Descartes' application of mathematical techniques to problems in physical science, and also has much of interest to say about the
nature of sense-perception and the relation between mind and body.

Descartes' philosophical masterpiece, the *Meditations on First Philosophy (Meditationes de prima philosophia)* was written in Latin during the
period 1638–40, when the philosopher was living in North Holland. The
work was completed by April 1640, and was first published in Paris in
1641. A second edition appeared in Amsterdam the following year, and a
French translation (by the Duc de Luynes) was released in 1647. The
subtitle of the 1642 edition tells the reader that the work contains a
demonstration of 'the existence of God and the distinction between the
human soul and the body', but Descartes makes it clear in a letter that he
chose the title 'Meditations on First Philosophy' to indicate that the
discussion 'is not confined to God and the soul, but treats in general of all
the first things to be discovered by philosophizing'. The *Meditations* is a
vividly dramatic account of the rejection of preconceived opinions and the
search for the foundations of a reliable system of knowledge. Descartes
wrote in the Preface to the volume, 'I would not urge anyone to read this
book except those who are able and willing to meditate seriously along
with me'; and as the title suggests, the book is not a static exposition of
finished doctrines, but a set of mental exercises that each individual must
follow for himself. By so doing, Descartes maintained, each of us can
become indubitably convinced first of his own existence, then of the
existence of God, and finally of the essence of material things and the true
nature of the human mind.

Descartes later wrote of the *Meditations* that 'although this work is not

very large, the size of the volume was increased and the contents greatly
clarified by the addition of the objections that several very learned persons
sent me on the subject, and by the replies I made to them'. The first edition
of the *Meditations* contained six sets of Objections, with Descartes' Replies. The first set is by the Dutch theologian Johan de Kater (Caterus); the
second and sixth sets were compiled by Descartes' friend and principal
correspondent Friar Marin Mersenne; the third set is by the English
philosopher Thomas Hobbes, who had fled to France for political reasons
in 1640; the fourth set is by the brilliant theologian and logician Antoine
Arnauld (then only in his late twenties); and the fifth and most detailed set
is by the celebrated philosopher Pierre Gassendi. The second (1642) edition
of the *Meditations* included a very long and very hostile seventh set of
Objections by the Jesuit Pierre Bourdin. The Objections and Replies (from
which brief excerpts are included in this selection) help to pinpoint some of
the major philosophical difficulties in the *Meditations*, and Descartes'
Replies are often of great value for the interpretation of his views. (Readers
should note that the arrangement of Objections and Replies by topic has
been done specially for the present volume, and does not correspond with
the order to be found in the original texts.)

Descartes' *magnum opus*, the *Principles of Philosophy* (*Principia phi-
losophiae*) was written in Latin during the early 1640s and published in
Amsterdam in 1644. A French translation by Claude Picot was issued with
Descartes' approval in 1647. The work runs to four parts, each divided into
a large number of short sections or 'articles'; there are five hundred and
four in all. Part One expounds Descartes' metaphysical doctrines (though
they are presented in a very different fashion from that of the *Meditations*);
Part Two gives a full account of the principles of Cartesian physics; Part
Three provides a detailed explanation in accordance with those principles
of the nature of the universe; and Part Four deals similarly with a wide
variety of terrestrial phenomena. A further two parts were originally
planned, to deal respectively with plants and animals, and with man, but
these were never completed. The present selection comprises the whole of
Part One, and excerpts from Parts Two and Four. The great length of the
original work reflects Descartes' ambitious project of providing a complete university textbook which would rival and, he hoped, eventually
replace the traditional texts based on Aristotle. The *Principles* remains the
most comprehensive statement of the Cartesian system, and is a particularly valuable source for students of his philosophy of science.

The *Comments on a Certain Broadsheet* (often referred to in English as
the 'Notes against a programme' – a virtual transliteration of the original
Latin title *Notae in programma quoddam*) was published in Amsterdam
early in 1648. This short work (from which extracts are provided below)

was Descartes' response to a broadsheet published anonymously in 1647 by Henri de Roy (Henricus Regius), Professor of Medicine at the University of Utrecht. Regius had earlier been an enthusiastic supporter of the Cartesian system, but when he published his *Foundations of Physics* in 1646, Descartes complained that the book shamelessly lifted and often distorted many of his ideas (some from unpublished material on physiology to which Regius had gained access). The *Comments* provide a good illustration of the type of bitter academic controversy in which Descartes often became embroiled during the 1640s; they also give some interesting insights into his views on the nature of the mind, and in particular his doctrine of innate ideas – a topic which was to become a major philosophical issue during the century following Descartes' death.

Descartes' last philosophical work, *The Passions of the Soul*, was written in French, printed in Holland, and published in Amsterdam and Paris in 1649 under the title *Les Passions de l'âme*. This work, like the *Principles*, is composed of a large number of short articles (two hundred and twelve in all); the first fifty articles, which form Part One of the work, are translated below. Defying the narrow classifications of the modern academic world, the *Passions* is a treatise on physiology-cum-psychology-cum-ethics, and was written at the urging of Princess Elizabeth of Bohemia, who, in a letter of 6 May 1643, had raised the crucial question 'how can the soul of man, being only a thinking substance, determine the bodily spirits to perform voluntary actions?' A long correspondence ensued, and in response to Elizabeth's further acute questioning, Descartes produced a short treatise which became the nucleus for the final published work. Very few have been satisfied with Descartes' theory of the interaction of the soul and body via the pineal gland in the brain, but the *Passions* nonetheless gives us a vivid picture of Descartes' view of human nature – that mysterious compound of two incompatible substances, mind and body. It also has much to say about the achievement of happiness – something which Descartes saw as the most precious fruit to be gathered from a sound philosophical system. Two months before the publication of the *Passions*, Descartes set sail on his ill-fated voyage to Stockholm, in response to the invitation of Queen Christina. Suffering from the rigours of the Swedish winter and the tedium of his courtly duties (which included giving lessons to the Queen at five o'clock in the morning), he contracted pneumonia and died on 11 February 1650, just over a month short of his fifty-fourth birthday.

NOTE ON THE TRANSLATIONS

The translations which appear below are taken from our two-volume translation, *The Philosophical Writings of Descartes*, published by Cambridge University Press in 1985 (known as CSM). We have taken the opportunity of making a number of minor revisions and corrections for the present edition. The translations are based on the texts to be found in the standard twelve-volume edition of Descartes by Adam and Tannery (known as AT),[1] and the reader will find running marginal references to the relevant volume of AT throughout the present work. (The marginal references are placed within brackets where they do not mark the beginning of a page in AT.) In each case our translations of Descartes' work are made from the original language in which they were composed; where subsequent translations approved by Descartes provide important additional material this has also been translated, but in footnotes or within diamond brackets to distinguish it from the original material. The work of translation is divided as follows: John Cottingham is responsible for the *Meditations* and *Principles*, Robert Stoothoff for the *Discourse, Optics* and *Passions*, and Dugald Murdoch for the *Rules* and *Comments on a Certain Broadsheet*. All the members of the team have, however, scrutinised each other's work and made numerous suggestions, many of which have found their way into the final version. We have included a short chronological table of Descartes' life and works, and we hope that the comprehensive index to be found at the end of the volume will be of assistance to those working on particular topics in Descartes.

J.C.

1 *Oeuvres de Descartes*, eds. Ch. Adam and P. Tannery (revised edition, Paris: Vrin/CNRS 1964–76).

Chronological table of Descartes' life and works

1596   born at La Haye near Tours on 31 March

1606–14   attends Jesuit college of La Flèche in Anjou[1]

1616   takes doctorate in law at University of Poitiers

1618   goes to Holland; joins army of Prince Maurice of Nassau; meets Isaac Beeckman; composes a short treatise on music, the *Compendium Musicae*

1619   travels in Germany; 10 November: has vision of new mathematical and scientific system

1622   returns to France; during next few years spends time in Paris, but also travels in Europe

1628   composes *Rules for the Direction of our Native Intelligence*; leaves for Holland, which is to be his home until 1649, though with frequent changes of address

1629   begins working on *The World*

1633   condemnation of Galileo; abandons plans to publish *The World*

1635   birth of Descartes' natural daughter Francine, baptized 7 August (died 1640)

1637   publishes *Discourse on the Method*, with *Optics*, *Meteorology* and *Geometry*

1641   *Meditations on First Philosophy* published, together with *Objections and Replies* (first six sets)

1642   second edition of *Meditations* published, with all seven sets of *Objections and Replies* and *Letter to Dinet*

1643   Cartesian philosophy condemned at the University of Utrecht; Descartes' long correspondence with Princess Elizabeth of Bohemia begins

1644   visits France; *Principles of Philosophy* published

1647   awarded a pension by King of France; publishes *Comments on a Certain Broadsheet*; begins work on *Description of the Human Body*

1648   interviewed by Frans Burman at Egmond-Binnen (*Conversation with Burman*)

1649   goes to Sweden on invitation of Queen Christina; *The Passions of the Soul* published

1650   dies at Stockholm on 11 February

1 Descartes is known to have stayed at La Flèche for eight or nine years, but the exact dates of his arrival and departure are uncertain. Baillet places Descartes' admission in 1604, the year of the College's foundation (A. Baillet, *La vie de M. Des-Cartes* (1691), vol. 1, p. 18).

Rules for the Direction of
our Native Intelligence

RULE ONE

The aim of our studies should be to direct the mind with a view to forming true and sound judgements about whatever comes before it.

The sciences as a whole are nothing other than human wisdom, which always remains one and the same, however different the subjects to which it is applied, it being no more altered by them than sunlight is by the variety of the things it shines on. Hence there is no need to impose any restrictions on our mental powers; for the knowledge of one truth does not, like skill in one art, hinder us from discovering another; on the contrary it helps us. . . . It must be acknowledged that all the sciences are so closely interconnected that it is much easier to learn them all together than to separate one from the other. If, therefore, someone seriously wishes to investigate the truth of things, he ought not to select one science in particular, for they are all interconnected and interdependent. . . .

RULE TWO

We should attend only to those objects of which our minds seem capable of having certain and indubitable cognition.

All knowledge[1] is certain and evident cognition. Someone who has doubts about many things is no wiser than one who has never given them a thought; indeed, he appears less wise if he has formed a false opinion about any of them. Hence it is better never to study at all than to occupy ourselves with objects which are so difficult that we are unable to distinguish what is true from what is false, and are forced to take the doubtful as certain; for in such matters the risk of diminishing our knowledge is greater than our hope of increasing it. So, in accordance with this Rule, we reject all such merely probable cognition and resolve to believe only what is perfectly known and incapable of being doubted. . . .

 Nevertheless, if we adhere strictly to this Rule, there will be very few

1 Lat. *scientia*, Descartes' term for systematic knowledge based on indubitable foundations.

I

things which we can get down to studying. For there is hardly any question in the sciences about which clever men have not frequently disagreed. ... Accordingly, if my reckoning is correct, out of all the sciences so far devised, we are restricted to just arithmetic and geometry if we (364) stick to this Rule.... So if we seriously wish to propose rules for ourselves which will help us scale the heights of human knowledge, we must include, as one of our primary rules, that we should take care not to waste our time by neglecting easy tasks and occupying ourselves only with difficult matters....

Of all the sciences so far discovered, arithmetic and geometry alone are, as we said above, free from any taint of falsity or uncertainty. If we are to give a careful estimate of the reason why this should be so, we 365   should bear in mind that there are two ways of arriving at a knowledge of things – through experience and through deduction. Moreover, we must note that while our experiences of things are often deceptive, the deduction or pure inference of one thing from another can never be performed wrongly by an intellect which is in the least degree rational, though we may fail to make the inference if we do not see it. Furthermore, those chains with which dialecticians[1] suppose they regulate human reason seem to me to be of little use here, though I do not deny that they are very useful for other purposes. In fact none of the errors to which men – men, I say, not the brutes – are liable is ever due to faulty inference; they are due only to the fact that men take for granted certain poorly understood observations, or lay down rash and groundless judgements.

These considerations make it obvious why arithmetic and geometry prove to be much more certain than other disciplines: they alone are concerned with an object so pure and simple that they make no assumptions that experience might render uncertain; they consist entirely in deducing conclusions by means of rational arguments. They are therefore the easiest and clearest of all the sciences and have just the sort of object we are looking for....

(366)   RULE THREE

Concerning objects proposed for study, we ought to investigate what we can clearly and evidently intuit[2] or deduce with certainty, and not what other people have thought or what we ourselves conjecture. For knowledge[3] can be attained in no other way.

1 'Dialectic' is Descartes' term for scholastic logic.
2 Lat. *intueri*, literally 'to look at, gaze at'; used by Descartes as a technical term for immediate intellectual apprehension.
3 Lat. *scientia*; see footnote on p. 1 above.

We would be well-advised not to mix any conjectures into the judgements (367) we make about the truth of things. It is most important to bear this point in mind. The main reason why we can find nothing in ordinary philosophy which is so evident and certain as to be beyond dispute is that students of the subject first of all are not content to acknowledge what is clear and 368 certain, but on the basis of merely probable conjectures venture also to make assertions on obscure matters about which nothing is known; they then gradually come to have complete faith in these assertions, indiscriminately mixing them up with others that are true and evident. The result is that the only conclusions they can draw are ones which apparently rest on some such obscure proposition, and which are accordingly uncertain.

But in case we in turn should slip into the same error, let us now review all the actions of the intellect by means of which we are able to arrive at a knowledge of things with no fear of being mistaken. We recognize only two: intuition and deduction.

By 'intuition' I do not mean the fluctuating testimony of the senses or the deceptive judgement of the imagination as it botches things together, but the conception of a clear and attentive mind, which is so easy and distinct that there can be no room for doubt about what we are understanding. Alternatively, and this comes to the same thing, intuition is the indubitable conception of a clear and attentive mind which proceeds solely from the light of reason. Because it is simpler, it is more certain than deduction, though deduction, as we noted above, is not something a man can perform wrongly. Thus everyone can mentally intuit that he exists, that he is thinking, that a triangle is bounded by just three lines, and a sphere by a single surface, and the like. Perceptions such as these are more numerous than most people realize, disdaining as they do to turn their minds to such simple matters....

The self-evidence and certainty of intuition is required not only for (369) apprehending single propositions, but also for any train of reasoning whatever. Take for example, the inference that 2 plus 2 equals 3 plus 1: not only must we intuitively perceive that 2 plus 2 makes 4, and that 3 plus 1 makes 4, but also that the original proposition follows necessarily from the other two.

There may be some doubt here about our reason for suggesting another mode of knowing in addition to intuition, *viz.* deduction, by which we mean the inference of something as following necessarily from some other propositions which are known with certainty. But this distinction had to be made, since very many facts which are not self-evident are known with certainty, provided they are inferred from true and known principles through a continuous and uninterrupted movement of thought in which each individual proposition is clearly intuited. This is similar to the way in which we know that the last link in

370 a long chain is connected to the first: even if we cannot take in at one glance all the intermediate links on which the connection depends, we can have knowledge of the connection provided we survey the links one after the other, and keep in mind that each link from first to last is attached to its neighbour. Hence we are distinguishing mental intuition from certain deduction on the grounds that we are aware of a movement or a sort of sequence in the latter but not in the former, and also because immediate self-evidence is not required for deduction, as it is for intuition; deduction in a sense gets its certainty from memory. It follows that those propositions which are immediately inferred from first principles can be said to be known in one respect through intuition, and in another respect through deduction. But the first principles themselves are known only through intuition, and the remote conclusions only through deduction....

371   RULE FOUR

We need a method if we are to investigate the truth of things.

By 'a method' I mean reliable rules which are easy to apply, and such that if
372 one follows them exactly, one will never take what is false to be true or fruitlessly expend one's mental efforts, but will gradually and constantly increase one's knowledge[1] till one arrives at a true understanding of everything within one's capacity.... The method cannot go so far as to teach us how to perform the actual operations of intuition and deduction, since these are the simplest of all and quite basic. If our intellect were not already able to perform them, it would not comprehend any of the rules of the method, however easy they might be....

(373)   So useful is this method that without it the pursuit of learning would, I think, be more harmful than profitable. Hence I can readily believe that the great minds of the past were to some extent aware of it, guided to it even by nature alone. For the human mind has within it a sort of spark of the divine, in which the first seeds of useful ways of thinking are sown, seeds which, however neglected and stifled by studies which impede them, often bear fruit of their own accord. This is our experience in the simplest of sciences, arithmetic and geometry: we are well aware that the geometers of antiquity employed a sort of analysis which they went on to apply to the solution of every problem, though they begrudged revealing it to posterity....

374   I shall have much to say below about figures and numbers, for no other disciplines can yield illustrations as evident and certain as these. But if one attends closely to my meaning, one will readily see that ordinary mathe-

---

1 Lat. *scientia*; see footnote on p. 1 above.

matics is far from my mind here, that it is quite another discipline I am expounding, and that these illustrations are more its outer garments than inner parts. This discipline should contain the primary rudiments of human reason and extend to the discovery of truths in any field whatever....

In the present age some very gifted men have tried to revive this method, 377) for the method seems to me to be none other than the art which goes by the outlandish name of 'algebra' – or at least it would be if algebra were divested of the multiplicity of numbers and incomprehensible figures which overwhelm it and instead possessed that abundance of clarity and simplicity which I believe the true mathematics ought to have. It was these thoughts which made me turn from the particular studies of arithmetic and geometry to a general investigation of mathematics. I began my investigation by inquiring what exactly is generally meant by the term 'mathematics'[1] and why it is that, in addition to arithmetic and geometry, sciences such as astronomy, music, optics, mechanics, among others, are called branches of mathematics. To answer this it is not enough just to look at the etymology of the word, for, since the word 'mathematics' has the same meaning as 'discipline',[2] these subjects have as much right to be called 'mathematics' as geometry has. Yet it is evident that almost anyone with the slightest education can easily tell the difference in any context between what relates to mathematics and what to the other disciplines. When I considered the matter more closely, I came to see that the exclusive 378 concern of mathematics is with questions of order or measure and that it is irrelevant whether the measure in question involves numbers, shapes, stars, sounds, or any other object whatever. This made me realize that there must be a general science which explains all the points that can be raised concerning order and measure irrespective of the subject-matter, and that this science should be termed *mathesis universalis*[3] – a venerable term with a well-established meaning – for it covers everything that entitles these other sciences to be called branches of mathematics....

Aware how slender my powers are, I have resolved in my search for knowledge of things to adhere unswervingly to a definite order, always 379 starting with the simplest and easiest things and never going beyond them till there seems to be nothing further which is worth achieving where they are concerned. Up to now, therefore, I have devoted all my energies to this universal mathematics, so that I think I shall be able in due course to tackle the somewhat more advanced sciences, without my efforts being premature....

1 Lat. *mathesis*, from the Greek μάθησις, literally 'learning'.
2 Lat. *disciplina*, from *discere*, 'to learn'.
3 I.e. 'universal mathematics'.

RULE FIVE

The whole method consists entirely in the ordering and arranging of the objects on which we must concentrate our mind's eye if we are to discover some truth. We shall be following this method exactly if we first reduce complicated and obscure propositions step by step to simpler ones, and then, starting with the intuition of the simplest ones of all, try to ascend through the same steps to a knowledge of all the rest.

This one Rule covers the most essential points in the whole of human endeavour. Anyone who sets out in quest of knowledge of things must
380 follow this Rule as closely as he would the thread of Theseus if he were to enter the Labyrinth.... But the order that is required here is often so obscure and complicated that not everyone can make out what it is; hence it is virtually impossible to guard against going astray unless one carefully observes the message of the following Rule.

381

RULE SIX

In order to distinguish the simplest things from those that are complicated and to set them out in an orderly manner, we should attend to what is most simple in each series of things in which we have directly deduced some truths from others, and should observe how all the rest are more, or less, or equally removed from the simplest.

Although the message of this Rule may not seem very novel, it contains nevertheless the main secret of my method; and there is no more useful Rule in this whole treatise. For it instructs us that all things can be arranged serially in various groups, not in so far as they can be referred to some ontological genus (such as the categories into which philosophers divide things[1]), but in so far as some things can be known on the basis of others. Thus when a difficulty arises, we can see at once whether it will be worth looking at any others first, and if so which ones and in what order.

In order to be able to do this correctly, we should note first that everything, with regard to its possible usefulness to our project, may be termed either 'absolute' or 'relative' – our project being, not to inspect the isolated natures of things, but to compare them with each other so that some may be known on the basis of others.

I call 'absolute' whatever has within it the pure and simple nature in question; that is, whatever is viewed as being independent, a cause, simple, universal, single, equal, similar, straight, and other qualities of
382 that sort. I call this the simplest and the easiest thing when we can make use of it in solving problems.

1 For example, the Aristotelian categories of substance, quality, quantity, relation, etc.

The 'relative', on the other hand, is what shares the same nature, or at least something of the same nature, in virtue of which we can relate it to the absolute and deduce it from the absolute in a definite series of steps. The concept of the 'relative' involves other terms besides, which I call 'relations': these include whatever is said to be dependent, an effect, composite, particular, many, unequal, dissimilar, oblique, etc. The further removed from the absolute such relative attributes are, the more mutually dependent relations of this sort they contain. This Rule points out that all these relations should be distinguished, and the interconnections between them, and their natural order, should be noted, so that given the last term we should be able to reach the one that is absolute in the highest degree, by passing through all the intermediate ones....

We should note, secondly, that there are very few pure and simple (383) natures which we can intuit straight off and *per se* (independently of any others) either in our sensory experience or by means of a light innate within us. We should, as I said, attend carefully to the simple natures which can be intuited in this way, for these are the ones which in each series we term simple in the highest degree. As for all the other natures, we can apprehend them only by deducing them from those which are simple in the highest degree, either immediately and directly, or by means of two or three or more separate inferences....

The third and last point to note is that we should not begin our studies (384) by investigating difficult matters. Before tackling any specific problems we ought first to make a random selection of truths which happen to be at hand, and ought then to see whether we can deduce some other truths from them step by step, and from these still others, and so on in logical sequence. This done, we should reflect attentively on the truths we have discovered and carefully consider why it was we were able to discover some of these truths sooner and more easily than others, and what these truths are....

RULE SEVEN (387)

In order to make our knowledge complete, every single thing relating to our undertaking must be surveyed in a continuous and wholly uninterrupted sweep of thought, and be included in a sufficient and well-ordered enumeration.

It is necessary to observe the points proposed in this Rule if we are to admit as certain those truths which, we said above, are not deduced immediately from first and self-evident principles. For this deduction sometimes requires such a long chain of inferences that when we arrive at such a truth it is not easy to recall the entire route which led us to it. That is why we say that a continuous movement of thought is needed to make good any weakness of memory....

(388)   In addition, this movement must nowhere be interrupted. Frequently those who attempt to deduce something too swiftly and from remote initial premises do not go over the entire chain of intermediate conclusions very carefully, but pass over many of the steps without due consideration. But, whenever even the smallest link is overlooked, the chain is immediately broken, and the certainty of the conclusion entirely collapses.

We maintain furthermore that enumeration is required for the completion of our knowledge.[1] The other Rules do indeed help us resolve most questions, but it is only with the aid of enumeration that we are able to make a true and certain judgement about whatever we apply our minds to. By means of enumeration nothing will wholly escape us and we shall be seen to have some knowledge on every question.

In this context enumeration, or induction, consists in a thorough investigation of all the points relating to the problem at hand, an investigation which is so careful and accurate that we may conclude with manifest certainty that we have not inadvertently overlooked anything.

389   So even though the object of our inquiry eludes us, provided we have made an enumeration, we shall be wiser at least to the extent that we shall perceive with certainty that it could not possibly be discovered by any method known to us....

We should note, moreover, that by 'sufficient enumeration' or 'induction' we just mean the kind of enumeration which renders the truth of our conclusions more certain than any other kind of proof (simple intuition excepted) allows...

(390)   The enumeration should sometimes be complete, and sometimes distinct, though there are times when it need be neither. That is why I said only that the enumeration must be sufficient. For if I wish to determine by enumeration how many kinds of corporeal entity there are or how many are in some way perceivable by the senses, I shall not assert that there are just so many and no more, unless I have previously made sure I have included them all in my enumeration and have distinguished one from another. But if I wish to show in the same way that the rational soul is not corporeal, there is no need for the enumeration to be complete; it will be sufficient if I group all bodies together into several classes so as to demonstrate that the rational soul cannot be assigned to any of these....

---

1 Lat. *scientia*; see footnote on p. 1 above.

RULE EIGHT   (392)

If in the series of things to be examined we come across something which our intellect is unable to intuit sufficiently well, we must stop at that point, and refrain from the superfluous task of examining the remaining items.

The most useful inquiry we can make at this stage is to ask: What is human (397) knowledge and what is its scope? We are at present treating this as one single question, which in our view is the first question of all that should be   398 examined by means of the Rules described above... In order to see how the above points apply to the problem before us, we shall first divide into two parts whatever is relevant to the question; for the question ought to relate either to us, who have the capacity for knowledge, or to the actual things it is possible to know. We shall discuss these two parts separately.

Within ourselves we are aware that, while it is the intellect alone that is capable of knowledge,[1] it can be helped or hindered by three other faculties, *viz.* imagination, sense-perception, and memory. We must therefore look at these faculties in turn, to see in what respect each of them could be a hindrance, so that we may be on our guard, and in what respect an asset, so that we may make full use of their resources. We   399 shall discuss this part of the question by way of a sufficient enumeration, as the following Rule will make clear.

We should then turn to the things themselves; and we should deal with these only in so far as they are within the reach of the intellect. In that respect we divide them into absolutely simple natures and complex or composite natures. Simple natures must all be either spiritual or corporeal, or belong to each of these categories. As for composite natures, there are some which the intellect experiences as composite before it decides to determine anything about them: but there are others which are put together by the intellect itself. All these points will be explained at greater length in Rule Twelve, where it will be demonstrated that there can be no falsity save in composite natures which are put together by the intellect. In view of this, we divide natures of the latter sort into two further classes, *viz.* those that are deduced from natures which are the most simple and self-evident (which we shall deal with throughout the next book), and those that presuppose others which experience shows us to be composite in reality....

---

1 Lat. *scientia*; see footnote on p. 1 above.

RULE NINE

(400)

We must concentrate our mind's eye totally upon the most insignificant and easiest of matters, and dwell on them long enough to acquire the habit of intuiting the truth distinctly and clearly.

We have given an account of the two operations of our intellect, intuition and deduction, on which we must, as we said, exclusively rely in our acquisition of knowledge. In this and the following Rule we shall proceed to explain how we can make our employment of intuition and deduction more skilful and at the same time how to cultivate two special mental faculties, *viz.* perspicacity in the distinct intuition of particular things and discernment in the methodical deduction of one thing from another.

401   We can best learn how mental intuition is to be employed by comparing it with ordinary vision. If one tries to look at many objects at one glance, one sees none of them distinctly. Likewise, if one is inclined to attend to many things at the same time in a single act of thought, one does so with a confused mind. Yet craftsmen who engage in delicate operations, and are used to fixing their eyes on a single point, acquire through practice the ability to make perfect distinctions between things, however minute and delicate. The same is true of those who never let their thinking be distracted by many different objects at the same time, but always devote their whole attention to the simplest and easiest of matters: they become perspicacious....

402   Everyone ought therefore to acquire the habit of encompassing in his thought at one time facts which are very simple and very few in number – so much so that he never thinks he knows something unless he intuits it just as distinctly as any of the things he knows most distinctly of all.... There is, I think, one point above all others which I must stress here, which is that everyone should be firmly convinced that the sciences, however abstruse, are to be deduced only from matters which are easy and highly accessible, and not from those which are grand and obscure....

RULE TEN

(403)   *In order to acquire discernment we should exercise our native intelligence by investigating what others have already discovered, and methodically survey even the most insignificant products of human skill, especially those which display or presuppose order.*

(404)   Since not all minds have such a natural disposition to puzzle things out by their own exertions, the message of this Rule is that we must not take up the more difficult and arduous issues immediately, but must first tackle the simplest and least exalted arts, and especially those in which order prevails

– such as weaving and carpet-making, or the more feminine arts of embroidery, in which threads are interwoven in an infinitely varied pattern. Number-games and any games involving arithmetic, and the like, belong here. It is surprising how much all these activities exercise our native intelligence, provided of course we discover them for ourselves and not from others....

RULE ELEVEN   407

If, after intuiting a number of simple propositions, we deduce something else from them, it is useful to run through them in a continuous and completely uninterrupted train of thought, to reflect on their relations to one another, and to form a distinct and, as far as possible, simultaneous conception of several of them. For in this way our knowledge becomes much more certain, and our intellectual capacity is enormously increased.

Two things are required for mental intuition: first, the proposition intuited must be clear and distinct; second, the whole proposition must be understood all at once, and not bit by bit. But when we think of the process of deduction as we did in Rule Three, it does not seem to take place all at once: inferring one thing from another involves a kind of movement of our mind. In that passage, then, we were justified in distinguishing intuition from deduction. But if we look on deduction as a completed process, as we   408
did in Rule Seven, then it no longer signifies a movement but rather the completion of a movement. That is why we are supposing that the deduction is made through intuition when it is simple and transparent, but not when it is complex and involved. When the latter is the case, we call it 'enumeration' or 'induction', since the intellect cannot simultaneously grasp it as a whole, and its certainty in a sense depends on memory, which must retain the judgements we have made on the individual parts of the enumeration if we are to derive a single conclusion from them taken as a whole....

As we have said, conclusions which embrace more than we can grasp in a single intuition depend for their certainty on memory, and since memory is weak and unstable, it must be refreshed and strengthened through this continuous and repeated movement of thought. Say, for instance, in virtue of several operations, I have discovered the relation between the first and the second magnitude of a series, then the relation between the second and the third and the third and fourth, and lastly the fourth and fifth: that does   409
not necessarily enable me to see what the relation is between the first and the fifth, and I cannot deduce it from the relations I already know unless I remember all of them. That is why it is necessary that I run over them again

and again in my mind until I can pass from the first to the last so quickly that memory is left with practically no role to play, and I seem to be intuiting the whole thing at once....

(410) ## RULE TWELVE

Finally we must make use of all the aids which intellect, imagination, sense-perception, and memory afford in order, firstly, to intuit simple propositions distinctly; secondly, to combine correctly the matters under investigation with what we already know, so that they too may be known; and thirdly, to find out what things should be compared with each other so that we make the most thorough use of all our human powers.

411 This Rule sums up everything that has been said above, and sets out a general lesson the details of which remain to be explained as follows.

Where knowledge of things is concerned, only two factors need to be considered: ourselves, the knowing subjects, and the things which are the objects of knowledge. As for ourselves, there are only four faculties which we can use for this purpose, *viz.* intellect, imagination, sense-perception and memory. It is of course only the intellect that is capable of perceiving the truth, but it has to be assisted by imagination, sense-perception and memory if we are not to omit anything which lies within our power. As for the objects of knowledge, it is enough if we examine the following three questions: What presents itself to us spontaneously? How can one thing be known on the basis of something else? What conclusions can be drawn from each of these? This seems to me to be a complete enumeration and to omit nothing which is within the range of human endeavour....

(417) With respect to the second factor, our aim is to distinguish carefully the notions of simple things from those which are composed of them, and in both cases to try to see where falsity can come in, so that we may guard against it, and to see what can be known with certainty, so that we may concern ourselves exclusively with that. To this end, as before, certain assumptions must be made in this context which perhaps not everyone will accept. But even if they are thought to be no more real than the imaginary circles which astronomers use to describe the phenomena they study, this matters little, provided they help us to pick out the kind of apprehension of any given thing that may be true and to distinguish it from the kind that may be false.

418 We state our view, then, in the following way. First, when we consider things in the order that corresponds to our knowledge of them, our view

of them must be different from what it would be if we were speaking of them in accordance with how they exist in reality. If, for example, we consider some body which has extension and shape, we shall indeed admit that, with respect to the thing itself, it is one single and simple entity. For, viewed in that way, it cannot be said to be a composite made up of corporeal nature, extension and shape, since these constituents have never existed in isolation from each other. Yet with respect to our intellect we call it a composite made up of these three natures, because we understood each of them separately before we were in a position to judge that the three of them are encountered at the same time in one and the same subject. That is why, since we are concerned here with things only in so far as they are perceived by the intellect, we term 'simple' only those things which we know so clearly and distinctly that they cannot be divided by the mind into others which are more distinctly known. Shape, extension and motion, etc. are of this sort; all the rest we conceive to be in a sense composed out of these. This point is to be taken in a very general sense, so that not even the things that we occasionally abstract from these simples are exceptions to it. We are abstracting, for example, when we say that shape is the limit of an extended thing, conceiving by the term 'limit' something more general than shape, since we can talk of the limit of a duration, the limit of a motion, etc. But, even if the sense of the term 'limit' is derived by abstraction from the notion of shape, that is no reason to regard it as simpler than shape. On the contrary, since the term 'limit' is also applied to other things – such as the limit of a duration or a motion, etc., things totally different in kind from shape – it must have been abstracted from these as well. Hence, it is something compounded out of many quite different natures, and the term 'limit' does not have a univocal application in all these cases.   419

Secondly, those things which are said to be simple with respect to our intellect are, on our view, either purely intellectual or purely material, or common to both. Those simple natures which the intellect recognizes by means of a sort of innate light, without the aid of any corporeal image, are purely intellectual. That there is a number of such things is certain: it is impossible to form any corporeal idea which represents for us what knowledge or doubt or ignorance is, or the action of the will, which may be called 'volition', and the like; and yet we have real knowledge of all of these, knowledge so easy that in order to possess it all we need is some degree of rationality. Those simple natures, on the other hand, which are recognized to be present only in bodies – such as shape, extension and motion, etc. – are purely material. Lastly, those simples are to be termed 'common' which are ascribed indifferently, now to corporeal things, now to spirits – for instance, existence, unity, duration and the like. To this class we must also refer those common notions which are, as it were, links that connect other simple natures together, and whose self-evidence is the basis for all the rational inferences we make. Examples of these are: 'Things that are the same as a third thing are the same as each other'; 'Things that cannot be related in the same way to a third thing are different in some respect.' These common notions can be known either by

420 the pure intellect or by the intellect as it intuits the images of material things.

Moreover, it is as well to count among the simple natures the corresponding privations and negations, in so far as we understand these. For when I intuit what nothing is, or an instant, or rest, my apprehension is as much genuine knowledge as my understanding what existence is, or duration, or motion. This way of conceiving of things will be helpful later on in enabling us to say that all the rest of what we know is put together out of these simple natures. Thus, if I judge that a certain shape is not moving, I shall say that my thought is in some way composed of shape and rest; and similarly in other cases.

Thirdly, these simple natures are all self-evident and never contain any falsity. This can easily be shown if we distinguish between the faculty by which our intellect intuits and knows things and the faculty by which it makes affirmative or negative judgements. For it can happen that we think we are ignorant of things we really know, as for example when we suspect that they contain something else which eludes us, something beyond what we intuit or reach in our thinking, even though we are mistaken in thinking this. For this reason, it is evident that we are mistaken if we ever judge that we lack complete knowledge of any one of these simple natures. For if we have even the slightest grasp of it in our mind – which we surely must have, on the assumption that we are making a judgement about it – it must follow that we have complete

421 knowledge of it. Otherwise it could not be said to be simple, but a composite made up of that which we perceive in it and that of which we judge we are ignorant.

Fourthly, the conjunction between these simple things is either necessary or contingent. The conjunction is necessary when one of them is somehow implied (albeit confusedly) in the concept of the other so that we cannot conceive of either of them distinctly if we judge them to be separate from each other. It is in this way that shape is conjoined with extension, motion with duration or time, etc., because we cannot conceive of a shape which is completely lacking in extension, or a motion wholly lacking in duration. Similarly, if I say that 4 and 3 make 7, the composition is a necessary one, for we do not have a distinct conception of the number 7 unless in a confused sort of way we include 3 and 4 in it.

In the same way, whatever we demonstrate concerning figures or numbers necessarily links up with that of which it is affirmed. This necessity applies not just to things which are perceivable by the senses but to others as well. If, for example, Socrates says that he doubts everything, it necessarily follows that he understands at least that he is doubting, and hence that he knows that something can be true or false, etc.; for there is a necessary connection between these facts and the nature of doubt. The union between such things, however, is contingent when the relation conjoining them is not an inseparable one. This is the case when we say that a body is animate, that a man is dressed, etc. Again, there are many instances of things which are necessarily conjoined, even though most people count them as contingent, failing to notice the relation between them: for example the proposition, 'I am, therefore God exists', or 'I understand, therefore I have a mind distinct from my body.' Finally, we must note that very many necessary propositions, when converted, are contingent. Thus from the fact that I exist I may conclude with certainty that God exists, but from the fact that God exists I cannot legitimately assert that I too exist.   422

Fifthly, it is not possible for us ever to understand anything beyond those simple natures and a certain mixture or compounding of one with another. Indeed, it is often easier to attend at once to several mutually conjoined natures than to separate one of them from the others. For example, I can have knowledge of a triangle, even though it has never occurred to me that this knowledge involves knowledge also of the angle, the line, the number three, shape, extension, etc. But that does not preclude our saying that the nature of a triangle is composed of these other natures and that they are better known than the triangle, for it is just these natures that we understand to be present in it. Perhaps there are many additional natures implicitly contained in the triangle which escape our notice, such as the size of the angles being equal to two right angles, the innumerable relations between the sides and the angles, the size of its surface area, etc.

Sixthly, those natures which we call 'composite' are known by us either because we learn from experience what sort they are, or because we ourselves put them together. Our experience consists of whatever we perceive by means of the senses, whatever we learn from others, and in general whatever reaches our intellect either from external sources or from its own reflexive self-contemplation. We should note here that the intellect can never be deceived by any experience, provided that when the object is presented to it, it intuits it in a fashion exactly corresponding to the way in which it possesses the object, either within itself or in the imagination. Furthermore, it must not judge that the imagination   423 faithfully represents the objects of the senses, or that the senses take on the true shapes of things, or in short that external things always are just as they appear to be. In all such cases we are liable to go wrong, as we do for example when we take as gospel truth a story which someone has told us; or as someone who has jaundice does when, owing to the yellow tinge of his eyes, he thinks everything is coloured yellow; or again, as we do when our imagination is impaired (as it is in depression) and we think that its disordered images represent real things. But the understanding of the wise man will not be deceived in such cases: while he will judge that whatever comes to him from his imagination really is depicted in it, he will never assert that it passes, complete and unaltered, from the external world to his senses, and from his senses to the corporeal imagination[1], unless he already has some other grounds for claiming to know this. But whenever we believe that an object of our understanding contains something of which the mind has no immediate perceptual experience, then it is we ourselves who are responsible for its composition. In the same way, when someone who has jaundice is convinced that the things he sees are yellow, this thought of his will be composite, consisting partly of what his corporeal imagination represents to him and partly of the assumption he is making on his own account, *viz.* that the colour looks yellow not owing to any defect of vision but because the things he sees really are yellow. It follows from this that we can go wrong only when we ourselves compose in some way the objects of our belief.

424   Seventhly, this composition can come about in three ways: through impulse, through conjecture or through deduction. It is a case of composition through impulse when, in forming judgements about things, our native intelligence leads us to believe something, not because good reasons convince us of it, but simply because we are caused to believe it, either by some superior power, or by our free will, or by a disposition of the corporeal imagination. The first cause is never a source of error, the second rarely, the third almost always; but the first of these is irrelevant in this context, since it does not come within the scope of method. An example of composition by way of conjecture would be our surmising that above the air there is nothing but a very pure ether, much thinner than air, on the grounds that water, being further from the centre of the globe than earth, is a thinner substance than earth, and air, which rises to greater heights than water, is thinner still. Nothing that we put together in this way really deceives us, so long as we judge it to be merely probable, and never assert it to be true; nor for that matter does it make us any the wiser.

Deduction, therefore, remains as our sole means of compounding things in a way that enables us to be certain of their truth. Yet even with

---

1 The part of the brain where the physical processes associated with imagining take place.

deduction there can be many drawbacks. If, say, we conclude that a given space full of air is empty, on the grounds that we do not perceive anything in it, either by sight, touch, or any other sense, then we are incorrectly conjoining the nature of a vacuum with the nature of this space. This is just what happens when we judge that we can deduce something general and necessary from something particular and contingent. But it is within our power to avoid this error, *viz.* by never   425 conjoining things unless we intuit that the conjunction of one with the other is wholly necessary, as we do for example when we deduce that nothing which lacks extension can have a shape, on the grounds that there is a necessary connection between shape and extension, and so on.

From all these considerations we may draw several conclusions. First, we have explained distinctly and, I think, by an adequate enumeration, what at the outset we were able to present only in a confused and rough-and-ready way, *viz.* that there are no paths to certain knowledge of the truth accessible to men save manifest intuition and necessary deduction....

Second, we need take no great pains to discover these simple natures, because they are self-evident enough. What requires effort is distinguishing one from another, and intuiting each one separately with steadfast mental gaze....

Third, the whole of human knowledge[1] consists uniquely in our   (427) achieving a distinct perception of how all these simple natures contribute to the composition of other things. This is a very useful point to note, since whenever some difficulty is proposed for investigation, almost everyone gets stuck right at the outset, uncertain as to which thoughts he ought to concentrate his mind on, yet quite convinced that he ought to seek some new kind of entity previously unknown to him....

Lastly, from what has been said it follows that we should not regard some branches of our knowledge of things as more obscure than others, since they are all of the same nature and consist simply in the putting   428 together of self-evident facts....

For the rest, in case anyone should fail to see the interconnection between our Rules, we divide everything that can be known into simple propositions and problems. As for simple propositions, the only rules we provide are those which prepare our cognitive powers for a more distinct intuition of any given object and for a more discerning examination of it. For these simple propositions must occur to us spontaneously; they cannot be sought out. We have covered simple propositions in the   429 preceding twelve Rules, and everything that might in any way facilitate the exercise of reason has, we think, been presented in them. As for

---

1 Lat. *scientia*; see footnote on p. 1 above.

problems, however, some can be understood perfectly, even though we do not know the solutions to them, while others are not perfectly understood.... We must note that a problem is to be counted as perfectly understood only if we have a distinct perception of the following three points: first, what the criteria are which enable us to recognize what we are looking for when we come upon it; second, what exactly is the basis from which we ought to deduce it; third, how it is to be proved that the two are so mutually dependent that the one cannot alter in any respect without there being a corresponding alteration in the other. So now that we possess all the premises, the only thing that remains to be shown is how the conclusion is to be found. This is not a matter of drawing a single deduction from a single, simple fact, for, as we have already pointed out, that can be done without the aid of rules; it is, rather, a matter of deriving a single fact which depends on many interconnected facts, and of doing this in such a methodical way that no greater intellectual capacity is required than is needed for the simplest inference. Problems of this sort are for the most part abstract, and arise almost exclusively in arithmetic and geometry, which is why they will seem to ignorant people to be of little use....

430

RULE THIRTEEN

If we perfectly understand a problem we must abstract it from every superfluous conception, reduce it to its simplest terms and, by means of an enumeration, divide it up into the smallest possible parts.

We view the whole matter in the following way. First, in every problem there must be something unknown; otherwise there would be no point in posing the problem. Secondly, this unknown something must be delineated in some way, otherwise there would be nothing to point us to one line of investigation as opposed to any other. Thirdly, the unknown something can be delineated only by way of something else which is already known. These conditions hold also for imperfect problems. If, for example, the problem concerns the nature of the magnet, we already understand what is meant by the words 'magnet' and 'nature', and it is this knowledge which determines us to adopt one line of inquiry rather than another, etc. But if the problem is to be perfect, we want it to be determinate in every respect, so that we are not looking for anything beyond what can be deduced from the data....

431

Furthermore, the problem should be reduced to the simplest terms according to Rules Five and Six, and it should be divided up according to Rule Seven. Thus if I carry out many observations in my research on the magnet, I shall run through them separately one after another. Again, if

432

the subject of my research is sound, as in the case above, I shall make separate comparisons between strings A and B, then between A and C, etc., with a view to including all of them together in a sufficient enumeration. With respect to the terms of a given problem, these three points are the only ones which the pure intellect has to observe before embarking on the final solution of the problem, for which the following eleven Rules may be required....

In every problem, of course, there has to be something unknown – (434) otherwise the inquiry would be pointless. Nevertheless this unknown something must be delineated by definite conditions, which point us   435 decidedly in one direction of inquiry rather than another. These conditions should, in our view, be gone into right from the very outset. We shall do this if we concentrate our mind's eye on intuiting each individual condition distinctly, looking carefully to see to what extent each condition delimits the unknown object of our inquiry. For in this context the human mind is liable to go wrong in one or other of two ways: it may assume something beyond the data required to define the problem, or on the other hand it may leave something out....[1]

1 Rules Fourteen to Twenty-one have been omitted.

Discourse on the Method

of rightly conducting one's reason and seeking the truth in the sciences

If this discourse seems too long to be read at a sitting you may divide it into six parts. In the first you will find various considerations regarding the sciences; in the second, the principal rules of the method which the author has sought; in the third, some of the moral rules he has derived from this method; in the fourth, the arguments by which he proves the existence of God and the human soul, which are the foundations of his metaphysics; in the fifth, the order of the questions in physics that he has investigated and, in particular, the explanation of the movement of the heart and of some other difficulties pertaining to medicine, and also the difference between our soul and that of the beasts; and in the last, the things he believes necessary in order to make further progress in the investigation of nature than he has made, and the reasons which made him write this discourse.

PART ONE

Good sense is the best distributed thing in the world: for everyone thinks
himself so well endowed with it that even those who are the hardest to
please in everything else do not usually desire more of it than they
possess. In this it is unlikely that everyone is mistaken. It indicates rather
that the power of judging well and of distinguishing the true from the
false – which is what we properly call 'good sense' or 'reason' – is
naturally equal in all men, and consequently that the diversity of our
opinions does not arise because some of us are more reasonable than
others but solely because we direct our thoughts along different paths
and do not attend to the same things. For it is not enough to have a good
mind; the main thing is to apply it well. The greatest souls are capable of
the greatest vices as well as the greatest virtues; and those who proceed
but very slowly can make much greater progress, if they always follow
the right path, than those who hurry and stray from it.

For my part, I have never presumed my mind to be in any way more
perfect than that of the ordinary man; indeed, I have often wished to
have as quick a wit, or as sharp and distinct an imagination, or as ample
or prompt a memory as some others. And apart from these, I know of no

other qualities which serve to perfect the mind; for, as regards reason or sense, since it is the only thing that makes us men and distinguishes us from the beasts, I am inclined to believe that it exists whole and complete in each of us. Here I follow the common opinion of the philosophers, who say there are differences of degree only between the *accidents*, and not between the *forms* (or natures) of *individuals* of the same *species*. 3

But I say without hesitation that I consider myself very fortunate to have happened upon certain paths in my youth which led me to considerations and maxims from which I formed a method whereby, it seems to me, I can increase my knowledge gradually and raise it little by little to the highest point allowed by the mediocrity of my mind and the short duration of my life. Now I always try to lean towards diffidence rather than presumption in the judgements I make about myself; and when I cast a philosophical eye upon the various activities and undertakings of mankind, there are almost none which I do not consider vain and useless. Nevertheless I have already reaped such fruits from this method that I cannot but feel extremely satisfied with the progress I think I have already made in the search for truth, and I cannot but entertain such hopes for the future as to venture the opinion that if any purely human occupation has solid worth and importance, it is the one I have chosen.

In other towns or love room — not among people.

Yet I may be wrong: perhaps what I take for gold and diamonds is nothing but a bit of copper and glass. I know how much we are liable to err in matters that concern us, and also how much the judgements of our friends should be distrusted when they are in our favour. I shall be glad, nevertheless, to reveal in this discourse what paths I have followed, and to represent my life in it as if in a picture, so that everyone may judge it for himself; and thus, learning from public response the opinions held of it, I shall add a new means of self-instruction to those I am accustomed to using. 4

My present aim, then, is not to teach the method which everyone must follow in order to direct his reason correctly, but only to reveal how I have tried to direct my own. One who presumes to give precepts must think himself more skilful than those to whom he gives them; and if he makes the slightest mistake, he may be blamed. But I am presenting this work only as a history or, if you prefer, a fable in which, among certain examples worthy of imitation, you will perhaps also find many others that it would be right not to follow; and so I hope it will be useful for some without being harmful to any, and that everyone will be grateful to me for my frankness.

man made

From my childhood I enjoyed the benefits of a literary education; and

because I was persuaded that by this means one could acquire a clear and
certain knowledge of all that is useful in life, I was extremely eager to learn.
But as soon as I had completed the course of study at the end of which one
is normally admitted to the ranks of the learned, I completely changed my
opinion. For I found myself beset by so many doubts and errors that I came
to think I had gained nothing from my attempts to become educated but

5   increasing recognition of my ignorance. And yet I was at one of the most
famous schools in Europe, where I thought there must be learned men if
they existed anywhere on earth. There I had learned everything that the
others were learning; moreover, not content with the subjects they taught
us, I had gone through all the books that fell into my hands concerning the
subjects that are considered most abstruse and unusual. At the same time, I
knew how the others judged me, and I saw that they did not regard me as
inferior to my fellow students, even though several among them were
already destined to take the place of our teachers. And finally, the age in
which we live seemed to me to be as flourishing, and as rich in good minds,
as any before it. This made me feel free to judge all others by reference to
myself and think there was no knowledge in the world such as I had
previously been led to hope for.

I did not, however, cease to value the exercises done in the Schools. I
knew that the languages learned there are necessary for understanding
the works of the ancients; that the charm of fables awakens the mind,
while the memorable deeds told in histories uplift it and help to shape
one's judgement if they are read with discretion; that reading good books
is like having a conversation with the most distinguished men of past ages
– indeed, a rehearsed conversation in which these authors reveal to us
only the best of their thoughts; that oratory has incomparable powers

6   and beauties; that poetry has quite ravishing delicacy and sweetness; that
mathematics contains some very subtle devices which serve as much to
satisfy the curious as to further all the arts and lessen man's labours; that
writings on morals contain many very useful teachings and exhortations
to virtue; that theology instructs us how to reach heaven; that philosophy
gives us the means of speaking plausibly about any subject and of
winning the admiration of the less learned; that jurisprudence, medicine,
and other sciences bring honours and riches to those who cultivate them;
and, finally, that it is good to have examined all these subjects, even those
full of superstition and falsehood, in order to know their true value and
guard against being deceived by them.

But I thought I had already given enough time to languages and
likewise to reading the works of the ancients, both their histories and
their fables. For conversing with those of past centuries is much the same
as travelling. It is good to know something of the customs of various

peoples, so that we may judge our own more soundly and not think that everything contrary to our own ways is ridiculous and irrational, as those who have seen nothing of the world ordinarily do. But one who spends too much time travelling eventually becomes a stranger in his own country; and one who is too curious about the practices of past ages usually remains quite ignorant about those of the present. Moreover, fables make us imagine many events as possible when they are not. And even the most accurate histories, while not altering or exaggerating the importance of matters to make them more worthy of being read, at any rate almost always omit the baser and less notable events; as a result, the other events appear in a false light, and those who regulate their conduct by examples drawn from these works are liable to fall into the excesses of the knights-errant in our tales of chivalry, and conceive plans beyond their powers.

I valued oratory highly and loved poetry; but I thought both were gifts of the mind rather than fruits of study. Those with the strongest reasoning and the most skill at ordering their thoughts so as to make them clear and intelligible are always the most persuasive, even if they speak only low Breton and have never learned rhetoric. And those with the most pleasing conceits and the ability to express them with the most embellishment and sweetness would still be the best poets, even if they knew nothing of the theory of poetry.

Above all I delighted in mathematics, because of the certainty and self-evidence of its reasonings. But I did not yet notice its real use; and since I thought it was of service only in the mechanical arts, I was surprised that nothing more exalted had been built upon such firm and solid foundations. On the other hand, I compared the moral writings of the ancient pagans to very proud and magnificent palaces built only on sand and mud. They extol the virtues, and make them appear more estimable than anything else in the world; but they do not adequately explain how to recognize a virtue, and often what they call by this fine name is nothing but a case of callousness, or vanity, or desperation, or parricide.

I revered our theology, and aspired as much as anyone else to reach heaven. But having learned as an established fact that the way to heaven is open no less to the most ignorant than to the most learned, and that the revealed truths which guide us there are beyond our understanding, I would not have dared submit them to my weak reasonings; and I thought that to undertake an examination of them and succeed, I would need to have some extraordinary aid from heaven and to be more than a mere man.

Regarding philosophy, I shall say only this: seeing that it has been cultivated for many centuries by the most excellent minds and yet there is still no point in it which is not disputed and hence doubtful, I was not so presumptuous as to hope to achieve any more in it than others had done. And, considering how many diverse opinions learned men may maintain on a single question – even though it is impossible for more than one to be true – I held as well-nigh false everything that was merely probable.

9   As for the other sciences, in so far as they borrow their principles from philosophy I decided that nothing solid could have been built upon such shaky foundations. Neither the honour nor the riches they offered was enough to induce me to learn them. For my circumstances did not, thank God, oblige me to augment my fortune by making science my profession; and although I did not profess to scorn glory, like a Cynic, yet I thought very little of the glory which I could hope to acquire only through false pretences. Finally, as for the false sciences, I thought that I already knew their worth well enough not to be liable to be deceived by the promises of an alchemist or the predictions of an astrologer, the tricks of a magician or the frauds and boasts of those who profess to know more than they do.

That is why, as soon as I was old enough to emerge from the control of my teachers, I entirely abandoned my literary studies. Resolving to seek no knowledge other than that which could be found in myself or else in the great book of the world, I spent the rest of my youth travelling, visiting courts and armies, mixing with people of diverse temperaments and ranks, gathering various experiences, testing myself in the situations which fortune offered me, and at all times reflecting upon whatever came my way so as to derive some profit from it. For it seemed to me that much more truth could be found in the reasonings which a man makes concerning matters that concern him than in those which some scholar

10   makes in his study about speculative matters. For the consequences of the former will soon punish the man if he judges wrongly, whereas the latter have no practical consequences and no importance for the scholar except that perhaps the further they are from common sense the more pride he will take in them, since he will have had to use so much more skill and ingenuity in trying to render them plausible. And it was always my most earnest desire to learn to distinguish the true from the false in order to see clearly into my own actions and proceed with confidence in this life.

It is true that, so long as I merely considered the customs of other men, I found hardly any reason for confidence, for I observed in them almost as much diversity as I had found previously among the opinions of philosophers. In fact the greatest benefit I derived from these observations was that they showed me many things which, although seeming very extravagant and ridiculous to us, are nevertheless commonly accepted and approved in other great nations; and so I learned not to believe too firmly anything of which I had been persuaded only by example and custom. Thus I gradually freed myself from many errors which may obscure our natural light and make us less capable of heeding reason. But after I had spent some years pursuing these studies in the book of the world and trying to gain some experience, I resolved one day to undertake studies within myself too and to use all the powers of my mind in choosing the paths I should follow. In this I have had much more success, I think, than I would have had if I had never left my country or my books.

11

PART TWO

At that time I was in Germany, where I had been called by the wars that are not yet ended there. While I was returning to the army from the coronation of the Emperor, the onset of winter detained me in quarters where, finding no conversation to divert me and fortunately having no cares or passions to trouble me, I stayed all day shut up alone in a stove-heated room, where I was completely free to converse with myself about my own thoughts.[1] Among the first that occurred to me was the thought that there is not usually so much perfection in works composed of several parts and produced by various different craftsmen as in the works of one man. Thus we see that buildings undertaken and completed by a single architect are usually more attractive and better planned than those which several have tried to patch up by adapting old walls built for different purposes. Again, ancient cities which have gradually grown from mere villages into large towns are usually ill-proportioned, compared with those orderly towns which planners lay out as they fancy on level ground. Looking at the buildings of the former individually, you will often find as much art in them, if not more, than in those of the latter; but in view of their arrangement – a tall one here, a small one there – and the way they make the streets crooked and irregular, you would say it is chance, rather than the will of men using reason, that placed them so. And when you consider that there have always been certain officials whose job is to see that private buildings embellish public places, you will understand how difficult it is to make something perfect by working only on what others have produced. Again, I thought, peoples who have grown gradually from a half-savage to a civilized state, and have made their laws only in so far as they were forced to by the inconvenience of crimes and quarrels, could not be so well governed as

12

1 In 1619 Descartes attended the coronation of Ferdinand II in Frankfurt, which took place from 20 July to 9 September. The mentioned army was that of the Catholic Duke Maximilian of Bavaria. It is thought that Descartes was detained in a village near Ulm. His day of solitary reflection in a stove-heated room was, according to Baillet, 10 November 1619.

those who from the beginning of their society have observed the basic
laws laid down by some wise law-giver. Similarly, it is quite certain that
the constitution of the true religion, whose articles have been made by
God alone, must be incomparably better ordered than all the others. And
to speak of human affairs, I believe that if Sparta was at one time very
flourishing, this was not because each of its laws in particular was good
(seeing that some were very strange and even contrary to good morals),
but because they were devised by a single man and hence all tended to the
same end.[1] And so I came to think that the sciences contained in books, at
least those involving merely probable arguments and having no demonstrative basis, being built up and developed little by little from the opinions
of many different persons, do not get so close to the truth as do the simple
reasonings which a man of good sense, using his natural powers, can carry
13   out in dealing with whatever objects he may come across. So, too, I
reflected that we were all children before being men and had to be governed for some time by our appetites and our teachers, which were often
opposed to each other and neither of which, perhaps, always gave us the
best advice; hence I thought it virtually impossible that our judgements
should be as unclouded and firm as they would have been if we had had the
full use of our reason from the moment of our birth, and if we had always
been guided by it alone.

  Admittedly, we never see people pulling down all the houses of a city
for the sole purpose of rebuilding them in a different style to make the
streets more attractive; but we do see many individuals having their
houses pulled down in order to rebuild them, some even being forced to
do so when the houses are in danger of falling down and their
foundations are insecure. This example convinced me that it would be
unreasonable for an individual to plan to reform a state by changing it
from the foundations up and overturning it in order to set it up again; or
again for him to plan to reform the body of the sciences or the established
order of teaching them in the schools. But regarding the opinions to
which I had hitherto given credence, I thought that I could not do better
than undertake to get rid of them, all at one go, in order to replace them
14   afterwards with better ones, or with the same ones once I had squared
them with the standards of reason. I firmly believed that in this way I
would succeed in conducting my life much better than if I built only upon
old foundations and relied only upon principles that I had accepted in my
youth without ever examining whether they were true. For although I
noted various difficulties in this undertaking, they were not insurmount-
able. Nor could they be compared with those encountered in the reform

---

1 By tradition the constitution of Sparta was attributed to Lycurgus.

of even minor matters affecting public institutions. These large bodies are too difficult to raise up once overthrown, or even to hold up once they begin to totter, and their fall cannot but be a hard one. Moreover, any imperfections they may possess – and their very diversity suffices to ensure that many do possess them – have doubtless been much smoothed over by custom; and custom has even prevented or imperceptibly corrected many imperfections that prudence could not so well provide against. Finally, it is almost always easier to put up with their imperfections than to change them, just as it is much better to follow the main roads that wind through mountains, which have gradually become smooth and convenient through frequent use, than to try to take a more direct route by clambering over rocks and descending to the foot of precipices.

That is why I cannot by any means approve of those meddlesome and restless characters who, called neither by birth nor by fortune to the management of public affairs, are yet forever thinking up some new reform. And if I thought this book contained the slightest ground for 15 suspecting me of such folly, I would be very reluctant to permit its publication. My plan has never gone beyond trying to reform my own thoughts and construct them upon a foundation which is all my own. If I am sufficiently pleased with my work to present you with this sample of it, this does not mean that I would advise anyone to imitate it. Those on whom God has bestowed more of his favours will perhaps have higher aims; but I fear that even my aim may be too bold for many people. The simple resolution to abandon all the opinions one has hitherto accepted is not an example that everyone ought to follow. The world is largely composed of two types of minds for whom it is quite unsuitable. First, there are those who, believing themselves cleverer than they are, cannot avoid precipitate judgements and never have the patience to direct all their thoughts in an orderly manner; consequently, if they once took the liberty of doubting the principles they accepted and of straying from the common path, they could never stick to the track that must be taken as a short-cut, and they would remain lost all their lives. Secondly, there are those who have enough reason or modesty to recognize that they are less capable of distinguishing the true from the false than certain others by whom they can be taught; such people should be content to follow the opinions of these others rather than seek better opinions themselves.

For myself, I would undoubtedly have been counted among the latter if 16 I had had only one teacher or if I had never known the differences that have always existed among the opinions of the most learned. But in my college days I discovered that nothing can be imagined which is too strange or incredible to have been said by some philosopher; and since then I have recognized through my travels that those with views quite contrary to ours are not on that account barbarians or savages, but that many of them make use of reason as much or more than we do. I thought, too, how the same man, with the same mind, if brought up from infancy among the French or Germans, develops otherwise than he would if he had always lived among the Chinese or cannibals; and how, even in our fashions of dress, the very thing that pleased us ten years ago, and will perhaps please us again ten years hence, now strikes us as extravagant and ridiculous. Thus it is custom and example that persuade us, rather than any certain knowledge. And yet a majority vote is worthless as a proof of truths that are at all difficult to discover; for a single man is much more likely to hit upon them than a group of people. I was, then, unable to choose anyone whose opinions struck me as preferable to those of all others, and I found myself as it were forced to become my own guide.

17 But, like a man who walks alone in the dark, I resolved to proceed so slowly, and to use such circumspection in all things, that even if I made but little progress I should at least be sure not to fall. Nor would I begin rejecting completely any of the opinions which may have slipped into my mind without having been introduced there by reason, until I had first spent enough time in planning the work I was undertaking and in seeking the true method of attaining the knowledge of everything within my mental capabilities.

When I was younger, my philosophical studies had included some logic, and my mathematical studies some geometrical analysis and algebra. These three arts or sciences, it seemed, ought to contribute something to my plan. But on further examination I observed with regard to logic that syllogisms and most of its other techniques are of less use for learning things than for explaining to others the things one already knows or even, as in the art of Lully, for speaking without judgement about matters of which one is ignorant.[1] And although logic does contain many excellent and true precepts, these are mixed up with so many others which are harmful or superfluous that it is almost as difficult to distinguish them as it is to carve a Diana or a Minerva from an unhewn block of marble. As to the analysis of the ancients and the algebra of the moderns, they cover only highly abstract matters, which seem to have no use. Moreover the former is so closely tied to the examination of figures

18 that it cannot exercise the intellect without greatly tiring the imagination; and the latter is so confined to certain rules and symbols that the end result is a confused and obscure art which encumbers the mind, rather

---

1 Raymond Lully (1232–1315) was a Catalan theologian whose *Ars Magna* purported to provide a universal method of discovery.

than a science which cultivates it. For this reason I thought I had to seek some other method comprising the advantages of these three subjects but free from their defects. Now a multiplicity of laws often provides an excuse for vices, so that a state is much better governed when it has only a few laws which are strictly observed; in the same way, I thought, in place of the large number of rules that make up logic, I would find the following four to be sufficient, provided that I made a strong and unswerving resolution never to fail to observe them.

The first was never to accept anything as true if I did not have evident knowledge of its truth: that is, carefully to avoid precipitate conclusions and preconceptions, and to include nothing more in my judgements than what presented itself to my mind so clearly and so distinctly that I had no occasion to call it into doubt.

The second, to divide each of the difficulties I examined into as many parts as possible and as may be required in order to resolve them better.

The third, to direct my thoughts in an orderly manner, by beginning with the simplest and most easily known objects in order to ascend little by little, step by step, to knowledge of the most complex, and by supposing some order even among objects that have no natural order of precedence. 19

And the last, throughout to make enumerations so complete, and reviews so comprehensive, that I could be sure of leaving nothing out.

Those long chains composed of very simple and easy reasonings, which geometers customarily use to arrive at their most difficult demonstrations, had given me occasion to suppose that all the things which come within the scope of human knowledge are interconnected in the same way. And I thought that, provided we refrain from accepting anything as true which is not, and always keep to the order required for deducing one thing from another, there can be nothing too remote to be reached in the end or too well hidden to be discovered. I had no great difficulty in deciding which things to begin with, for I knew already that it must be with the simplest and most easily known. Reflecting, too, that of all those who have hitherto sought after truth in the sciences, mathematicians alone have been able to find any demonstrations – that is to say, certain and evident reasonings – I had no doubt that I should begin with the very things that they studied. From this, however, the only advantage I hoped to gain was to accustom my mind to nourish itself on truths and not to be satisfied with bad reasoning. Nor did I have any intention of trying to learn all the special sciences commonly called 'mathematics'.[1] For I saw that, despite the diversity of their objects, they agree in considering nothing but the 20 various relations or proportions that hold between these objects. And so I

---

1 These are subjects with a theoretical basis in mathematics, such as astronomy, music and optics.

thought it best to examine only such proportions in general, supposing them to hold only between such items as would help me to know them more easily. At the same time I would not restrict them to these items, so that I could apply them the better afterwards to whatever others they might fit. Next I observed that in order to know these proportions I would need sometimes to consider them separately, and sometimes merely to keep them in mind or understand many together. And I thought that in order the better to consider them separately I should suppose them to hold between lines, because I did not find anything simpler, nor anything that I could represent more distinctly to my imagination and senses. But in order to keep them in mind or understand several together, I thought it necessary to designate them by the briefest possible symbols. In this way I would take over all that is best in geometrical analysis and in algebra, using the one to correct all the defects of the other.

In fact, I venture to say that by strictly observing the few rules I had chosen, I became very adept at unravelling all the questions which come within the scope of these two sciences. So much so, in fact, that in the two or three months I spent in examining them – beginning with the simplest and most general and using each truth I found as a rule for finding further truths – not only did I solve many problems which I had previously thought very difficult, but also it seemed to me towards the end that even in those cases where I was still in the dark I could determine by what means and to what extent it was possible to find a solution. This claim will not appear too arrogant if you consider that since there is only one truth concerning any matter, whoever discovers this truth knows as much about it as can be known. For example, if a child who has been taught arithmetic does a sum following the rules, he can be sure of having found everything the human mind can discover regarding the sum he was considering. In short, the method which instructs us to follow the correct order, and to enumerate exactly all the relevant factors, contains everything that gives certainty to the rules of arithmetic.

But what pleased me most about this method was that by following it I was sure in every case to use my reason, if not perfectly, at least as well as was in my power. Moreover, as I practised the method I felt my mind gradually become accustomed to conceiving its objects more clearly and distinctly; and since I did not restrict the method to any particular subject-matter, I hoped to apply it as usefully to the problems of the other sciences as I had to those of algebra. Not that I would have dared to try at the outset to examine every problem that might arise, for that would itself have been contrary to the order which the method prescribes. But observing that the principles of these sciences must all be derived from

philosophy, in which I had not yet discovered any certain ones, I thought 22
that first of all I had to try to establish some certain principles in
philosophy. And since this is the most important task of all, and the one
in which precipitate conclusions and preconceptions are most to be
feared, I thought that I ought not try to accomplish it until I had reached a
more mature age than twenty-three, as I then was, and until I had first
spent a long time in preparing myself for it. I had to uproot from my
mind all the wrong opinions I had previously accepted, amass a variety of
experiences to serve as the subject-matter of my reasonings, and practise
constantly my self-prescribed method in order to strengthen myself more
and more in its use.

PART THREE

Now, before starting to rebuild your house, it is not enough simply to
pull it down, to make provision for materials and architects (or else train
yourself in architecture), and to have carefully drawn up the plans; you
must also provide yourself with some other place where you can live
comfortably while building is in progress. Likewise, lest I should remain
indecisive in my actions while reason obliged me to be so in my
judgements, and in order to live as happily as I could during this time, I
formed for myself a provisional moral code consisting of just three or
four maxims, which I should like to tell you about.

The first was to obey the laws and customs of my country, holding 23
constantly to the religion in which by God's grace I had been instructed
from my childhood, and governing myself in all other matters according
to the most moderate and least extreme opinions – the opinions
commonly accepted in practice by the most sensible of those with whom I
should have to live. For I had begun at this time to count my own
opinions as worthless, because I wished to submit them all to examination, and so I was sure I could do no better than follow those of the most
sensible men. And although there may be men as sensible among the
Persians or Chinese as among ourselves, I thought it would be most
useful for me to be guided by those with whom I should have to live. I
thought too that in order to discover what opinions they really held I had
to attend to what they did rather than what they said. For with our
declining standards of behaviour, few people are willing to say everything that they believe; and besides, many people do not know what they
believe, since believing something and knowing that one believes it are
different acts of thinking, and the one often occurs without the other.
Where many opinions were equally well accepted, I chose only the most
moderate, both because these are always the easiest to act upon and

probably the best (excess being usually bad), and also so that if I made a mistake, I should depart less from the right path than I would if I chose one extreme when I ought to have pursued the other. In particular, I counted as excessive all promises by which we give up some of our freedom. It was not that I disapproved of laws which remedy the inconstancy of weak minds by allowing us to make vows or contracts that oblige perseverance in some worthy project (or even, for the security of commerce, in some indifferent one). But I saw nothing in the world which remained always in the same state, and for my part I was determined to make my judgements more and more perfect, rather than worse. For these reasons I thought I would be sinning against good sense if I were to take my previous approval of something as obliging me to regard it as good later on, when it had perhaps ceased to be good or I no longer regarded it as such.

My second maxim was to be as firm and decisive in my actions as I could, and to follow even the most doubtful opinions, once I had adopted them, with no less constancy than if they had been quite certain. In this respect I would be imitating a traveller who, upon finding himself lost in a forest, should not wander about turning this way and that, and still less stay in one place, but should keep walking as straight as he can in one direction, never changing it for slight reasons even if mere chance made him choose it in the first place; for in this way, even if he does not go exactly where he wishes, he will at least end up in a place where he is likely to be better off than in the middle of a forest. Similarly, since in everyday life we must often act without delay, it is a most certain truth that when it is not in our power to discern the truest opinions, we must follow the most probable. Even when no opinions appear more probable than any others, we must still adopt some; and having done so we must then regard them not as doubtful, from a practical point of view, but as most true and certain, on the grounds that the reason which made us adopt them is itself true and certain. By following this maxim I could free myself from all the regrets and remorse which usually trouble the consciences of those weak and faltering spirits who allow themselves to set out on some supposedly good course of action which later, in their inconstancy, they judge to be bad.

My third maxim was to try always to master myself rather than fortune, and change my desires rather than the order of the world. In general I would become accustomed to believing that nothing lies entirely within our power except our thoughts, so that after doing our best in dealing with things external to us, whatever we fail to achieve is absolutely impossible so far as we are concerned. This alone, I thought, would be sufficient to prevent me from desiring in future something I could not get, and so to make me content. For our will naturally tends to desire only what our intellect represents to it as somehow possible; and so it is certain that if we consider all external goods as equally beyond our power, we shall not regret the absence of goods which seem to be our birthright when we are deprived of them through no fault of our own, any more than we regret not possessing the kingdom of China or of Mexico. Making a virtue of necessity, as they say, we shall not desire to be healthy when ill or free when imprisoned, any more than we now desire to have bodies of a material as indestructible as diamond or wings to fly like the birds. But I admit that it takes long practice and repeated meditation to become accustomed to seeing everything in this light. In this, I believe, lay the secret of those philosophers who in earlier times were able to escape from the dominion of fortune and, despite suffering and poverty, rival their gods in happiness. Through constant reflection upon the limits prescribed for them by nature, they became perfectly convinced that nothing was in their power but their thoughts, and this alone was sufficient to prevent them from being attracted to other things. Their mastery over their thoughts was so absolute that they had reason to count themselves richer, more powerful, freer and happier than other men who, because they lack this philosophy, never achieve such mastery over all their desires, however favoured by nature and fortune they may be.

Finally, to conclude this moral code, I decided to review the various occupations which men have in this life, in order to try to choose the best. Without wishing to say anything about the occupations of others, I thought I could do no better than to continue with the very one I was engaged in, and devote my whole life to cultivating my reason and advancing as far as I could in the knowledge of the truth, following the method I had prescribed for myself. Since beginning to use this method I had felt such great satisfaction that I thought one could not have any sweeter or purer enjoyment in this life. Every day I discovered by its means truths which, it seemed to me, were quite important and were generally unknown by other men; and the satisfaction they gave me so filled my mind that nothing else mattered to me. Besides, the sole basis of the foregoing three maxims was the plan I had to continue my self-instruction. For since God has given each of us a light to distinguish truth from falsehood, I should not have thought myself obliged to rest content with the opinions of others for a single moment if I had not intended in due course to examine them using my own judgement; and I could not have avoided having scruples about following these opinions, if I had not hoped to take every opportunity to discover better ones, in case there were any. Lastly, I could not have limited my desires, or been happy, had I not been following a path by which I thought I was sure to acquire all the knowledge of which I was capable, and in this way all the true goods within my reach. For since our will tends to pursue or avoid only what our intellect represents to it as good or bad, we need only to judge well in order to act well, and to judge as well as we can in order to do our best – that is to say, in order to acquire all the virtues and in general all the other goods we can acquire. And when we are certain of this, we cannot fail to be happy.

Once I had established these maxims and set them on one side together with the truths of faith, which have always been foremost among my beliefs, I judged that I could freely undertake to rid myself of all the rest of my opinions. As I expected to be able to achieve this more readily by talking with other men than by staying shut up in the stove-heated room where I had had all these thoughts, I set out on my travels again before the end of winter. Throughout the following nine years I did nothing but roam about in the world, trying to be a spectator rather than an actor in all the comedies that are played out there. Reflecting especially upon the points in every subject which might make it suspect and give occasion for us to make mistakes, I kept uprooting from my mind any errors that might previously have slipped into it. In doing this I was not copying the sceptics, who doubt only for the sake of doubting and pretend to be always undecided; on the contrary, my whole aim was to reach certainty – to cast aside the loose earth and sand so as to come upon rock or clay. In this I think I was quite successful. For I tried to expose the falsity or uncertainty of the propositions I was examining by clear and certain arguments, not by weak conjectures; and I never encountered any proposition so doubtful that I could not draw from it some quite certain conclusion – if only the conclusion that it contained nothing certain. And, just as in pulling down an old house we usually keep the remnants for use in building a new one, so in destroying all those opinions of mine that I judged ill-founded I made various observations and acquired many experiences which I have since used in establishing more certain opinions. Moreover, I continued practising the method I had prescribed for myself. Besides taking care in general to conduct all my thoughts according to its rules, I set aside some hours now and again to apply it more particularly to mathematical problems. I also applied it to certain other problems which I could put into something like mathematical form by detaching them from all the principles of the other sciences, which I did not find sufficiently secure (as you will see I have done in many problems discussed later in this book).[1] Thus, while appearing to live like those concerned only to lead an agreeable and blameless life, who take

1 Here Descartes is referring to the scientific problems which he deals with in the essays published with the *Discourse on the Method*.

care to keep their pleasures free from vices, and who engage in every honest pastime in order to enjoy their leisure without boredom, I never stopped pursuing my project, and I made perhaps more progress in the knowledge of the truth than I would have if I had done nothing but read books or mix with men of learning.

Those nine years passed by, however, without my taking any side regarding the questions which are commonly debated among the learned, or beginning to search for the foundations of any philosophy more certain than the commonly accepted one. The example of many fine intellects who had previously had this project, but had not, I thought, met with success, made me imagine the difficulties to be so great that I would not have dared to embark upon it so soon if I had not noticed that some people were spreading the rumour that I had already completed it. I cannot say what basis they had for this opinion. If I contributed anything to it by my conversation, it must have been because I confessed my ignorance more ingenuously than is customary for those with a little learning, and perhaps also because I displayed the reasons I had for doubting many things which others regard as certain, rather than because I boasted of some learning. But as I was honest enough not to wish to be taken for what I was not, I thought I had to try by every means to become worthy of the reputation that was given me. Exactly eight years ago this desire made me resolve to move away from any place where I might have acquaintances and retire to this country, where the long duration of the war has led to the establishment of such order that the armies maintained here seem to serve only to make the enjoyment of the fruits of peace all the more secure.[1] Living here, amidst this great mass of busy people who are more concerned with their own affairs than curious about those of others, I have been able to lead a life as solitary and withdrawn as if I were in the most remote desert, while lacking none of the comforts found in the most populous cities.

PART FOUR

I do not know whether I should tell you of the first meditations that I had there, for they are perhaps too metaphysical and uncommon for everyone's taste. And yet, to make it possible to judge whether the foundations I have chosen are firm enough, I am in a way obliged to speak of them. For a long time I had observed, as noted above, that in practical life it is sometimes necessary to act on opinions as if they were indubitable, even when one knows that they are quite uncertain. But since I now wished to devote myself solely to the search for truth, I thought it necessary to do the

1 Descartes settled in Holland in 1629. The war was that conducted by the United Provinces against Spain from 1572 to 1648.

very opposite and reject as if absolutely false everything in which I could imagine the least doubt, in order to see if I was left believing anything that was entirely indubitable. Thus, because our senses sometimes deceive us, I decided to suppose that nothing was such as they led us to imagine. And since there are men who make mistakes in reasoning, committing logical fallacies concerning the simplest questions in geometry, and because I judged that I was as prone to error as anyone else, I rejected as unsound all the arguments I had previously taken as demonstrative proofs. Lastly, considering that the very thoughts we have while awake may also occur while we sleep without any of them being at that time true, I resolved to pretend that all the things that had ever entered my mind were no more true than the illusions of my dreams. But immediately I noticed that while I was endeavouring in this way to think that everything was false, it was necessary that I, who was thinking this, was something. And observing that this truth '*I am thinking, therefore I exist*' was so firm and sure that all the most extravagant suppositions of the sceptics were incapable of shaking it, I decided that I could accept it without scruple as the first principle of the philosophy I was seeking.

Next I examined attentively what I was. I saw that while I could pretend that I had no body and that there was no world and no place for me to be in, I could not for all that pretend that I did not exist. I saw on the contrary that from the mere fact that I thought of doubting the truth of other things, it followed quite evidently and certainly that I existed; whereas if I had merely ceased thinking, even if everything else I had ever imagined had been true, I should have had no reason to believe that I existed. From this I knew I was a substance whose whole essence or nature is solely to think, and which does not require any place, or depend on any material thing, in order to exist. Accordingly this 'I' – that is, the soul by which I am what I am – is entirely distinct from the body, and indeed is easier to know than the body, and would not fail to be whatever it is, even if the body did not exist.

After this I considered in general what is required of a proposition in order for it to be true and certain; for since I had just found one that I knew to be such, I thought that I ought also to know what this certainty consists in. I observed that there is nothing at all in the proposition '*I am thinking, therefore I exist*' to assure me that I am speaking the truth, except that I see very clearly that in order to think it is necessary to exist. So I decided that I could take it as a general rule that the things we conceive very clearly and very distinctly are all true; only there is some difficulty in recognizing which are the things that we distinctly conceive.

Next, reflecting upon the fact that I was doubting and that consequently my being was not wholly perfect (for I saw clearly that it is a greater perfection to know than to doubt), I decided to inquire into the source of my ability to think of something more perfect than I was; and I recognized very clearly that this had to come from some nature that was 34 in fact more perfect. Regarding the thoughts I had of many other things outside me, like the heavens, the earth, light, heat and numerous others, I had no such difficulty in knowing where they came from. For I observed nothing in them that seemed to make them superior to me; and so I could believe that, if they were true, they depended on my nature in so far as it had any perfection, and if they were not true, I got them from nothing – in other words, they were in me because I had some defect. But the same could not hold for the idea of a being more perfect than my own. For it was manifestly impossible to get this from nothing; and I could not have got it from myself since it is no less contradictory that the more perfect should result from the less perfect, and depend on it, than that something should proceed from nothing. So there remained only the possibility that the idea had been put into me by a nature truly more perfect than I was and even possessing in itself all the perfections of which I could have any idea, that is – to explain myself in one word – by God. To this I added that since I knew of some perfections that I did not possess, I was not the only being which existed (here, by your leave, I shall freely use some scholastic terminology), but there had of necessity to be some other, more perfect being on which I depended and from which I had acquired all that I possessed. For if I had existed alone and independently of every other being, so that I had got from myself what little of the perfect being I 35 participated in, then for the same reason I could have got from myself everything else I knew I lacked, and thus been myself infinite, eternal, immutable, omniscient, omnipotent; in short, I could have had all the perfections which I could observe to be in God. For, according to the arguments I have just advanced, in order to know the nature of God, as far as my own nature was capable of knowing it, I had only to consider, for each thing of which I found in myself some idea, whether or not it was a perfection to possess it; and I was sure that none of those which indicated any imperfection was in God, but that all the others were. Thus I saw that doubt, inconstancy, sadness and the like could not be in God, since I myself would have been very glad to be free from them. Besides this, I had ideas of many corporeal things capable of being perceived by the senses; for even if I were to suppose that I was dreaming and that whatever I saw or imagined was false, yet I could not deny that the ideas were truly in my mind. But since I had already recognized very clearly from my own case that the intellectual nature is distinct from the corporeal, and as I observed that all composition is evidence of dependence and that dependence is manifestly a defect, I concluded that it could not be a perfection in God to be composed of these two natures, and consequently that he was not composed of them. But if there were any bodies in the world, or any intelligences or other natures that were not wholly perfect, their being must depend on God's power in such a manner that they could not subsist for a single moment without him.

After that, wishing to seek other truths, I considered the object studied by geometers. I conceived of this as a continuous body, or a space indefinitely extended in length, breadth and height or depth, and divisible into different parts which may have various shapes and sizes, and may be moved or transposed in every way: for all this is assumed by geometers in their object of study. I went through some of their simpler demonstrations and noted that the great certainty which everyone ascribes to them is founded solely on their being conceived as evident (in accordance with the rule stated above). I noted also that there was nothing at all in these demonstrations which assured me of the existence of their object. For example, I saw clearly that the three angles of any given triangle must equal two right angles; yet for all that, I saw nothing which assured me that there existed any triangle in the world. Whereas when I looked again at the idea I had of a perfect being, I found that this included existence in the same way as – or even more evidently than – the idea of a triangle includes the equality of its three angles to two right angles, or the idea of a sphere includes the equidistance of all the points on the surface from the centre. Thus I concluded that it is at least as certain as any geometrical proof that God, who is this perfect being, is or exists.

But many are convinced that there is some difficulty in knowing God, and even in knowing what their soul is. The reason for this is that they never raise their minds above things which can be perceived by the senses: they are so used to thinking of things only by imagining them (a way of thinking specially suited to material things) that whatever is unimaginable seems to them unintelligible. This is sufficiently obvious from the fact that even the scholastic philosophers take it as a maxim that there is nothing in the intellect which has not previously been in the senses; and yet it is certain that the ideas of God and of the soul have never been in the senses. It seems to me that trying to use one's imagination in order to understand these ideas is like trying to use one's eyes in order to hear sounds or smell odours – though there is this difference, that the sense of sight gives us no less assurance of the reality of its objects than do the senses of smell and hearing, while neither our imagination nor our senses could ever assure us of anything without the intervention of our intellect.

Finally, if there are still people who are not sufficiently convinced of the existence of God and of their soul by the arguments I have proposed,

I would have them know that everything else of which they may think themselves more sure – such as their having a body, there being stars and an earth, and the like – is less certain. For although we have a moral certainty[1] about these things, so that it seems we cannot doubt them without being extravagant, nevertheless when it is a question of metaphysical certainty, we cannot reasonably deny that there are adequate grounds for not being entirely sure about them. We need only observe that in sleep we may imagine in the same way that we have a different body and see different stars and a different earth, without there being any of these things. For how do we know that the thoughts which come to us in dreams are any more false than the others, seeing that they are often no less lively and distinct? However much the best minds study this question, I do not believe they will·be able to give any reason sufficient to remove this doubt unless they presuppose the existence of God. For in the first place, what I took just now as a rule, namely that everything we conceive very clearly and very distinctly is true, is assured only for the reasons that God is or exists, that he is a perfect being, and that everything in us comes from him. It follows that our ideas or notions, being real things and coming from God, cannot be anything but true, in every respect in which they are clear and distinct. Thus, if we frequently have ideas containing some falsity, this can happen only because there is something confused and obscure in them, for in that respect they participate in nothingness, that is, they are in us in this confused state only because we are not wholly perfect. And it is evident that it is no less contradictory that falsity or imperfection as such should proceed from God than that truth or perfection should proceed from nothingness. But if we did not know that everything real and true within us comes from a perfect and infinite being then, however clear and distinct our ideas were, we would have no reason to be sure that they had the perfection of being true.

But once the knowledge of God and the soul has made us certain of this rule, it is easy to recognize that the things we imagine in dreams should in no way make us doubt the truth of the thoughts we have when awake. For if one happened even in sleep to have some very distinct idea (if, say, a geometer devised some new proof), one's being asleep would not prevent the idea from being true. And as to the most common error of our dreams, which consists in their representing various objects to us in the same way as our external senses do, it does not matter that this gives us occasion to doubt the truth of such ideas, for often they can also mislead us without our being asleep – as when those with jaundice see

1 See footnote 2, p. 210 below.

everything coloured yellow, or when stars or other very distant bodies appear to us much smaller than they are. For after all, whether we are awake or asleep, we ought never to let ourselves be convinced except by the evidence of our reason. It will be observed that I say 'our reason', not

40 'our imagination' or 'our senses'. Even though we see the sun very clearly, we must not judge on that account that it is only as large as we see it; and we can distinctly imagine a lion's head on a goat's body without having to conclude from this that a chimera exists in the world. For reason does not insist that what we thus see or imagine is true. But it does insist that all our ideas or notions must have some foundation of truth; for otherwise it would not be possible that God, who is all-perfect and all-truthful, should have placed them in us. And our reasonings are never so evident or complete in sleep as in waking life, although sometimes our imaginings in sleep are as lively and distinct as in waking life, or more so. Hence reason also demands that, since our thoughts cannot all be true because we are not wholly perfect, what truth they do possess must inevitably be found in the thoughts we have when awake, rather than in our dreams.

PART FIVE

I would gladly go on and reveal the whole chain of other truths that I deduced from these first ones. But in order to do this I would have to discuss many questions that are being debated among the learned, and I do not wish to quarrel with them. So it will be better, I think, for me not to do this, and merely to say in general what these questions are, so as to let those who are wiser decide whether it would be useful for the public

41 to be informed more specifically about them. I have always remained firm in the resolution I had taken to assume no principle other than the one I have just used to demonstrate the existence of God and of the soul, and to accept nothing as true which did not seem to me clearer and more certain than the demonstrations of the geometers had hitherto seemed. And yet I venture to say that I have found a way to satisfy myself within a short time about all the principal difficulties usually discussed in philosophy. What is more, I have noticed certain laws which God has so established in nature, and of which he has implanted such notions in our minds, that after adequate reflection we cannot doubt that they are exactly observed in everything which exists or occurs in the world. Moreover, by considering what follows from these laws it seems to me that I have discovered many truths more useful and important than anything I had previously learned or even hoped to learn.

I endeavoured to explain the most important of these truths in a treatise which certain considerations prevent me from publishing, and I know of no better way to make them known than by summarizing its contents.[1] My aim was to include in it everything I thought I knew about the nature of material things before I began to write it. Now a painter cannot represent all the different sides of a solid body equally well on his flat canvas, and so he chooses one of the principal ones, sets it facing the light, and shades the others so as to make them stand out only when viewed from the perspective of the chosen side. In just the same way, fearing that I could not put everything I had in mind into my discourse, I undertook merely to expound quite fully what I understood about light. Then, as the occasion arose, I added something about the sun and fixed stars, because almost all light comes from them; about the heavens, because they transmit light; about planets, comets and the earth, because they reflect light; about terrestrial bodies in particular, because they are either coloured or transparent or luminous; and finally about man, because he observes these bodies. But I did not want to bring these matters too much into the open, for I wished to be free to say what I thought about them without having either to follow or to refute the accepted opinions of the learned. So I decided to leave our world wholly for them to argue about, and to speak solely of what would happen in a new world. I therefore supposed that God now created, somewhere in imaginary spaces, enough matter to compose such a world; that he variously and randomly agitated the different parts of this matter so as to form a chaos as confused as any the poets could invent; and that he then did nothing but lend his regular concurrence to nature, leaving it to act according to the laws he established. First of all, then, I described this matter, trying to represent it so that there is absolutely nothing, I think, which is clearer and more intelligible, with the exception of what has just been said about God and the soul. In fact I expressly supposed that this matter lacked all those forms or qualities about which they dispute in the Schools, and in general that it had only those features the knowledge of which was so natural to our souls that we could not even pretend not to know them. Further, I showed what the laws of nature were, and without basing my arguments on any principle other than the infinite perfections of God, I tried to demonstrate all those laws about which we could have any doubt, and to show that they are such that, even if God created many worlds, there could not be any in which they failed to be observed. After this, I showed how, in consequence of these laws, the greater part of the matter of this chaos had to become disposed and arranged in a certain way, which made it resemble our heavens; and how, at the same time,

---

1 The treatise of which *The World* and the *Treatise on Man* are parts. See AT XI 3ff; CSM I 79ff.

some of its parts had to form an earth, some planets and comets, and others a sun and fixed stars. Here I dwelt upon the subject of light, explaining at some length the nature of the light that had to be present in the sun and the stars, how from there it travelled instantaneously across the immense distances of the heavens, and how it was reflected from the planets and comets to the earth. To this I added many points about the substance, position, motions and all the various qualities of these heavens and stars; and I thought I had thereby said enough to show that for anything observed in the heavens and stars of our world, something wholly similar had to appear, or at least could appear, in those of the

44   world I was describing. From that I went on to speak of the earth in particular: how, although I had expressly supposed that God had put no gravity into the matter of which it was formed, yet all its parts tended exactly towards its centre; how, there being water and air on its surface, the disposition of the heavens and heavenly bodies (chiefly the moon), had to cause an ebb and flow similar in all respects to that observed in our seas, as well as a current of both water and air from east to west like the one we observe between the tropics; how mountains, seas, springs and rivers could be formed naturally there, and how metals could appear in mines, plants grow in fields, and generally how all the bodies we call 'mixed' or 'composite' could come into being there. Among other things, I took pains to make everything belonging to the nature of fire very clearly understandable, because I know nothing else in the world, apart from the heavenly bodies, that produces light. Thus I made clear how it is formed and fuelled, how sometimes it possesses only heat without light, and sometimes light without heat; how it can produce different colours and various other qualities in different bodies; how it melts some bodies and hardens others; how it can consume almost all bodies, or turn them into ashes and smoke; and finally how it can, by the mere force of its

45   action, form glass from these ashes – something I took particular pleasure in describing since it seems to me as wonderful a transmutation as any that takes place in nature.

Yet I did not wish to infer from all this that our world was created in the way I proposed, for it is much more likely that from the beginning God made it just as it had to be. But it is certain, and it is an opinion commonly accepted among theologians, that the act by which God now preserves it is just the same as that by which he created it. So, even if in the beginning God had given the world only the form of a chaos, provided that he established the laws of nature and then lent his concurrence to enable nature to operate as it normally does, we may believe without impugning the miracle of creation that by this means alone all purely material things could in the course of time have come to be just as we now see them. And their nature is much easier to conceive if we see them develop gradually in this way than if we consider them only in their completed form.

From the description of inanimate bodies and plants I went on to describe animals, and in particular men. But I did not yet have sufficient knowledge to speak of them in the same manner as I did of the other things – that is, by demonstrating effects from causes and showing from what seeds and in what manner nature must produce them. So I contented myself with supposing that God formed the body of a man exactly like our own both in the outward shape of its limbs and in the internal arrangement of its organs, using for its composition nothing but the matter that I had described. I supposed, too, that in the beginning God did not place in this body any rational soul or any other thing to serve as a vegetative or sensitive soul, but rather that he kindled in its heart one of those fires without light which I had already explained, and whose nature I understood to be no different from that of the fire which heats hay when it has been stored before it is dry, or which causes new wine to seethe when it is left to ferment from the crushed grapes. And when I looked to see what functions would occur in such a body I found precisely those which may occur in us without our thinking of them, and hence without any contribution from our soul (that is, from that part of us, distinct from the body, whose nature, as I have said previously, is simply to think). These functions are just the ones in which animals without reason may be said to resemble us. But I could find none of the functions which, depending on thought, are the only ones that belong to us as men; though I found all these later on, once I had supposed that God created a rational soul and joined it to this body in a particular way which I described.

But so that you might see how I dealt with this subject, I shall give my explanation of the movement of the heart and the arteries.[1]

*   *   *

I explained all these matters in sufficient detail in the treatise I previously intended to publish.[2] And then I showed what structure the nerves and muscles of the human body must have in order to make the animal spirits inside them strong enough to move its limbs – as when we see severed heads continue to move about and bite the earth although they are no longer alive. I also indicated what changes must occur in

1 We omit the passage containing this explanation. It is summarized in the *Passions*, art. 7–9 (below, pp. 220–1).
2 See footnote p. 41 above.

the brain in order to cause waking, sleep and dreams; how light, sounds, smells, tastes, heat and the other qualities of external objects can imprint various ideas on the brain through the mediation of the senses; and how hunger, thirst, and the other internal passions can also send their ideas there. And I explained which part of the brain must be taken to be the 'common' sense,[1] where these ideas are received; the memory, which preserves them; and the corporeal imagination, which can change them in various ways, form them into new ideas, and, by distributing the animal spirits to the muscles, make the parts of this body move in as many different ways as the parts of our bodies can move without being guided by the will, and in a manner which is just as appropriate to the objects of the senses and the internal passions. This will not seem at all strange to those who know how many kinds of automatons, or moving machines, the skill of man can construct with the use of very few parts, in comparison with the great multitude of bones, muscles, nerves, arteries, veins and all the other parts that are in the body of any animal. For they will regard this body as a machine which, having been made by the hand of God, is incomparably better ordered than any machine that can be devised by man, and contains in itself movements more wonderful than those in any such machine.

I made special efforts to show that if any such machines had the organs and outward shape of a monkey or of some other animal that lacks reason, we should have no means of knowing that they did not possess entirely the same nature as these animals; whereas if any such machines bore a resemblance to our bodies and imitated our actions as closely as possible for all practical purposes, we should still have two very certain means of recognizing that they were not real men. The first is that they could never use words, or put together other signs, as we do in order to declare our thoughts to others. For we can certainly conceive of a machine so constructed that it utters words, and even utters words which correspond to bodily actions causing a change in its organs (e.g. if you touch it in one spot it asks what you want of it, if you touch it in another it cries out that you are hurting it, and so on). But it is not conceivable that such a machine should produce different arrangements of words so as to give an appropriately meaningful answer to whatever is said in its presence, as the dullest of men can do. Secondly, even though such machines might do some things as well as we do them, or perhaps even better, they would inevitably fail in others, which would reveal that they were acting not through understanding but only from the disposition of their organs. For whereas reason is a universal instrument which can be used in all kinds of situations, these organs need some particular

1 See footnote, p. 120 below.

disposition for each particular action; hence it is for all practical purposes impossible for a machine to have enough different organs to make it act in all the contingencies of life in the way in which our reason makes us act.

Now in just these two ways we can also know the difference between man and beast. For it is quite remarkable that there are no men so dull-witted or stupid – and this includes even madmen – that they are incapable of arranging various words together and forming an utterance from them in order to make their thoughts understood; whereas there is no other animal, however perfect and well-endowed it may be, that can do the like. This does not happen because they lack the necessary organs, for we see that magpies and parrots can utter words as we do, and yet they cannot speak as we do: that is, they cannot show that they are thinking what they are saying. On the other hand, men born deaf and dumb, and thus deprived of speech-organs as much as the beasts or even   58 more so, normally invent their own signs to make themselves understood by those who, being regularly in their company, have the time to learn their language. This shows not merely that the beasts have less reason than men, but that they have no reason at all. For it patently requires very little reason to be able to speak; and since as much inequality can be observed among the animals of a given species as among human beings, and some animals are more easily trained than others, it would be incredible that a superior specimen of the monkey or parrot species should not be able to speak as well as the stupidest child – or at least as well as a child with a defective brain – if their souls were not completely different in nature from ours. And we must not confuse speech with the natural movements which express passions and which can be imitated by machines as well as by animals. Nor should we think, like some of the ancients, that the beasts speak, although we do not understand their language. For if that were true, then since they have many organs that correspond to ours, they could make themselves understood by us as well as by their fellows. It is also a very remarkable fact that although many animals show more skill than we do in some of their actions, yet the same animals show none at all in many others; so what they do better does not prove that they have any intelligence, for if it did then they would have more intelligence than any of us and would excel us in everything. It   59 proves rather that they have no intelligence at all, and that it is nature which acts in them according to the disposition of their organs. In the same way a clock, consisting only of wheels and springs, can count the hours and measure time more accurately than we can with all our wisdom.

After that, I described the rational soul, and showed that, unlike the other things of which I had spoken, it cannot be derived in any way from the potentiality of matter, but must be specially created.[1] And I showed how it is not sufficient for it to be lodged in the human body like a helmsman in his ship, except perhaps to move its limbs, but that it must be more closely joined and united with the body in order to have, besides this power of movement, feelings and appetites like ours and so constitute a real man. Here I dwelt a little upon the subject of the soul, because it is of the greatest importance. For after the error of those who deny God, which I believe I have already adequately refuted, there is none that leads weak minds further from the straight path of virtue than that of imagining that the souls of the beasts are of the same nature as ours, and hence that after this present life we have nothing to fear or to hope for, any more than flies and ants. But when we know how much the beasts differ from us, we understand much better the arguments which prove that our soul is of a nature entirely independent of the body, and consequently that it is not bound to die with it. And since we cannot see any other causes which destroy the soul, we are naturally led to conclude that it is immortal.

PART SIX

It is now three years since I reached the end of the treatise that contains all these things. I was beginning to revise it in order to put it in the hands of a publisher, when I learned that some persons to whom I defer and who have hardly less authority over my actions than my own reason has over my thoughts, had disapproved of a physical theory published a little while before by someone else.[2] I will not say that I accepted this theory, but only that before their condemnation I had noticed nothing in it that I could imagine to be prejudicial either to religion or to the state, and hence nothing that would have prevented me from publishing it myself, if reason had convinced me of it. This made me fear that there might be some mistake in one of my own theories, in spite of the great care I had always taken never to adopt any new opinion for which I had no certain demonstration, and never to write anything that might work to anyone's disadvantage. That was enough to make me change my previous decision to publish my views. For although I had had very strong reasons for this decision, my inclination, which has always made me dislike the business of writing books, prompted me to find excuses enough for deciding otherwise. The reasons, on one side and the other, are such that not only do I have some interest in stating them here, but also the public may be interested to know what they are.

1 The section of the *Treatise on Man* referred to here has not survived.
2 Galileo, whose *Dialogue Concerning the Two Chief World Systems* was published in 1632 and condemned by the Congregation of the Holy Office in 1633.

I have never made much of the products of my own mind; and so long as the only fruits I gathered from the method I use were my own satisfaction regarding certain difficulties in the speculative sciences, or else my attempts to govern my own conduct by the principles I learned from it, I did not think I was obliged to write anything about it. For as regards conduct, everyone is so full of his own wisdom that we might find as many reformers as heads if permission to institute change in these matters were granted to anyone other than those whom God has set up as sovereigns over his people or those on whom he has bestowed sufficient grace and zeal to be prophets. As regards my speculations, although they pleased me very much, I realized that other people had their own which perhaps pleased them more. But as soon as I had acquired some general notions in physics and had noticed, as I began to test them in various particular problems, where they could lead and how much they differ from the principles used up to now, I believed that I could not keep them secret without sinning gravely against the law which obliges us to do all in our power to secure the general welfare of mankind. For they opened my eyes to the possibility of gaining knowledge which would be very useful in life, and of discovering a practical philosophy which might replace the speculative philosophy taught in the schools. Through this 62 philosophy we could know the power and action of fire, water, air, the stars, the heavens and all the other bodies in our environment, as distinctly as we know the various crafts of our artisans; and we could use this knowledge – as the artisans use theirs – for all the purposes for which it is appropriate, and thus make ourselves, as it were, the lords and masters of nature. This is desirable not only for the invention of innumerable devices which would facilitate our enjoyment of the fruits of the earth and all the goods we find there, but also, and most importantly, for the maintenance of health, which is undoubtedly the chief good and the foundation of all the other goods in this life. For even the mind depends so much on the temperament and disposition of the bodily organs that if it is possible to find some means of making men in general wiser and more skilful than they have been up till now, I believe we must look for it in medicine. It is true that medicine as currently practised does not contain much of any significant use; but without intending to disparage it, I am sure there is no one, even among its practitioners, who would not admit that all we know in medicine is almost nothing in comparison with what remains to be known, and that we might free ourselves from innumerable diseases, both of the body and of the mind, and perhaps even from the infirmity of old age, if we had sufficient knowledge of their causes and of all the remedies that nature has provided. Intending as I did to devote my life to the pursuit of such 63 indispensable knowledge, I discovered a path which would, I thought, inevitably lead us to it, unless prevented by the brevity of life or the lack of observations.[1] And I judged that the best remedy against these two obstacles was to communicate faithfully to the public what little I had discovered, and to urge the best minds to try and make further progress by helping with the necessary observations, each according to his inclination and ability, and by communicating to the public everything they learn. Thus, by building upon the work of our predecessors and combining the lives and labours of many, we might make much greater progress working together than anyone could make on his own.

I also noticed, regarding observations, that the further we advance in our knowledge, the more necessary they become. At the beginning, rather than seeking those which are more unusual and highly contrived, it is better to resort only to those which, presenting themselves spontaneously to our senses, cannot be unknown to us if we reflect even a little. The reason for this is that the more unusual observations are apt to mislead us when we do not yet know the causes of the more common ones, and the factors on which they depend are almost always so special and so minute that it is very difficult to discern them. But the order I have adopted in this regard is the following. First I tried to discover in general the 64   principles or first causes of everything that exists or can exist in the world. To this end I considered nothing but God alone, who created the world; and I derived these principles only from certain seeds of truth which are naturally in our souls. Next I examined the first and most ordinary effects deducible from these causes. In this way, it seems to me, I discovered the heavens, the stars, and an earth; and, on the earth, water, air, fire, minerals, and other such things which, being the most common of all and the simplest, are consequently the easiest to know. Then, when I sought to descend to more particular things, I encountered such a variety that I did not think the human mind could possibly distinguish the forms or species of bodies that are on the earth from an infinity of others that might be there if it had been God's will to put them there; nor could it relate them to our purposes except by progressing to the causes by way of the effects and making use of many special observations. And now, reviewing in my mind all the objects that have ever been present to my senses, I venture to say that I have never noticed anything in them which I could not explain quite easily by the principles I had discovered. But I must also admit that the power of nature is so ample and so vast, and these principles so simple and so general, that I notice hardly any particular

---

1 Fr. *expériences*, a term which Descartes often uses when talking of scientific observations, and which sometimes comes close to meaning 'experiments' in the modern sense (its root being derived from Lat. *experiri*, 'to test').

effect of which I do not know at once that it can be deduced from the principles in many different ways – and my greatest difficulty is usually to discover in which of these ways it depends on them. I know no other means to discover this than by seeking further observations whose outcomes vary according to which of these ways provides the correct explanation. Moreover, I have now reached a point where I think I can see quite clearly what line we should follow in making most of the observations which serve this purpose; but I see also that they are of such a kind and so numerous that neither my dexterity nor my income (were it even a thousand times greater than it is) could suffice for all of them. And so the advances I make in the knowledge of nature will depend henceforth on the opportunities I get to make more or fewer of these observations. I resolved to make this known in the treatise I had written, and to show clearly how the public could benefit from such knowledge. This would oblige all who desire the general well-being of mankind – that is, all who are really virtuous, not virtuous only in appearance or merely in repute – both to communicate to me the observations they have already made and to assist me in seeking those which remain to be made.

Since then, however, other considerations have made me change my mind. I have come to think that I must continue writing down anything I consider at all important, when I discover its truth, and that I should take as much care over these writings as I would if I intended to have them published. For this will give me all the more reason to examine them closely, as undoubtedly we always look more carefully at something we think is to be seen by others than at something we do only for ourselves; and often what seemed true to me when I first conceived it has looked false when I tried to put it on paper. This plan will also ensure both that I lose no opportunity to benefit the public if I can, and that if my writings have any value, those who get them after my death can make the most appropriate use of them. But I was determined not to agree to their publication during my lifetime, so that neither the opposition and controversy they might arouse, nor the reputation they might gain for me, would make me lose any of the time I planned to devote to my self-instruction. Every man is indeed bound to do what he can to procure the good of others, and a man who is of no use to anyone else is strictly worthless. Nevertheless it is also true that our concern ought to extend beyond the present, and that it is good to neglect matters which may profit the living when we aim to do other things which will benefit posterity even more. In any case I am willing to acknowledge that the little I have learned so far is almost nothing in comparison with that which I do not know but which I hope to be able to learn. Those who gradually discover the truth in the sciences are like people who become

66

class- IN
BACON

67

rich and find they have less trouble making large profits than they had in making much smaller ones when they were poorer. Or they may be compared with military commanders, whose forces tend to grow in proportion to their victories, but who need more skill to maintain their position after losing a battle than they do to take towns and provinces after winning one. For attempting to overcome all the difficulties and errors that prevent our arriving at knowledge of the truth is indeed a matter of fighting battles: we lose a battle whenever we accept some false opinion concerning an important question of general significance, and we need much more skill afterwards to regain our former position than we do to make good progress when we already have principles which are well-founded. For my part, if I have hitherto discovered a number of truths in the sciences (and I trust that the contents of this volume warrant the judgement that I have discovered some), I may say that they are merely the results and consequences of some five or six fundamental difficulties which I surmounted and which I count as so many battles where I had fortune on my side. I even venture to say that I think I need to win only two or three further such battles in order to achieve my aims completely, and that my age is not so far advanced that I may not in the normal course of nature still

68   have the time to do this. But the more hopeful I am of being able to use my remaining years effectively, the more I think I am obliged to plan my time carefully; and many occasions for wasting time would undoubtedly arise if I published the fundamental principles of my physics. For although these principles are almost all so evident that they need only to be understood to be believed, and although I think I can demonstrate all of them, yet since it is impossible that they should accord with all the diverse opinions of other men, I foresee that I should often be distracted by the controversies they would arouse.

   It may be claimed that such controversies would be useful. Not only would they make me aware of my mistakes, but also they would enable others to have a better understanding of anything worthwhile that I may have discovered; and, just as many people are able to see more than one person can on his own, so these others might begin to make use of my discoveries and help me with theirs. But although I recognize that I am extremely prone to error, and I almost never trust the first thoughts that come to me, at the same time my acquaintance with the objections that may be raised prevents me from expecting any benefit from them. For I have already had frequent experience of the judgements both of those I held to be my friends and of some I thought indifferent towards me, and even of certain others whose malice and envy would, I knew, make them eager enough to reveal what affection would hide from my friends. But it has rarely happened that an objection has been raised which I had not

wholly foreseen, except when it was quite wide of the mark. Thus I have 69
almost never encountered a critic of my views who did not seem to be
either less rigorous or less impartial than myself. Nor have I ever observed
that any previously unknown truth has been discovered by means of the
disputations practised in the schools. For so long as each side strives for
victory, more effort is put into establishing plausibility than in weighing
reasons for and against; and those who have long been good advocates do
not necessarily go on to make better judges.

As for the benefit that others might gain from the communication of
my thoughts, this could not be so very great. For I have not yet taken
them sufficiently far: I need to add many things to them before applying
them in practice. And I think I can say without vanity that if anyone is
capable of making these additions it must be myself rather than someone
else – not that there may not be many minds in the world incomparably
better than mine, but because no one can conceive something so well, and
make it his own, when he learns it from someone else as when he
discovers it himself. This is especially true in the case under consideration. I have often explained some of my opinions to highly intelligent
persons who seemed to understand them quite distinctly when I told
them about them; but, when they repeated them, I observed that they
almost always changed them in such a way that I could no longer
acknowledge them as my own. For this reason I should like to beg future 70
generations never to believe that I am the source of an opinion they hear
unless I have published it myself. I do not wonder at the absurdities
attributed to all the ancient philosophers whose writings we do not
possess; nor do I conclude from these attributions that their thoughts
were highly unreasonable. As they were some of the best minds of their
time, I conclude rather that their thoughts have been misreported. We see
too that it has almost never happened that any of their followers has
surpassed them; and I am sure that Aristotle's most enthusiastic contem-
porary followers would count themselves fortunate if they had as much
knowledge of nature as he had, even on the condition that they should
never know any more. They are like ivy, which never seeks to climb
higher than the trees which support it, and often even grows downward
after reaching the tree-tops. For it seems to me that they too take
downward steps, or become somehow less knowledgeable than if they
refrained from study, when, not content with knowing everything which
is intelligibly explained in their author's writings, they wish in addition to
find there the solution to many problems about which he says nothing
and about which perhaps he never thought. But this manner of philosophizing is very convenient for those with only mediocre minds, for the
obscurity of the distinctions and principles they use makes it possible for

them to speak about everything as confidently as if they knew it, and to defend all they say against the most subtle and clever thinkers without anyone having the means to convince them that they are wrong. In this they seem to resemble a blind man who, in order to fight without disadvantage against someone who can see, lures him into the depths of a very dark cellar. These philosophers, I may say, have an interest in my refraining from publishing the principles of the philosophy I use. For my principles are so very simple and evident that in publishing them I should, as it were, be opening windows and admitting daylight into that cellar where they have gone down to fight. But even the best minds have no reason to wish to know my principles. For if they want to be able to speak about everything and acquire the reputation of being learned, they will achieve this more readily by resting content with plausibility, which can be found without difficulty in all kinds of subjects, than by seeking the truth; for the truth comes to light only gradually in certain subjects, and it obliges us frankly to confess our ignorance where other subjects are concerned. But if they prefer the knowledge of some few truths to the vanity of appearing ignorant of nothing (and undoubtedly the former is preferable), and if they wish to follow a plan similar to mine, then in that case I need tell them nothing more than I have already said in this discourse. For if they are capable of making further progress than I have made, they will be all the more capable of discovering for themselves everything I think I have discovered. Inasmuch as I have examined everything in an orderly manner, it is certain that what still remains for me to discover is in itself more difficult and more hidden than anything I have thus far been able to discover; and they would have much less pleasure in learning it from me than in learning it for themselves. Besides, by investigating easy matters first and then moving on gradually to more difficult ones, they will acquire habits more useful to them than all my instructions could be. For my part, I am convinced that if from my youth I had been taught all the truths I have since sought to demonstrate, and so had learned them without any difficulty, I should perhaps never have known any others; or at least I should never have acquired the habit and facility, which I think I have, for always finding new truths whenever I apply myself in searching for them. In short, if there was ever a task which could not be completed so well by someone other than the person who began it, it is the one on which I am working.

True, as regards observations which may help in this work, one man could not possibly make them all. But he could not effectively use hands other than his own, except by employing artisans, or other persons whom he could pay and who would be led by the hope of gain (a most effective motive) to do precisely what he ordered them to do. For voluntary helpers, who might offer their assistance from curiosity or a desire to learn, usually promise more than they achieve and make fine proposals which never come to anything. In addition, they would inevitably wish to be rewarded by having certain difficulties explained to them, or at any rate by compliments and useless conversation, which could not but waste a lot of his time. And as for the observations that others have already made, even if they were willing to communicate them to him (something which those who call them 'secrets' would never do), they are for the most part bound up with so many details or superfluous ingredients that it would be very hard for him to make out the truth in them. Besides, he would find almost all of these observations to be so badly explained or indeed so mistaken – because those who made them were eager to have them appear to conform with their principles – that it would simply not be worthwhile for him to spend the time required to pick out those which he might find useful. So if there were someone in the world whom we knew for sure to be capable of making discoveries of the greatest possible importance and public utility, and whom other men accordingly were eager to help in every way to achieve his ends, I do not see how they could do anything for him except to contribute towards the expenses of the observations that he would need and, further, prevent unwelcome visitors from wasting his free time. But I am not so presumptuous that I wish to promise anything extraordinary, nor do I entertain thoughts so vain as the supposition that the public ought to take a great interest in my projects. Apart from that, I am not so mean-spirited that I would willingly accept from anyone a favour that I might be thought not to deserve.

All these considerations taken together caused me to decide, three years ago, that I did not wish to publish the treatise I had ready then, and made me resolve not to publish any other work during my lifetime which was so general in scope or by which the foundations of my physics might be understood. Since then, however, two further reasons have compelled me to include here some essays on particular topics and to give to the public some account of my actions and plans. The first is that, if I failed to do so, then many who knew of my earlier intention to publish certain writings might suppose that my reasons for not doing so were more discreditable to me than they are. I am not excessively fond of glory – indeed if I may say so, I dislike it – in so far as I regard it as opposed to that tranquillity which I value above everything else. At the same time I have never tried to conceal my actions as if they were crimes, or taken many precautions to remain unknown. For if I had done this I thought I would do myself an injustice, and moreover that would have given me a certain sort of disquiet, which again would have been opposed to the perfect peace of mind I am seeking. And since my indifference as to whether I was well-known or not made it unavoidable that I should gain some sort of reputation, I thought I ought to do my best at least to avoid

75   getting a bad one. The other reason compelling me to write this is that every day I am becoming more and more aware of the delay which my project of self-instruction is suffering because of the need for innumerable observations which I cannot possibly make without the help of others. Although I do not flatter myself with any expectation that the public will share my interests, yet at the same time I am unwilling to be so unfaithful to myself as to give those who come after me cause to reproach me one day on the grounds that I could have left them many far better things if I had not been so remiss in making them understand how they could contribute to my projects.

   I thought it convenient for me to choose certain subjects which, without being highly controversial and without obliging me to reveal more of my principles than I wished, would nevertheless show quite clearly what I can, and what I cannot, achieve in the sciences. I cannot tell if I have succeeded in this, and I do not wish to anticipate anyone's judgements about my writings by speaking about them myself. But I shall be very glad if they are examined. In order to provide more opportunity for this, I beg all who have any objections to take the trouble to send them to my publisher, and when he informs me about them I shall attempt to append my reply at the same time, so that readers can see both sides together, and decide the truth all the more easily. I do not promise to make very long replies, but only to acknowledge my errors very

76   frankly if I recognize them; and where I cannot see them I shall simply say what I consider is required for defending what I have written, without introducing any new material, so as to avoid getting endlessly caught up in one topic after another.

   Should anyone be shocked at first by some of the statements I make at the beginning of the *Optics* and the *Meteorology* because I call them 'suppositions' and do not seem to care about proving them, let him have the patience to read the whole book attentively, and I trust that he will be satisfied. For I take my reasonings to be so closely interconnected that just as the last are proved by the first, which are their causes, so the first are proved by the last, which are their effects. It must not be supposed that I am here committing the fallacy which logicians call 'arguing in a circle'. For as experience renders most of these effects quite certain, the causes from which I deduce them serve not so much to prove them as to explain them; indeed, quite to the contrary, it is the causes which are proved by the effects. And I have called them 'suppositions' simply to make it known that I think I can deduce them from the primary truths I have expounded above; but I have deliberately avoided carrying out these deductions in order to prevent certain ingenious persons from taking the opportunity to construct, on what they believe to be my principles, some extravagant philosophy for which I shall be blamed. These persons imagine that they can learn in a single day what it has taken someone else twenty years to think out, as soon as he has told them only two or three words about it; whereas the more penetrating and acute they are, the more prone to error they are and the less capable of truth. As to the opinions that are wholly mine, I do not apologize for their novelty. If the reasons for them are properly considered, I am sure they will be found to be so simple and so much in agreement with common sense as to appear less extraordinary and strange than any other views that people may hold on the same subjects. I do not boast of being the first to discover any of them, but I do claim to have accepted them not because they have, or have not, been expressed by others, but solely because reason has convinced me of them. 77

If artisans are not immediately able to put into operation the invention explained in the *Optics*, I do not think it can on that account be said to be defective.[1] For much skill and practice are needed for making and adjusting the machines I have described, and although my description does not omit any details, I should be no less astonished if they succeeded at the first attempt than if someone could learn to play the lute excellently in a single day simply by being given a good fingering chart. And if I am writing in French, my native language, rather than Latin, the language of my teachers, it is because I expect that those who use only their natural reason in all its purity will be better judges of my opinions than those who give credence only to the writings of the ancients. As to those who combine good sense with application – the only judges I wish to have – I am sure they will not be so partial to Latin that they will refuse to listen to my arguments because I expound them in the vernacular. 78

For the rest, I do not wish to speak here in detail about the further progress I hope to make in the sciences, or to commit myself in the eyes of the public by making any promise that I am not sure of fulfilling. I will say only that I have resolved to devote the rest of my life to nothing other than trying to acquire some knowledge of nature from which we may derive rules in medicine which are more reliable than those we have had up till now. Moreover, my inclination makes me so strongly opposed to all other projects, and especially to those which can be useful to some persons only by harming others, that if circumstances forced me to engage in any such pursuit, I do not think I would be capable of succeeding in it. Of this I make here a public declaration, fully recogniz-

---

1 Here Descartes refers to the method of cutting lenses described in Discourse 10 of the *Optics*.

ing that it cannot serve to make me eminent in the world; but then I have no desire to be such. And I shall always hold myself more obliged to those by whose favour I enjoy uninterrupted leisure than to any who might offer me the most honourable positions in the world.

Optics

DISCOURSE ONE
Light

The conduct of our life depends entirely on our senses, and since sight is the noblest and most comprehensive of the senses, inventions which serve to increase its power are undoubtedly among the most useful there can be. And it is difficult to find any such inventions which do more to increase the power of sight than those wonderful telescopes which, though in use for only a short time, have already revealed a greater number of new stars and other new objects above the earth than we had seen there before. Carrying our vision much further than our forebears could normally extend their imagination, these telescopes seem to have opened the way for us to attain a knowledge of nature much greater and more perfect than they possessed . . . But inventions of any complexity do (82) not reach their highest degree of perfection right away, and this one is still sufficiently problematical to give me cause to write about it. And since the construction of the things of which I shall speak must depend on the skill of craftsmen, who usually have little formal education, I shall try to make myself intelligible to everyone; and I shall try not to omit 83 anything, or to assume anything that requires knowledge of other sciences. This is why I shall begin by explaining light and light-rays; then, having briefly described the parts of the eye, I shall give a detailed account of how vision comes about; and, after noting all the things which are capable of making vision more perfect, I shall show how they can be aided by the inventions which I shall describe.

Now since my only reason for speaking of light here is to explain how its rays enter into the eye, and how they may be deflected by the various bodies they encounter, I need not attempt to say what is its true nature. It will, I think, suffice if I use two or three comparisons in order to facilitate that conception of light which seems most suitable for explaining all those of its properties that we know through experience and for then deducing all the other properties that we cannot observe so easily. In this I am imitating the astronomers, whose suppositions are almost all false or uncertain, but who nevertheless draw many very true and certain consequences from them because they are related to various observations they have made.

No doubt you have had the experience of walking at night over rough ground without a light, and finding it necessary to use a stick in order to guide yourself. You may then have been able to notice that by means of this stick you could feel the various objects situated around you, and that you could even tell whether they were trees or stones or sand or water or grass or mud or any other such thing. It is true that this kind of sensation is somewhat confused and obscure in those who do not have long practice with it. But consider it in those born blind, who have made use of it all their lives: with them, you will find, it is so perfect and so exact that one might almost say that they see with their hands, or that their stick is the organ of some sixth sense given to them in place of sight. In order to draw a comparison from this, I would have you consider the light in bodies we call 'luminous' to be nothing other than a certain movement, or very rapid and lively action, which passes to our eyes through the medium of the air and other transparent bodies, just as the movement or resistance of the bodies encountered by a blind man passes to his hand by means of his stick. In the first place this will prevent you from finding it strange that this light can extend its rays instantaneously from the sun to us. For you know that the action by which we move one end of a stick must pass instantaneously to the other end, and that the action of light would have to pass from the heavens to the earth in the same way, even though the distance in this case is much greater than that between the ends of a stick. Nor will you find it strange that by means of this action we can see all sorts of colours. You may perhaps even be prepared to believe that in the bodies we call 'coloured' the colours are nothing other than the various ways in which the bodies receive light and reflect it against our eyes. You have only to consider that the differences a blind man notices between trees, rocks, water and similar things by means of his stick do not seem any less to him than the differences between red, yellow, green and all the other colours seem to us. And yet in all those bodies the differences are nothing other than the various ways of moving the stick or of resisting its movements. Hence you will have reason to conclude that there is no need to suppose that something material passes from objects to our eyes to make us see colours and light, or even that there is something in the objects which resembles the ideas or sensations that we have of them. In just the same way, when a blind man feels bodies, nothing has to issue from the bodies and pass along his stick to his hand; and the resistance or movement of the bodies, which is the sole cause of the sensations he has of them, is nothing like the ideas he forms of them. By this means, your mind will be delivered from all those little images flitting through the air, called 'intentional forms',[1] which so exercise the imagination of the philosophers. You will even find it easy to settle the current philosophical debate concerning the origin of the action which causes visual perception. For, just as our blind man can feel the bodies around him not only through the action of these bodies when they move against his stick, but also through the action of his hand when they do nothing but resist the stick, so we must acknowledge that the objects of sight can be perceived not only by means of the action in them which is directed towards our eyes, but also by the action in our eyes which is directed towards them. Nevertheless, because the latter action is nothing other than light, we must note that it is found only in the eyes of those creatures which can see in the dark, such as cats, whereas a man normally sees only through the action which comes from the objects. For experience shows us that these objects must be luminous or illuminated in order to be seen, and not that our eyes must be luminous or illuminated in order to see them. But because our blind man's stick differs greatly from the air and the other transparent bodies through the medium of which we see, I must make use of yet another comparison.

86

Consider a wine-vat at harvest time, full to the brim with half-pressed grapes, in the bottom of which we have made one or two holes through which the unfermented wine can flow.[2] Now observe that, since there is no vacuum in nature (as nearly all philosophers acknowledge), and yet there are many pores in all the bodies we perceive around us (as experience can show quite clearly), it is necessary that these pores be filled with some very subtle and very fluid matter, which extends without interruption from the heavenly bodies to us. Now, if you compare this subtle matter with the wine in the vat, and compare the less fluid or coarser parts of the air and the other transparent bodies with the bunches of grapes which are mixed in with the wine, you will readily understand the following. The parts of wine at one place tend to go down in a straight line through one hole at the very instant it is opened, and at the same time through the other hole, while the parts at other places also tend at the same time to go down through these two holes, without these actions being impeded by each other or by the resistance of the bunches of grapes in the vat. This happens even though the bunches support each other and so do not tend in the least to go down through the holes, as does the wine, and at the same time they can even be moved in many other ways by the bunches which press upon them. In the same way, all the parts of the subtle matter in contact with the side of the sun facing us

87

1 A reference to the scholastic doctrine that material objects transmit to the soul 'forms' or 'images' (Fr. *espèces*, Lat. *species*) resembling them.
2 A diagram of the wine-vat is omitted here.

tend in a straight line towards our eyes at the very instant they are opened, without these parts impeding each other, and even without their being impeded by the coarser parts of the transparent bodies which lie between them. This happens whether these bodies move in other ways – like the air which is almost always agitated by some wind – or are

88   motionless – say, like glass or crystal. And note here that it is necessary to distinguish between the movement and the action or tendency to move. For we may very easily conceive that the parts of wine at one place should tend towards one hole and at the same time towards the other, even though they cannot actually move towards both holes at the same time, and that they should tend exactly in a straight line towards one and towards the other, even though they cannot move exactly in a straight line because of the bunches of grapes which are between them. In the same way, considering that the light of a luminous body must be regarded as being not so much its movement as its action, you must think of the rays of light as nothing other than the lines along which this action tends. Thus there is an infinity of such rays which come from all the points of a luminous body towards all the points of the bodies it illuminates, just as you can imagine an infinity of straight lines along which the actions coming from all the points of the surface of the wine tend towards one hole, and an infinity of others along which the actions coming from the same points tend also towards the other hole, without either impeding the other.

Moreover, these rays must always be imagined to be exactly straight when they pass through a single transparent body which is uniform throughout. But when they meet certain other bodies, they are liable to be deflected by them, or weakened, in the same way that the movement

89   of a ball or stone thrown into the air is deflected by the bodies it encounters. For it is very easy to believe that the action or tendency to move (which, I have said, should be taken for light) must in this respect obey the same laws as the movement itself. In order that I may give a complete account of this third comparison, consider that a ball passing through the air may encounter bodies that are soft or hard or fluid. If the bodies are soft, they completely stop the ball and check its movement, as when it strikes linen sheets or sand or mud. But if they are hard, they send the ball in another direction without stopping it, and they do so in many different ways. For their surface may be quite even and smooth, or rough and uneven; if even, either flat or curved; if uneven, its unevenness may consist merely in its being composed of many variously curved parts, each quite smooth in itself, or also in its having many different angles or points, or some parts harder than others, or parts which are moving (their movements being varied in a thousand imaginable ways). And it must be noted that the ball, besides moving in the simple and ordinary way which

takes it from one place to another, may move in yet a second way, turning on its axis, and that the speed of the latter movement may have many different relations with that of the former. Thus, when many balls coming from the same direction meet a body whose surface is completely smooth and even, they are reflected uniformly and in the same order, so 90 that if this surface is completely flat they keep the same distance between them after having met it as they had beforehand; and if it is curved inward or outward they come towards each other or go away from each other in the same order, more or less, on account of this curvature . . . It (91) is necessary to consider, in the same manner, that there are bodies which break up the light-rays that meet them and take away all their force (namely bodies called 'black', which have no colour other than that of shadows); and there are others which cause the rays to be reflected, some in the same order as they receive them (namely bodies with highly polished surfaces, which can serve as mirrors, both flat and curved), and others in many directions in complete disarray. Among the latter, again, some 92 bodies cause the rays to be reflected without bringing about any other change in their action (namely bodies we call 'white'), and others bring about an additional change similar to that which the movement of a ball undergoes when we graze it (namely bodies which are red, or yellow, or blue or some other such colour). For I believe I can determine the nature of each of these colours, and reveal it experimentally; but this goes beyond the limits of my subject.[1] All I need to do here is to point out that the light-rays falling on bodies which are coloured and not polished are usually reflected in every direction even if they come from only a single direction... Finally, consider that the rays are also deflected, in the same way as the ball just described, when they fall obliquely on the surface of a 93 transparent body and penetrate this body more or less easily than the body from which they come. This mode of deflection is called 'refraction'.[1]

DISCOURSE FOUR

The senses in general 109

Now I must tell you something about the nature of the senses in general, the more easily to explain that of sight in particular. We know for certain that it is the soul which has sensory awareness, and not the body. For when the soul is distracted by an ecstasy or deep contemplation, we see that the whole body remains without sensation, even though it has various objects touching it. And we know that it is not, properly speaking, because of its presence in the parts of the body which function as organs of the external senses that the soul has sensory awareness, but

---

1 Discourses Two and Three are omitted here.

because of its presence in the brain, where it exercises the faculty called the 'common' sense.[1] For we observe injuries and diseases which attack the brain alone and impede all the senses generally, even though the rest of the body continues to be animated. We know, lastly, that it is through the nerves that the impressions formed by objects in the external parts of the body reach the soul in the brain. For we observe various accidents which cause injury only to a nerve, and destroy sensation in all the parts of the body to which this nerve sends its branches, without causing it to

(112) diminish elsewhere...[2] We must take care not to assume – as our philosophers commonly do – that in order to have sensory awareness the soul must contemplate certain images[3] transmitted by objects to the brain; or at any rate we must conceive the nature of these images in an entirely different manner from that of the philosophers. For since their conception of the images is confined to the requirement that they should resemble the objects they represent, the philosophers cannot possibly show us how the images can be formed by the objects, or how they can be received by the external sense organs and transmitted by the nerves to the brain. Their sole reason for positing such images was that they saw how easily a picture can stimulate our mind to conceive the objects depicted in it, and so it seemed to them that the mind must be stimulated to conceive the objects that affect our senses in the same way – that is, by little pictures formed in our head. We should, however, recall that our mind can be stimulated by many things other than images – by signs and words, for example, which in no way resemble the things they signify And if, in order to depart as little as possible from accepted views, we prefer to maintain that the objects which we perceive by our senses really

113   send images of themselves to the inside of our brain, we must at least observe that in no case does an image have to resemble the object it represents in all respects, for otherwise there would be no distinction between the object and its image. It is enough that the image resembles its object in a few respects. Indeed the perfection of an image often depends on its not resembling its object as much as it might. You can see this in the case of engravings: consisting simply of a little ink placed here and there on a piece of paper, they represent to us forests, towns, people, and even battles and storms; and although they make us think of countless different qualities in these objects, it is only in respect of shape that there is any real resemblance. And even this resemblance is very imperfect, since engravings represent to us bodies of varying relief and depth on a

---

1 See footnote, p. 120 below.
2 There follows an account of the function of the nerves and animal spirits in producing sensation and movement. Cf. *Treatise on Man*, AT XI 132ff and *Passions*, pp. 221–8 below.
3 See footnote, p. 59 above.

surface which is entirely flat. Moreover, in accordance with the rules of perspective they often represent circles by ovals better than by other circles, squares by rhombuses better than by other squares, and similarly for other shapes. Thus it often happens that in order to be more perfect as an image and to represent an object better, an engraving ought not to resemble it. Now we must think of the images formed in our brain in just the same way, and note that the problem is to know simply how they can enable the soul to have sensory awareness of all the various qualities of the objects to which they correspond – not to know how they can resemble these objects. For instance, when our blind man touches bodies 114 with his stick, they certainly do not transmit anything to him except in so far as they cause his stick to move in different ways according to the different qualities in them, thus likewise setting in motion the nerves in his hand, and then the regions of his brain where these nerves originate. This is what occasions his soul to have sensory awareness of just as many different qualities in these bodies as there are differences in the movements caused by them in his brain.

DISCOURSE FIVE

The images which are formed on the back of the eye

You see, then, that in order to have sensory awareness the soul does not need to contemplate any images resembling the things which it perceives. And yet, for all that, the objects we look at do imprint quite perfect images of themselves on the back of our eyes. This has been very ingeniously explained by the following comparison. Suppose a chamber is all shut up apart from a single hole, and a glass lens is placed in front of this hole with a white sheet stretched at a certain distance behind it so that the light coming from objects outside forms images on the sheet. Now it is said that the chamber represents the eye; the hole, the pupil; the 115 lens, the crystalline humour, or rather all the parts of the eye which cause some refraction; and the sheet, the internal membrane, which is composed of the optic nerve-endings.

But you may become more certain of this if, taking the eye of a newly dead person (or failing that, the eye of an ox or some other large animal), you carefully cut away the three surrounding membranes at the back so as to expose a large part of the humour without spilling any. Then cover the hole with some white body thin enough to let light pass through (e.g. a piece of paper or an egg-shell), and put this eye in the hole of a specially made shutter so that its front faces a place where there are various objects lit up by the sun, and its back faces the inside of the room where you are standing. (No light must enter the room except what comes through this eye, all of whose parts you know to be entirely transparent.) Having done this, if you look at the white body you will see there, not perhaps without wonder and pleasure, a picture representing in natural perspective all the objects outside – at any rate you will if you ensure that the eye keeps its natural shape, according to the distance of the objects (for if you squeeze it just a little more or less than you ought, the picture becomes less distinct) . . .

116
117

(124) Now, when you have seen this picture in the eye of a dead animal, and considered its causes, you cannot doubt that a quite similar picture is formed in the eye of a living person, on the internal membrane for which we substituted the white body – indeed, a much better one is formed there since the humours in this eye are full of animal spirits and so are more transparent and more exactly of the shape necessary for this to occur. (And also, perhaps in the eye of an ox the shape of the pupil, which is not round, prevents the picture from being so perfect.) . . .

(128) The images of objects are not only formed in this way at the back of the eye but also pass beyond into the brain...[1]

DISCOURSE SIX

130

Vision

Now, when this picture thus passes to the inside of our head, it still bears some resemblance to the objects from which it proceeds. As I have amply shown already, however, we must not think that it is by means of this resemblance that the picture causes our sensory awareness of these objects – as if there were yet other eyes within our brain with which we could perceive it. Instead we must hold that it is the movements composing this picture which, acting directly upon our soul in so far as it is united to our body, are ordained by nature to make it have such sensations. I will explain this in more detail. All the qualities which we perceive in the objects of sight can be reduced to six principal ones: light, colour, position, distance, size and shape. First, regarding light and colour (the only qualities belonging properly to the sense of sight), we must suppose our soul to be of such a nature that what makes it have the sensation of light is the force of the movements taking place in the regions of the brain where the optic nerve-fibres originate, and what makes it have the sensation of colour is the manner of these movements. Likewise, the movements in the nerves leading to the ears make the soul hear sounds; those in the nerves of the tongue make it taste flavours; and, in general, movements in the nerves anywhere in the body make the soul

131

1 Here Descartes repeats the account given in the *Treatise on Man*, AT XI 174ff; CSM I 105–6.

have a tickling sensation if they are moderate, and a pain when they are too violent. But in all this there need be no resemblance between the ideas which the soul conceives and the movements which cause these ideas. You will readily grant this if you note that people struck in the eye seem to see countless sparks and flashes before them, even though they shut their eyes or are in a very dark place; hence this sensation can be ascribed only to the force of the blow, which sets the optic nerve-fibres in motion as a bright light would do. The same force might make us hear a sound if it affected the ears, or feel pain if it affected some other part of the body. This is also confirmed by the fact that whenever you force your eyes to look at the sun, or at some other very bright light, they retain its impression for a short time afterwards, so that even with your eyes shut you seem to see various colours which change and pass from one to another as they fade away. This can only result from the fact that the optic nerve-fibres have been set in motion with extraordinary force, and so cannot come to rest as soon as they usually can. But the agitation remaining in them when the eyes are shut is not great enough to represent   132 the bright light that caused it, and thus it represents the less vivid colours. That these colours change as they fade away shows that their nature consists simply in the diversity of the movement, exactly as I have already suggested. And finally this is revealed by the frequent appearance of colours in transparent bodies, for it is certain that nothing can cause this except the various ways in which the light-rays are received in such bodies. One example is the appearance of a rainbow in the clouds, and a still clearer example is the likeness of a rainbow seen in a piece of glass cut on many sides.

But we must consider in detail what determines the quantity of the light which is seen, i.e. the quantity of the force with which each of the optic nerve-fibres is moved. For it is not always equal to the light which is in the objects, but varies in proportion to their distance and the size of the pupil, and also in proportion to the area at the back of the eye which may be occupied by the rays coming from each point of the object ... We   (133) must also consider that we cannot discriminate the parts of the bodies we are looking at except in so far as they differ somehow in colour; and distinct vision of these colours depends not only on the fact that all the rays coming from each point of the object converge in almost as many different points at the back of the eye, and on the fact that no rays reach the same points from elsewhere ... but also on the great number of optic nerve-fibres in the area which the image occupies at the back of the eye. For example, if an object is composed of ten thousand parts capable of   134 sending rays to a certain area at the back of the eye in ten thousand different ways, and consequently of making ten thousand colours simultaneously visible, these parts nevertheless will enable the soul to discriminate only at most a thousand colours, if we suppose that in this area there are only a thousand fibres of the optic nerve. Thus ten parts of the object, acting together upon each of the fibres, can move it in just one single way made up of all the ways in which they act, so that the area occupied by each fibre has to be regarded as if it were only a single point. This is why a field decked out in countless different colours often appears from a distance to be all white or all blue; why, in general, all bodies are seen less distinctly from a distance than close at hand; and finally why the greater the area which we can make the image of a single object occupy at the back of the eye, the more distinctly it can be seen. We shall need to take special note of this fact later on.

As regards position, that is, the orientation of each part of an object relative to our body, we perceive it by means of our eyes exactly as we do by means of our hands. Our knowledge of it does not depend on any image, nor on any action coming from the object, but solely on the position of the tiny parts of the brain where the nerves originate. For this position, which varies ever so slightly each time there is a change in the position of the limbs in which the nerves are embedded, is 135 ordained by nature to enable the soul not only to know the place occupied by each part of the body it animates relative to all the others, but also to shift attention from these places to any of those lying on straight lines which we can imagine to be drawn from the extremity of each part and extended to infinity. In the same way, when the blind man, of whom we have already spoken so much, turns his hand A towards E [Fig. 1], or again his hand C towards E, the nerves

Fig. 1

embedded in that hand cause a certain change in his brain, and through this change his soul can know not only the place A or C but also all the other places located on the straight line AE or CE; in this way his soul can turn its attention to the objects B and D, and determine the places they occupy without in any way knowing or thinking of those which his hands occupy. Similarly, when our eye or head is turned in some direction, our soul is informed of this by the change in the brain which is caused by the nerves embedded in the muscles used for these movements. ... You must not, therefore, find it strange that objects can be seen in their true position even though the picture they imprint upon the eye is inverted. This is just like our blind man's being able to feel, at one and the same time, the object B (to his right) by means of his left hand, and the object D (to his left) by means of his right hand. And as the blind man does not judge a body to be double although he touches it with his two hands, so too, when both our eyes are disposed in the manner required to direct our attention to one and the same place, they need only make us see a single object there, even though a picture of it is formed in each of our eyes.

The seeing of distance depends no more than does the seeing of position upon any images emitted from objects. Instead it depends in the first place on the shape of the body of the eye. For as we have said, for us to see things close to our eyes this shape must be slightly different from the shape which enables us to see things farther away; and as we adjust the shape of the eye according to the distance of objects, we change a certain part of our brain in a manner that is ordained by nature to make our soul perceive this distance. Ordinarily this happens without our reflecting upon it – just as, for example, when we clasp some body with our hand, we adjust our hand to its size and shape and thus feel it by means of our hand without needing to think of these movements. In the second place, we know distance by the relation of the eyes to one another. Our blind man holding the two sticks AE and CE (whose length I assume he does not know) and knowing only the distance between his two hands A and C and the size of the angles ACE and CAE, can tell from this knowledge, as if by a natural geometry, where the point E is. And similarly, when our two eyes A and B are turned towards point X, the length of the line AB and the size of the two angles XAB and XBA enable us to know where the point X is. We can do the same thing also with the aid of only one eye, by changing its position.[1] Thus, if we keep it turned towards X and place it first at point A and immediately afterwards at point B, this will be enough to make our imagination contain the magnitude of the line AC together with that of the two angles XAB and XBA, and thus enable us to perceive the distance from point X. And this is done by a mental act which, though only a very simple act of the imagination, involves a kind of reasoning quite similar to that used by surveyors when they measure inaccessible places by means of two different vantage points. We have yet another way of perceiving distance,

136

137

138

1 A diagram is omitted here.

namely by the distinctness or indistinctness of the shape seen, together with the strength or weakness of the light. Thus, if we gaze fixedly towards X [Fig. 2], the rays coming from objects 10 and 12 do not converge so exactly upon R or T, at the back of our eye, as they would if these objects were at points V and Y. From this we see that they are farther from us, or nearer to us, than X. Then, the light coming from object 10 to our eye is stronger than it would be if that object were near V, and from this we judge it to be nearer; and the light coming from object 12 is weaker than it would be if it were near Y, and so we judge it to be farther away. Finally, we may already have from another source an image of an object's size, or its position, or the distinctness of its shape and its colours, or merely the strength of the light coming from it; and this may enable us to imagine its distance, if not actually to see it. For example, when we observe from afar some body we are used to seeing close at hand, we judge its distance much better than we would if its size were less well known to us. If we are looking at a mountain lit up by sunlight beyond a forest covered in shadow, it is solely the position of the forest that makes us judge it the nearer. And when we look at two ships out at sea, one smaller than the other but proportionately nearer so that they appear equal in size, we can use the difference in their shapes and colours, and in the light they send to us, to judge which is the more distant.

139
140

Concerning the manner in which we see the size and shape of objects, I need not say anything in particular since it is wholly included in the way we see the distance and the position of their parts. That is, we judge their size by the knowledge or opinion that we have of their distance, compared with the size of the images they imprint on the back of the eye – and not simply by the size of these images. This is sufficiently obvious from the fact that the images imprinted by objects very close to us are a hundred times bigger than those imprinted by objects ten times farther away, and yet they do not make us see the objects a hundred times larger; instead they make the objects look almost the same size, at least if their distance does not deceive us. It is obvious too that we judge shape by the knowledge or opinion that we have of the position of the various parts of an object, and not by the resemblance of the pictures in our eyes. For these pictures usually contain only ovals and rhombuses when they make us see circles and squares.

141

But in order that you may have no doubts at all that vision works as I have explained it, I would again have you consider the reasons why it sometimes deceives us. First, it is the soul which sees, and not the eye; and it does not see directly, but only by means of the brain. That is why madmen and those who are asleep often see, or think they see, various

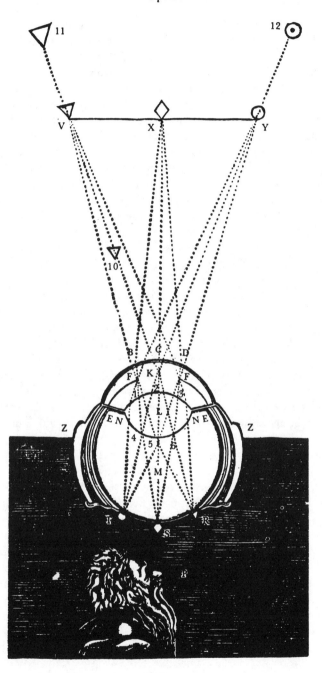

Fig. 2

objects which are nevertheless not before their eyes: namely, certain vapours disturb their brain and arrange those of its parts normally engaged in vision exactly as they would be if these objects were present. Then, because the impressions which come from outside pass to the 'common' sense by way of the nerves, if the position of these nerves is changed by any unusual cause, this may make us see objects in places (142) other than where they are ... Again, because we normally judge that the impressions which stimulate our sight come from places towards which we have to look in order to sense them, we may easily be deceived when they happen to come from elsewhere. Thus, those whose eyes are affected by jaundice, or who are looking through yellow glass or shut up in a room where no light enters except through such glass, attribute this colour to all the bodies they look at. And the person inside the dark room which I described earlier attributes to the white body the colours of the ,objects outside because he directs his sight solely upon that body. And if our eyes see objects through lenses and in mirrors, they judge them to be at points where they are not and to be smaller or larger than they are, or inverted as well as smaller (namely, when they are somewhat distant from the eyes). This occurs because the lenses and mirrors deflect the rays
143   coming from the objects, so that our eyes cannot see the objects distinctly except by making the adjustments necessary for looking towards the points in question.[1] This will readily be known by those who take the
144   trouble to examine the matter. In the same way they will see how far the ancients went wrong in their catoptrics when they tried to determine the location of the images in concave and convex mirrors. It should further be noted that all our methods for recognizing distance are highly unreliable. For the shape of the eye undergoes hardly any perceptible variation when the object is more than four or five feet away, and even when the object is nearer the shape varies so little that no very precise knowledge can be obtained from it. And if one is looking at an object at all far away, there is also hardly any variation in the angles between the line joining the two eyes (or two positions of the same eye) and the lines from the eyes to the object. As a consequence, even our 'common' sense seems incapable of receiving in itself the idea of a distance greater than approximately one or two hundred feet. This can be verified in the case of the moon and the sun. Although they are among the most distant bodies that we can see, and their diameters are to their distances roughly as one to a hundred, they normally appear to us as at most only one or two feet in diameter – although we know very well by reason that they are extremely large and extremely far away. This does not happen because we are unable to conceive them as any larger, since we quite well conceive towers and

1 A diagram is omitted here, and the text is slightly condensed.

mountains which are much larger. It happens, rather, because we cannot conceive them as more than one or two hundred feet away, and consequently their diameters cannot appear to us to be more than one or two feet. The position of these bodies also helps to mislead us. For usually, when they are very high in the sky at midday, they seem smaller than they do when they are rising or setting, and we can notice their distance more easily because there are various objects between them and our eyes. And, by measuring them with their instruments, the astronomers prove clearly that they appear larger at one time than at another not because they are seen to subtend a greater angle, but because they are judged to be farther away. It follows that the axiom of the ancient optics – which says that the apparent size of objects is proportional to the size of the angle of vision – is not always true. We are also deceived because white or luminous bodies, and generally all those which have a great power to stimulate the sense of sight, always appear just a little nearer and larger than they would if they had less such power. The reason why such bodies appear nearer is that the movement with which the pupil contracts to avoid their strong light is so connected with the movement which disposes the whole eye to see near objects distinctly – a movement by which we judge the distance of such objects – that the one hardly ever takes place without the other occurring to some extent as well. (In the same way, we cannot fully close the first two fingers of our hand without the third bending a little too, as if to close with the others.) The reason why these white or luminous bodies appear larger is not only that our estimation of their size depends on that of their distance, but also that they impress larger images on the back of the eye. For it must be noted that the back of the eye is covered by the ends of optic nerve-fibres which, though very small, still have some size. Thus each of them may be affected in one of its parts by one object and in other parts by other objects. But it is capable of being moved in only a single way at any given time; so when the smallest of its parts is affected by some very brilliant object, and the others by different objects that are less brilliant, the whole of it moves in accordance with the most brilliant object, presenting its image but not that of the others. Thus, suppose the ends of these little fibres are 1, 2, 3 [Fig. 3] and the

Fig. 3

rays which come, for example, from a star to trace an image on the back of the eye are spread over 1, and also slightly beyond over the six nerve-endings marked 2 (which I suppose are reached by no other rays except very weak ones from regions of the sky next to the star). In this case the image of the star will be spread over the whole area occupied by the six nerve-endings marked 2 and may even spread throughout that occupied by the twelve marked 3 if the disturbance is strong enough to be propagated to them as well. So you can see that the stars, while appearing rather small, nevertheless appear much larger than their extreme distance should cause them to appear. And even if they were not perfectly round,

147 they could not fail to appear so – just as a square tower seen from afar looks round, and all bodies that trace only very small images in the eye cannot trace there the shapes of their angles. Finally, as regards judgement of distance by size, shape, colour, or light, pictures drawn in perspective show how easy it is to make mistakes. For often the things depicted in such pictures appear to us to be farther off than they are because they are smaller, while their outlines are more blurred, and their colours darker or fainter, than we imagine they ought to be.[1]

1 The last four Discourses are omitted.

Synopsis of the following six Meditations

In the First Meditation reasons are provided which give us possible grounds for doubt about all things, especially material things, so long as we have no foundations for the sciences other than those which we have had up till now. Although the usefulness of such extensive doubt is not apparent at first sight, its greatest benefit lies in freeing us from all our preconceived opinions, and providing the easiest route by which the mind may be led away from the senses. The eventual result of this doubt *goal.* is to make it impossible for us to have any further doubts about what we subsequently discover to be true.

In the Second Meditation, the mind uses its own freedom and supposes the non-existence of all the things about whose existence it can have even the slightest doubt; and in so doing the mind notices that it is impossible that it should not itself exist during this time. This exercise is also of the greatest benefit, since it enables the mind to distinguish without difficulty what belongs to itself, i.e. to an intellectual nature, from what belongs to the body. But since some people may perhaps expect arguments for the immortality of the soul in this section, I think they should be warned here and now that I have tried not to put down anything which I could not 13 precisely demonstrate. Hence the only order which I could follow was that normally employed by geometers, namely to set out all the premisses on which a desired proposition depends, before drawing any conclusions about it. Now the first and most important prerequisite for knowledge of the immortality of the soul is for us to form a concept of the soul which is as clear as possible and is also quite distinct from every *soul separate from body* concept of body; and that is just what has been done in this section. A further requirement is that we should know that everything that we clearly and distinctly understand is true in a way which corresponds exactly to our understanding of it; but it was not possible to prove this before the Fourth Meditation. In addition we need to have a distinct concept of corporeal nature, and this is developed partly in the Second Meditation itself, and partly in the Fifth and Sixth Meditations. The inference to be drawn from these results is that all the things that we clearly and distinctly conceive of as different substances (as we do in the case of mind and body) are in fact substances which are really distinct one from the other; and this conclusion is drawn in the Sixth Meditation. This conclusion is confirmed in the same Meditation by the fact that we (cannot understand a body except as being divisible, while by contrast we cannot understand a mind except as being indivisible) For we cannot conceive of half of a mind, while we can always conceive of half of a body, however small; and this leads us to recognize that the natures of mind and body are not only different, but in some way opposite. But I have not pursued this topic any further in this book, first because these arguments are enough to show that the decay of the body does not imply the destruction of the mind, and are hence enough to give mortals the hope of an after-life, and secondly because the premises which lead to the conclusion that the soul is immortal depend on an account of the whole of physics. This is required for two reasons. (First,) we need to know that absolutely all substances, or things which must be created by God in order to exist, are by their nature incorruptible and cannot ever cease to exist unless they are reduced to nothingness by God's denying his concurrence[1] to them. Secondly, we need to recognize that body, taken in the general sense, is a substance, so that it too never perishes. But the human body, in so far as it differs from other bodies, is simply made up of a certain configuration of limbs and other accidents[2] of this sort; whereas the human mind is not made up of any accidents in this way, but is a pure substance. For even if all the accidents of the mind change, so that it has different objects of the understanding and different desires and sensations, it does not on that account become a different mind; whereas a human body loses its identity merely as a result of a change in the shape of some of its parts. And it follows from this that while the body can very easily perish, the mind[3] is immortal by its very nature.

In the Third Meditation I have explained quite fully enough, I think, my principal argument for proving the existence of God. But in order to draw my readers' minds away from the senses as far as possible, I was not willing to use any comparison taken from bodily things. So it may be that many obscurities remain; but I hope they will be completely removed later, in my Replies to the Objections. One such problem, among others, is how the idea of a supremely perfect being, which is in us, possesses so much objective[4] reality that it can come only from a cause which is supremely perfect. In the Replies this is illustrated by the comparison of a

---

1 The continuous divine action necessary to maintain things in existence.
2 Descartes here uses this scholastic term to refer to those features of a thing which may alter, e.g. the particular size, shape etc. of a body, or the particular thoughts, desires etc. of a mind.
3 '. . . or the soul of man, for I make no distinction between them' (added in French version).
4 For Descartes' use of this term, see Med. III, p. 90 below.

very perfect machine, the idea of which is in the mind of some engineer. Just as the objective intricacy belonging to the idea must have some cause, namely the scientific knowledge of the engineer, or of someone else who passed the idea on to him, so the idea of God which is in us must have God himself as its cause.

In the Fourth Meditation it is proved that everything that we clearly and distinctly perceive is true, and I also explain what the nature of falsity consists in. These results need to be known both in order to confirm what has gone before and also to make intelligible what is to come later. (But here it should be noted in passing that I do not deal at all with sin, i.e. the error which is committed in pursuing good and evil, but only with the error that occurs in distinguishing truth from falsehood. And there is no discussion of matters pertaining to faith or the conduct of life, but simply of speculative truths which are known solely by means of the natural light.)[1]

In the Fifth Meditation, besides an account of corporeal nature taken in general, there is a new argument demonstrating the existence of God. Again, several difficulties may arise here, but these are resolved later in the Replies to the Objections. Finally I explain the sense in which it is true that the certainty even of geometrical demonstrations depends on the knowledge of God.

Lastly, in the Sixth Meditation, the intellect is distinguished from the imagination; the criteria for this distinction are explained; the mind is proved to be really distinct from the body, but is shown, notwithstanding, to be so closely joined to it that the mind and the body make up a kind of unit; there is a survey of all the errors which commonly come from the senses, and an explanation of how they may be avoided; and, lastly, there is a presentation of all the arguments which enable the existence of material things to be inferred. The great benefit of these arguments is not, in my view, that they prove what they establish – namely that there really is a world, and that human beings have bodies and so on – since no sane person has ever seriously doubted these things. The point is that in considering these arguments we come to realize that they are not as solid or as transparent as the arguments which lead us to knowledge of our own minds and of God, so that the latter are the most certain and evident of all possible objects of knowledge for the human intellect. Indeed, this is the one thing that I set myself to prove in these Meditations. And for that reason I will not now go over the various other issues in the book which are dealt with as they come up.

---

1 Descartes added this passage on the advice of Arnauld (cf. AT VII 215; CSM II 151). He told Mersenne 'please put the words in brackets so that it can be seen that they have been added' (letter of 18 March 1641).

*in which are demonstrated the existence of God and the
distinction between the human soul and the body*

FIRST MEDITATION

What can be called into doubt

Some years ago I was struck by the large number of falsehoods that I had accepted as true in my childhood, and by the highly doubtful nature of the whole edifice that I had subsequently based on them. I realized that it was necessary, once in the course of my life, to demolish everything completely and start again right from the foundations if I wanted to establish anything at all in the sciences that was stable and likely to last. But the task looked an enormous one, and I began to wait until I should reach a mature enough age to ensure that no subsequent time of life would be more suitable for tackling such inquiries. This led me to put the project off for so long that I would now be to blame if by pondering over it any further I wasted the time still left for carrying it out. So today I 18 have expressly rid my mind of all worries and arranged for myself a clear stretch of free time. I am here quite alone, and at last I will devote myself sincerely and without reservation to the general demolition of my opinions.

But to accomplish this, it will not be necessary for me to show that all my opinions are false, which is something I could perhaps never manage. Reason now leads me to think that I should hold back my assent from opinions which are not completely certain and indubitable just as carefully as I do from those which are patently false. So, for the purpose of rejecting all my opinions, it will be enough if I find in each of them at least some reason for doubt. And to do this I will not need to run through them all individually, which would be an endless task. Once the foundations of a building are undermined, anything built on them collapses of its own accord; so I will go straight for the basic principles on which all my former beliefs rested.

Whatever I have up till now accepted as most true I have acquired either from the senses or through the senses. But from time to time I have found that the senses deceive, and it is prudent never to trust completely those who have deceived us even once.

Yet although the senses occasionally deceive us with respect to objects which are very small or in the distance, there are many other beliefs about which doubt is quite impossible, even though they are derived from the senses – for example, that I am here, sitting by the fire, wearing a winter dressing-gown, holding this piece of paper in my hands, and so on. Again, how could it be denied that these hands or this whole body are mine? Unless perhaps I were to liken myself to madmen, whose brains are so damaged by the persistent vapours of melancholia that they firmly maintain they are kings when they are paupers, or say they are dressed in purple when they are naked, or that their heads are made of earthenware, or that they are pumpkins, or made of glass. But such people are insane, and I would be thought equally mad if I took anything from them as a model for myself.

better than Madmen

A brilliant piece of reasoning! As if I were not a man who sleeps at night, and regularly has all the same experiences[1] while asleep as madmen do when awake – indeed sometimes even more improbable ones. How often, asleep at night, am I convinced of just such familiar events – that I am here in my dressing-gown, sitting by the fire – when in fact I am lying undressed in bed! Yet at the moment my eyes are certainly wide awake when I look at this piece of paper; I shake my head and it is not asleep; as I stretch out and feel my hand I do so deliberately, and I know what I am doing. All this would not happen with such distinctness to someone asleep. Indeed! As if I did not remember other occasions when I have been tricked by exactly similar thoughts while asleep! As I think about this more carefully, I see plainly that there are never any sure signs by means of which being awake can be distinguished from being asleep. The result is that I begin to feel dazed, and this very feeling only reinforces the notion that I may be asleep.

challenge

Suppose then that I am dreaming, and that these particulars – that my eyes are open, that I am moving my head and stretching out my hands – are not true. Perhaps, indeed, I do not even have such hands or such a body at all. Nonetheless, it must surely be admitted that the visions which come in sleep are like paintings, which must have been fashioned in the likeness of things that are real, and hence that at least these general kinds of things – eyes, head, hands and the body as a whole – are things which are not imaginary but are real and exist. For even when painters try to create sirens and satyrs with the most extraordinary bodies, they cannot give them natures which are new in all respects; they simply jumble up the limbs of different animals. Or if perhaps they manage to think up something so new that nothing remotely similar has ever been seen before – something which is therefore completely fictitious and unreal – at least the colours used in the composition must be real. By similar reasoning, although these general kinds of things – eyes, head, hands and so on – could be imaginary, it must at least be admitted that certain other even simpler and more universal things are real. These are

19

20

1 '. . . and in my dreams regularly represent to myself the same things' (French version).

as it were the real colours from which we form all the images of things, whether true or false, that occur in our thought.

This class appears to include corporeal nature in general, and its extension; the shape of extended things; the quantity, or size and number of these things; the place in which they may exist, the time through which they may endure,[1] and so on.

So a reasonable conclusion from this might be that physics, astronomy, medicine, and all other disciplines which depend on the study of composite things, are doubtful; while arithmetic, geometry and other subjects of this kind, which deal only with the simplest and most general things, regardless of whether they really exist in nature or not, contain something certain and indubitable. For whether I am awake or asleep, two and three added together are five, and a square has no more than four sides. It seems impossible that such transparent truths should incur any suspicion of being false.

And yet firmly rooted in my mind is the long-standing belief that there is an omnipotent God who made me the kind of creature that I am. How do I know that he has not brought it about that there is no earth, no sky, no extended thing, no shape, no size, no place, while at the same time ensuring that all these things appear to me to exist just as they do now? Moreover, since I sometimes consider that others go astray in cases where they think they have the most perfect knowledge, may I not similarly go wrong every time I add two and three or count the sides of a square, or in some even simpler matter, if that is imaginable? But perhaps God would not have wished me to be deceived in this way, since he is said to be supremely good. But if it were inconsistent with his goodness to have created me such that I am deceived all the time, it would seem equally foreign to his goodness to allow me to be deceived even occasionally; yet this last assertion cannot be made.[2]

Perhaps there may be some who would prefer to deny the existence of so powerful a God rather than believe that everything else is uncertain. Let us not argue with them, but grant them that everything said about God is a fiction. According to their supposition, then, I have arrived at my present state by fate or chance or a continuous chain of events, or by some other means; yet since deception and error seem to be imperfections, the less powerful they make my original cause, the more likely it is that I am so imperfect as to be deceived all the time. I have no answer to these arguments, but am finally compelled to admit that there is not one of my former beliefs about which a doubt may not properly be raised; and this is not a flippant or ill-considered conclusion, but is based

---

1 '. . . the place where they are, the time which measures their duration' (French version).
2 '. . . yet I cannot doubt that he does allow this' (French version).

on powerful and well thought-out reasons. So in future I must withhold **22**
my assent from these former beliefs just as carefully as I would from
obvious falsehoods, if I want to discover any certainty.[1]

But it is not enough merely to have noticed this; I must make an effort
to remember it. My habitual opinions keep coming back, and, despite my
wishes, they capture my belief, which is as it were bound over to them as
a result of long occupation and the law of custom. I shall never get out of
the habit of confidently assenting to these opinions, so long as I suppose
them to be what in fact they are, namely highly probable opinions –
opinions which, despite the fact that they are in a sense doubtful, as has
just been shown, it is still much more reasonable to believe than to deny.
In view of this, I think it will be a good plan to turn my will in completely the opposite direction and deceive myself, by pretending for a
time that these former opinions are utterly false and imaginary. I shall do
this until the weight of preconceived opinion is counter-balanced and the
distorting influence of habit no longer prevents my judgement from
perceiving things correctly. In the meantime, I know that no danger or
error will result from my plan, and that I cannot possibly go too far in my
distrustful attitude. This is because the task now in hand does not involve
action but merely the acquisition of knowledge.

I will suppose therefore that not God, who is supremely good and the
source of truth, but rather some malicious demon of the utmost power
and cunning has employed all his energies in order to deceive me. I shall
think that the sky, the air, the earth, colours, shapes, sounds and all
external things are merely the delusions of dreams which he has devised
to ensnare my judgement. I shall consider myself as not having hands or **23**
eyes, or flesh, or blood or senses, but as falsely believing that I have all
these things. I shall stubbornly and firmly persist in this meditation; and,
even if it is not in my power to know any truth, I shall at least do what is
in my power,[2] that is, resolutely guard against assenting to any falsehoods, so that the deceiver, however powerful and cunning he may be,
will be unable to impose on me in the slightest degree. But this is an
arduous undertaking, and a kind of laziness brings me back to normal
life. I am like a prisoner who is enjoying an imaginary freedom while
asleep; as he begins to suspect that he is asleep, he dreads being woken
up, and goes along with the pleasant illusion as long as he can. In the
same way, I happily slide back into my old opinions and dread being
shaken out of them, for fear that my peaceful sleep may be followed by
hard labour when I wake, and that I shall have to toil not in the light, but
amid the inextricable darkness of the problems I have now raised.

1 '. . . in the sciences' (added in French version).
2 '. . . nevertheless it is in my power to suspend my judgement' (French version).

SECOND MEDITATION

The nature of the human mind, and how it is better known than the body

So serious are the doubts into which I have been thrown as a result of yesterday's meditation that I can neither put them out of my mind nor see any way of resolving them. It feels as if I have fallen unexpectedly into a deep whirlpool which tumbles me around so that I can neither stand on the bottom nor swim up to the top. Nevertheless I will make an effort and once more attempt the same path which I started on yesterday. Anything which admits of the slightest doubt I will set aside just as if I had found it to be wholly false; and I will proceed in this way until I recognize something certain, or, if nothing else, until I at least recognize for certain that there is no certainty. Archimedes used to demand just one firm and immovable point in order to shift the entire earth; so I too can hope for great things if I manage to find just one thing, however slight, that is certain and unshakeable.

I will suppose then, that everything I see is spurious. I will believe that my memory tells me lies, and that none of the things that it reports ever happened. I have no senses. Body, shape, extension, movement and place are chimeras. So what remains true? Perhaps just the one fact that nothing is certain.

Yet apart from everything I have just listed, how do I know that there is not something else which does not allow even the slightest occasion for doubt? Is there not a God, or whatever I may call him, who puts into me[1] the thoughts I am now having? But why do I think this, since I myself may perhaps be the author of these thoughts? In that case am not I, at least, something? But I have just said that I have no senses and no body. This is the sticking point: what follows from this? Am I not so bound up with a body and with senses that I cannot exist without them? But I have convinced myself that there is absolutely nothing in the world, no sky, no earth, no minds, no bodies. Does it now follow that I too do not exist? No: if I convinced myself of something[2] then I certainly existed. But there is a deceiver of supreme power and cunning who is deliberately and constantly deceiving me. In that case I too undoubtedly exist, if he is deceiving me; and let him deceive me as much as he can, he will never bring it about that I am nothing so long as I think that I am something. So after considering everything very thoroughly, I must finally conclude that this proposition, *I am, I exist,* is necessarily true whenever it is put forward by me or conceived in my mind.

1 '. . . puts into my mind' (French version).
2 '. . . or thought anything at all' (French version).

But I do not yet have a sufficient understanding of what this 'I' is, that now necessarily exists. So I must be on my guard against carelessly taking something else to be this 'I', and so making a mistake in the very item of knowledge that I maintain is the most certain and evident of all. I will therefore go back and meditate on what I originally believed myself to be, before I embarked on this present train of thought. I will then subtract anything capable of being weakened, even minimally, by the arguments now introduced, so that what is left at the end may be exactly and only what is certain and unshakeable.

What then did I formerly think I was? A man. But what is a man? Shall I say 'a rational animal'? No; for then I should have to inquire what an animal is, what rationality is, and in this way one question would lead me down the slope to other harder ones, and I do not now have the time to waste on subtleties of this kind. Instead I propose to concentrate on what came into my thoughts spontaneously and quite naturally whenever I used to consider what I was. Well, the first thought to come to mind was that I had a face, hands, arms and the whole mechanical structure of limbs which can be seen in a corpse, and which I called the body. The next thought was that I was nourished, that I moved about, and that I engaged in sense-perception and thinking; and these actions I attributed to the soul. But as to the nature of this soul, either I did not think about this or else I imagined it to be something tenuous, like a wind or fire or ether, which permeated my more solid parts. As to the body, however, I had no doubts about it, but thought I knew its nature distinctly. If I had tried to describe the mental conception I had of it, I would have expressed it as follows: by a body I understand whatever has a determinable shape and a definable location and can occupy a space in such a way as to exclude any other body; it can be perceived by touch, sight, hearing, taste or smell, and can be moved in various ways, not by itself but by whatever else comes into contact with it. For, according to my judgement, the power of self-movement, like the power of sensation or of thought, was quite foreign to the nature of a body; indeed, it was a source of wonder to me that certain bodies were found to contain faculties of this kind.

But what shall I now say that I am, when I am supposing that there is some supremely powerful and, if it is permissible to say so, malicious deceiver, who is deliberately trying to trick me in every way he can? Can I now assert that I possess even the most insignificant of all the attributes which I have just said belong to the nature of a body? I scrutinize them, think about them, go over them again, but nothing suggests itself; it is tiresome and pointless to go through the list once more. But what about the attributes I assigned to the soul? Nutrition or movement? Since now I

26

27

He pulls the term soul out of a place that seems educated on the matter

do not have a body, these are mere fabrications. Sense-perception? This surely does not occur without a body, and besides, when asleep I have appeared to perceive through the senses many things which I afterwards realized I did not perceive through the senses at all. Thinking? At last I have discovered it – thought; this alone is inseparable from me. I am, I exist – that is certain. But for how long? For as long as I am thinking. For it could be that were I totally to cease from thinking, I should totally cease to exist. At present I am not admitting anything except what is necessarily true. I am, then, in the strict sense only a thing that thinks;[1] that is, I am a mind, or intelligence, or intellect, or reason – words whose meaning I have been ignorant of until now. But for all that I am a thing which is real and which truly exists. But what kind of a thing? As I have just said – a thinking thing.

What else am I? I will use my imagination.[2] I am not that structure of limbs which is called a human body. I am not even some thin vapour which permeates the limbs – a wind, fire, air, breath, or whatever I depict in my imagination; for these are things which I have supposed to be nothing. Let this supposition stand;[3] for all that I am still something. And yet may it not perhaps be the case that these very things which I am supposing to be nothing, because they are unknown to me, are in reality identical with the 'I' of which I am aware? I do not know, and for the moment I shall not argue the point, since I can make judgements only about things which are known to me. I know that I exist; the question is, what is this 'I' that I know? If the 'I' is understood strictly as we have been taking it, then it is quite certain that knowledge of it does not depend on things of whose existence I am as yet unaware; so it cannot depend on any of the things which I invent in my imagination. And this very word 'invent' shows me my mistake. It would indeed be a case of fictitious invention if I used my imagination to establish that I was something or other; for imagining is simply contemplating the shape or image of a corporeal thing. Yet now I know for certain both that I exist and at the same time that all such images and, in general, everything relating to the nature of body, could be mere dreams ⟨and chimeras⟩. Once this point has been grasped, to say 'I will use my imagination to get to know more distinctly what I am' would seem to be as silly as saying 'I

28

1 The word 'only' is most naturally taken as going with 'a thing that thinks', and this interpretation is followed in the French version. When discussing this passage with Gassendi, however, Descartes suggests that he meant the 'only' to govern 'in the strict sense'; cf. AT IXA 215; CSM II 276.
2 '. . . to see if I am not something more' (added in French version).
3 Lat. *maneat* ('let it stand'), first edition. The second edition has the indicative *manet*: 'The proposition still stands, *viz.* that I am nonetheless something.' The French version reads: 'without changing this supposition, I find that I am still certain that I am something'.

am now awake, and see some truth; but since my vision is not yet clear enough, I will deliberately fall asleep so that my dreams may provide a truer and clearer representation.' I thus realize that none of the things that the imagination enables me to grasp is at all relevant to this knowledge of myself which I possess, and that the mind must therefore be most carefully diverted from such things[1] if it is to perceive its own nature as distinctly as possible.

But what then am I? A thing that thinks. What is that? A thing that doubts, understands, affirms, denies, is willing, is unwilling, and also imagines and has sensory perceptions.

This is a considerable list, if everything on it belongs to me. But does it? Is it not one and the same 'I' who is now doubting almost everything, who nonetheless understands some things, who affirms that this one thing is true, denies everything else, desires to know more, is unwilling to be deceived, imagines many things even involuntarily, and is aware of many things which apparently come from the senses? Are not all these things just as true as the fact that I exist, even if I am asleep all the time, and even if he who created me is doing all he can to deceive me? Which of all these activities is distinct from my thinking? Which of them can be said to be separate from myself? The fact that it is I who am doubting and understanding and willing is so evident that I see no way of making it any clearer. But it is also the case that the 'I' who imagines is the same 'I'. For even if, as I have supposed, none of the objects of imagination are real, the power of imagination is something which really exists and is part of my thinking. Lastly, it is also the same 'I' who has sensory perceptions, or is aware of bodily things as it were through the senses. For example, I am now seeing light, hearing a noise, feeling heat. But I am asleep, so all this is false. Yet I certainly *seem* to see, to hear, and to be warmed. This cannot be false; what is called 'having a sensory perception' is strictly just this, and in this restricted sense of the term it is simply thinking.

From all this I am beginning to have a rather better understanding of what I am. But it still appears – and I cannot stop thinking this – that the corporeal things of which images are formed in my thought, and which the senses investigate, are known with much more distinctness than this puzzling 'I' which cannot be pictured in the imagination. And yet it is surely surprising that I should have a more distinct grasp of things which I realize are doubtful, unknown and foreign to me, than I have of that which is true and known – my own self. But I see what it is: my mind enjoys wandering off and will not yet submit to being restrained within the bounds of truth. Very well then; just this once let us give it a

29

30

1 '. . . from this manner of conceiving things' (French version).

completely free rein, so that after a while, when it is time to tighten the reins, it may more readily submit to being curbed.

Let us consider the things which people commonly think they understand most distinctly of all; that is, the bodies which we touch and see. I do not mean bodies in general – for general perceptions are apt to be somewhat more confused – but one particular body. Let us take, for example, this piece of wax. It has just been taken from the honeycomb; it has not yet quite lost the taste of the honey; it retains some of the scent of the flowers from which it was gathered; its colour, shape and size are plain to see; it is hard, cold and can be handled without difficulty; if you rap it with your knuckle it makes a sound. In short, it has everything which appears necessary to enable a body to be known as distinctly as possible. But even as I speak, I put the wax by the fire, and look: the residual taste is eliminated, the smell goes away, the colour changes, the shape is lost, the size increases; it becomes liquid and hot; you can hardly touch it, and if you strike it, it no longer makes a sound. But does the same wax remain? It must be admitted that it does; no one denies it, no one thinks otherwise. So what was it in the wax that I understood with such distinctness? Evidently none of the features which I arrived at by means of the senses; for whatever came under taste, smell, sight, touch or hearing has now altered – yet the wax remains.

Perhaps the answer lies in the thought which now comes to my mind; namely, the wax was not after all the sweetness of the honey, or the fragrance of the flowers, or the whiteness, or the shape, or the sound, but was rather a body which presented itself to me in these various forms a little while ago, but which now exhibits different ones. But what exactly is it that I am now imagining? Let us concentrate, take away everything which does not belong to the wax, and see what is left: merely something extended, flexible and changeable. But what is meant here by 'flexible' and 'changeable'? Is it what I picture in my imagination: that this piece of wax is capable of changing from a round shape to a square shape, or from a square shape to a triangular shape? Not at all; for I can grasp that the wax is capable of countless changes of this kind, yet I am unable to run through this immeasurable number of changes in my imagination, from which it follows that it is not the faculty of imagination that gives me my grasp of the wax as flexible and changeable. And what is meant by 'extended'? Is the extension of the wax also unknown? For it increases if the wax melts, increases again if it boils, and is greater still if the heat is increased. I would not be making a correct judgement about the nature of wax unless I believed it capable of being extended in many more different ways than I will ever encompass in my imagination. I must therefore admit that the nature of this piece of wax is in no way revealed by my imagination, but is perceived by the mind alone. (I am speaking of this particular piece of wax; the point is even clearer with regard to wax in general.) But what is this wax which is perceived by the mind alone?[1] It is of course the same wax which I see, which I touch, which I picture in my imagination, in short the same wax which I thought it to be from the start. And yet, and here is the point, the perception I have of it[2] is a case not of vision or touch or imagination – nor has it ever been, despite previous appearances – but of purely mental scrutiny; and this can be imperfect and confused, as it was before, or clear and distinct as it is now, depending on how carefully I concentrate on what the wax consists in.

bc saw it alter

But as I reach this conclusion I am amazed at how ⟨weak and⟩ prone to error my mind is. For although I am thinking about these matters within myself, silently and without speaking, nonetheless the actual words bring me up short, and I am almost tricked by ordinary ways of talking. We say that we see the wax itself, if it is there before us, not that we judge it to be there from its colour or shape; and this might lead me to conclude without more ado that knowledge of the wax comes from what the eye sees, and not from the scrutiny of the mind alone. But then if I look out of the window and see men crossing the square, as I just happen to have done, I normally say that I see the men themselves, just as I say that I see the wax. Yet do I see any more than hats and coats which could conceal automatons? I *judge* that they are men. And so something which I thought I was seeing with my eyes is in fact grasped solely by the faculty of judgement which is in my mind.

32

However, one who wants to achieve knowledge above the ordinary level should feel ashamed at having taken ordinary ways of talking as a basis for doubt. So let us proceed, and consider on which occasion my perception of the nature of the wax was more perfect and evident. Was it when I first looked at it, and believed I knew it by my external senses, or at least by what they call the 'common' sense[3] – that is, the power of imagination? Or is my knowledge more perfect now, after a more careful investigation of the nature of the wax and of the means by which it is known? Any doubt on this issue would clearly be foolish; for what distinctness was there in my earlier perception? Was there anything in it which an animal could not possess? But when I distinguish the wax from its outward forms – take the clothes off, as it were, and consider it naked – then although my judgement may still contain errors, at least my perception now requires a human mind.

If considered naked what is it?

But what am I to say about this mind, or about myself? (So far,

33

1 '...which can be conceived only by the understanding or the mind' (French version).
2 '... or rather the act whereby it is perceived' (added in French version).
3 See note p. 120 below. – *S Seußes*

remember, I am not admitting that there is anything else in me except a mind.) What, I ask, is this 'I' which seems to perceive the wax so distinctly? Surely my awareness of my own self is not merely much truer and more certain than my awareness of the wax, but also much more distinct and evident. For if I judge that the wax exists from the fact that I see it, clearly this same fact entails much more evidently that I myself also exist. It is possible that what I see is not really the wax; it is possible that I do not even have eyes with which to see anything. But when I see, or think I see (I am not here distinguishing the two), it is simply not possible that I who am now thinking am not something. By the same token, if I judge that the wax exists from the fact that I touch it, the same result follows, namely that I exist. If I judge that it exists from the fact that I imagine it, or for any other reason, exactly the same thing follows. And the result that I have grasped in the case of the wax may be applied to everything else located outside me. Moreover, if my perception of the wax seemed more distinct[1] after it was established not just by sight or touch but by many other considerations, it must be admitted that I now know myself even more distinctly. This is because every consideration whatsoever which contributes to my perception of the wax, or of any other body, cannot but establish even more effectively the nature of my own mind. But besides this, there is so much else in the mind itself which can serve to make my knowledge of it more distinct, that it scarcely seems worth going through the contributions made by considering bodily things.

34   I see that without any effort I have now finally got back to where I wanted. I now know that even bodies are not strictly perceived by the senses or the faculty of imagination but by the intellect alone, and that this perception derives not from their being touched or seen but from their being understood; and in view of this I know plainly that I can achieve an easier and more evident perception of my own mind than of anything else. But since the habit of holding on to old opinions cannot be set aside so quickly, I should like to stop here and meditate for some time on this new knowledge I have gained, so as to fix it more deeply in my memory.

THIRD MEDITATION

The existence of God

I will now shut my eyes, stop my ears, and withdraw all my senses. I will eliminate from my thoughts all images of bodily things, or rather, since

1 The French version has 'more clear and distinct' and, at the end of this sentence, 'more evidently, distinctly and clearly'.

this is hardly possible, I will regard all such images as vacuous, false and worthless. I will converse with myself and scrutinize myself more deeply; and in this way I will attempt to achieve, little by little, a more intimate knowledge of myself. I am a thing that thinks: that is, a thing that doubts, affirms, denies, understands a few things, is ignorant of many things,[1] is willing, is unwilling, and also which imagines and has sensory perceptions; for as I have noted before, even though the objects of my sensory experience and imagination may have no existence outside me, nonetheless the modes of thinking which I refer to as cases of sensory perception and imagination, in so far as they are simply modes of thinking, do exist within me – of that I am certain.

In this brief list I have gone through everything I truly know, or at least everything I have so far discovered that I know. Now I will cast around more carefully to see whether there may be other things within me which I have not yet noticed. I am certain that I am a thinking thing. Do I not therefore also know what is required for my being certain about anything? In this first item of knowledge there is simply a clear and distinct perception of what I am asserting; this would not be enough to make me certain of the truth of the matter if it could ever turn out that something which I perceived with such clarity and distinctness was false. So I now seem to be able to lay it down as a general rule that whatever I perceive very clearly and distinctly is true.[2]

Yet I previously accepted as wholly certain and evident many things which I afterwards realized were doubtful. What were these? The earth, sky, stars, and everything else that I apprehended with the senses. But what was it about them that I perceived clearly? Just that the ideas, or thoughts, of such things appeared before my mind. Yet even now I am not denying that these ideas occur within me. But there was something else which I used to assert, and which through habitual belief I thought I perceived clearly, although I did not in fact do so. This was that there were things outside me which were the sources of my ideas and which resembled them in all respects. Here was my mistake; or at any rate, if my judgement was true, it was not thanks to the strength of my perception.[3]

But what about when I was considering something very simple and straightforward in arithmetic or geometry, for example that two and three added together make five, and so on? Did I not see at least these things clearly enough to affirm their truth? Indeed, the only reason for my later judgement that they were open to doubt was that it occurred to me that perhaps some God could have given me a nature such that I was deceived even in matters which seemed most evident. And whenever my

1 The French version here inserts 'loves, hates'.
2 '... all the things which we conceive very clearly and very distinctly are true' (French version).
3 '... it was not because of any knowledge I possessed' (French version).

preconceived belief in the supreme power of God comes to mind, I cannot but admit that it would be easy for him, if he so desired, to bring it about that I go wrong even in those matters which I think I see utterly clearly with my mind's eye. Yet when I turn to the things themselves which I think I perceive very clearly, I am so convinced by them that I spontaneously declare: let whoever can do so deceive me, he will never bring it about that I am nothing, so long as I continue to think I am something; or make it true at some future time that I have never existed, since it is now true that I exist; or bring it about that two and three added together are more or less than five, or anything of this kind in which I see a manifest contradiction. And since I have no cause to think that there is a deceiving God, and I do not yet even know for sure whether there is a God at all, any reason for doubt which depends simply on this belief is a very slight and, so to speak, metaphysical one. But in order to remove even this slight reason for doubt, as soon as the opportunity arises I must examine whether there is a God, and, if there is, whether he can be a deceiver. For if I do not know this, it seems that I can never be quite certain about anything else.

37 First, however, considerations of order appear to dictate that I now classify my thoughts into definite kinds,[1] and ask which of them can properly be said to be the bearers of truth and falsity. Some of my thoughts are as it were the images of things, and it is only in these cases that the term 'idea' is strictly appropriate – for example, when I think of a man, or a chimera, or the sky, or an angel, or God. Other thoughts have various additional forms: thus when I will, or am afraid, or affirm, or deny, there is always a particular thing which I take as the object of my thought, but my thought includes something more than the likeness of that thing. Some thoughts in this category are called volitions or emotions, while others are called judgements.

Now as far as ideas are concerned, provided they are considered solely in themselves and I do not refer them to anything else, they cannot strictly speaking be false; for whether it is a goat or a chimera that I am imagining, it is just as true that I imagine the former as the latter. As for the will and the emotions, here too one need not worry about falsity; for even if the things which I may desire are wicked or even non-existent, that does not make it any less true that I desire them. Thus the only remaining thoughts where I must be on my guard against making a mistake are judgements. And the chief and most common mistake which

---

1 The opening of this sentence is greatly expanded in the French version: 'In order that I may have the opportunity of examining this without interrupting the order of meditating which I have decided upon, which is to start only from those notions which I find first of all in my mind and pass gradually to those which I may find later on, I must here divide my thoughts . . .'

is to be found here consists in my judging that the ideas which are in me resemble, or conform to, things located outside me. Of course, if I considered just the ideas themselves simply as modes of my thought, without referring them to anything else, they could scarcely give me any material for error.

Among my ideas, some appear to be innate, some to be adventitious,[1] and others to have been invented by me. My understanding of what a thing is, what truth is, and what thought is, seems to derive simply from my own nature. But my hearing a noise, as I do now, or seeing the sun, or feeling the fire, comes from things which are located outside me, or so I have hitherto judged. Lastly, sirens, hippogriffs and the like are my own invention. But perhaps all my ideas may be thought of as adventitious, or they may all be innate, or all made up; for as yet I have not clearly perceived their true origin.

But the chief question at this point concerns the ideas which I take to be derived from things existing outside me: what is my reason for thinking that they resemble these things? Nature has apparently taught me to think this. But in addition I know by experience that these ideas do not depend on my will, and hence that they do not depend simply on me. Frequently I notice them even when I do not want to: now, for example, I feel the heat whether I want to or not, and this is why I think that this sensation or idea of heat comes to me from something other than myself, namely the heat of the fire by which I am sitting. And the most obvious judgement for me to make is that the thing in question transmits to me its own likeness rather than something else.

I will now see if these arguments are strong enough. When I say 'Nature taught me to think this', all I mean is that a spontaneous impulse leads me to believe it, not that its truth has been revealed to me by some natural light. There is a big difference here. Whatever is revealed to me by the natural light – for example that from the fact that I am doubting it follows that I exist, and so on – cannot in any way be open to doubt. This is because there cannot be another faculty[2] both as trustworthy as the natural light and also capable of showing me that such things are not true. But as for my natural impulses, I have often judged in the past that they were pushing me in the wrong direction when it was a question of choosing the good, and I do not see why I should place any greater confidence in them in other matters.[3]

Then again, although these ideas do not depend on my will, it does not follow that they must come from things located outside me. Just as the

38

39

---

1 '... foreign to me and coming from outside' (French version).
2 '... or power for distinguishing truth from falsehood' (French version).
3 '... concerning truth and falsehood' (French version).

impulses which I was speaking of a moment ago seem opposed to my will even though they are within me, so there may be some other faculty not yet fully known to me, which produces these ideas without any assistance from external things; this is, after all, just how I have always thought ideas are produced in me when I am dreaming.

And finally, even if these ideas did come from things other than myself, it would not follow that they must resemble those things. Indeed, I think I have often discovered a great disparity ⟨between an object and its idea⟩ in many cases. For example, there are two different ideas of the sun which I find within me. One of them, which is acquired as it were from the senses and which is a prime example of an idea which I reckon to come from an external source, makes the sun appear very small. The other idea is based on astronomical reasoning, that is, it is derived from certain notions which are innate in me (or else it is constructed by me in some other way), and this idea shows the sun to be several times larger than the earth. Obviously both these ideas cannot resemble the sun which exists outside me; and reason persuades me that the idea which seems to have emanated most directly from the sun itself has in fact no resemblance to it at all.

40   All these considerations are enough to establish that it is not reliable judgement but merely some blind impulse that has made me believe up till now that there exist things distinct from myself which transmit to me ideas or images of themselves through the sense organs or in some other way.

But it now occurs to me that there is another way of investigating whether some of the things of which I possess ideas exist outside me. In so far as the ideas are ⟨considered⟩ simply ⟨as⟩ modes of thought, there is no recognizable inequality among them: they all appear to come from within me in the same fashion. But in so far as different ideas ⟨are considered as images which⟩ represent different things, it is clear that they differ widely. Undoubtedly, the ideas which represent substances to me amount to something more and, so to speak, contain within themselves more objective[1] reality than the ideas which merely represent modes or accidents. Again, the idea that gives me my understanding of a supreme God, eternal, infinite, ⟨immutable,⟩ omniscient, omnipotent and the creator of all things that exist apart from him, certainly has in it more objective reality than the ideas that represent finite substances.

---

1 '. . . i.e. participate by representation in a higher degree of being or perfection' (added in French version). According to the scholastic distinction invoked in the paragraphs that follow, the 'formal' reality of anything is its own intrinsic reality, while the 'objective' reality of an idea is a function of its representational content. Thus if an idea *A* represents some object *X* which is *F*, then *F*-ness will be contained 'formally' in *X* but 'objectively' in *A*.

Now it is manifest by the natural light that there must be at least as much ⟨reality⟩ in the efficient and total cause as in the effect of that cause. For where, I ask, could the effect get its reality from, if not from the cause? And how could the cause give it to the effect unless it possessed it? It follows from this both that something cannot arise from nothing, and also that what is more perfect – that is, contains in itself more reality – cannot arise from what is less perfect. And this is transparently true not only in the case of effects which possess ⟨what the philosophers call⟩ actual or formal reality, but also in the case of ideas, where one is considering only ⟨what they call⟩ objective reality. A stone, for example, which previously did not exist, cannot begin to exist unless it is produced by something which contains, either formally or eminently everything to be found in the stone;[1] similarly, heat cannot be produced in an object which was not previously hot, except by something of at least the same order ⟨degree or kind⟩ of perfection as heat, and so on. But it is also true that the *idea* of heat, or of a stone, cannot exist in me unless it is put there by some cause which contains at least as much reality as I conceive to be in the heat or in the stone. For although this cause does not transfer any of its actual or formal reality to my idea, it should not on that account be supposed that it must be less real.[2] The nature of an idea is such that of itself it requires no formal reality except what it derives from my thought, of which it is a mode.[3] But in order for a given idea to contain such and such objective reality, it must surely derive it from some cause which contains at least as much formal reality as there is objective reality in the idea. For if we suppose that an idea contains something which was not in its cause, it must have got this from nothing; yet the mode of being by which a thing exists objectively ⟨or representatively⟩ in the intellect by way of an idea, imperfect though it may be, is certainly not nothing, and so it cannot come from nothing.

And although the reality which I am considering in my ideas is merely objective reality, I must not on that account suppose that the same reality need not exist formally in the causes of my ideas, but that it is enough for it to be present in them objectively. For just as the objective mode of being belongs to ideas by their very nature, so the formal mode of being belongs to the causes of ideas – or at least the first and most important ones – by *their* very nature. And although one idea may perhaps originate from another, there cannot be an infinite regress here; eventually one

1 '. . . i.e. it will contain in itself the same things as are in the stone or other more excellent things' (added in French version). In scholastic terminology, to possess a property 'formally' is to possess it literally, in accordance with its definition; to possess it 'eminently' is to possess it in some higher form.
2 '. . . that this cause must be less real' (French version).
3 '. . . i.e. a manner or way of thinking' (added in French version).

41

42

must reach a primary idea, the cause of which will be like an archetype which contains formally ⟨and in fact⟩ all the reality ⟨or perfection⟩ which is present only objectively ⟨or representatively⟩ in the idea. So it is clear to me, by the natural light, that the ideas in me are like ⟨pictures, or⟩ images which can easily fall short of the perfection of the things from which they are taken, but which cannot contain anything greater or more perfect.

The longer and more carefully I examine all these points, the more clearly and distinctly I recognize their truth. But what is my conclusion to be? If the objective reality of any of my ideas turns out to be so great that I am sure the same reality does not reside in me, either formally or eminently, and hence that I myself cannot be its cause, it will necessarily follow that I am not alone in the world, but that some other thing which is the cause of this idea also exists. But if no such idea is to be found in me, I shall have no argument to convince me of the existence of anything apart from myself. For despite a most careful and comprehensive survey, this is the only argument I have so far been able to find.

Among my ideas, apart from the idea which gives me a representation of myself, which cannot present any difficulty in this context, there are ideas which variously represent God, corporeal and inanimate things, angels, animals and finally other men like myself.

As far as concerns the ideas which represent other men, or animals, or angels, I have no difficulty in understanding that they could be put together from the ideas I have of myself, of corporeal things and of God, even if the world contained no men besides me, no animals and no angels.

As to my ideas of corporeal things, I can see nothing in them which is so great ⟨or excellent⟩ as to make it seem impossible that it originated in myself. For if I scrutinize them thoroughly and examine them one by one, in the way in which I examined the idea of the wax yesterday, I notice that the things which I perceive clearly and distinctly in them are very few in number. The list comprises size, or extension in length, breadth and depth; shape, which is a function of the boundaries of this extension; position, which is a relation between various items possessing shape; and motion, or change in position; to these may be added substance, duration and number. But as for all the rest, including light and colours, sounds, smells, tastes, heat and cold and the other tactile qualities, I think of these only in a very confused and obscure way, to the extent that I do not even know whether they are true or false, that is, whether the ideas I have of them are ideas of real things or of non-things.[1] For although, as I have noted before, falsity in the strict sense, or formal falsity, can occur only in

---

1 '. . . chimerical things which cannot exist' (French version).

judgements, there is another kind of falsity, material falsity, which occurs in ideas, when they represent non-things as things. For example, the ideas which I have of heat and cold contain so little clarity and distinctness that   44
they do not enable me to tell whether cold is merely the absence of heat or vice versa, or whether both of them are real qualities, or neither is. And since there can be no ideas which are not as it were of things,[1] if it is true that cold is nothing but the absence of heat, the idea which represents it to me as something real and positive deserves to be called false; and the same goes for other ideas of this kind.

Such ideas obviously do not require me to posit a source distinct from myself. For on the one hand, if they are false, that is, represent non-things, I know by the natural light that they arise from nothing – that is, they are in me only because of a deficiency and lack of perfection in my nature. If on the other hand they are true, then since the reality which they represent is so extremely slight that I cannot even distinguish it from a non-thing, I do not see why they cannot originate from myself.

With regard to the clear and distinct elements in my ideas of corporeal things, it appears that I could have borrowed some of these from my idea of myself, namely substance, duration, number and anything else of this kind. For example, I think that a stone is a substance, or is a thing capable of existing independently, and I also think that I am a substance. Admittedly I conceive of myself as a thing that thinks and is not extended, whereas I conceive of the stone as a thing that is extended and does not think, so that the two conceptions differ enormously; but they seem to agree with respect to the classification 'substance'.[2] Again, I perceive that I now exist, and remember that I have existed for some time; moreover, I have various thoughts which I can count; it is in these ways that I acquire the ideas of duration and number which I can then   45
transfer to other things. As for all the other elements which make up the ideas of corporeal things, namely extension, shape, position and movement, these are not formally contained in me, since I am nothing but a thinking thing; but since they are merely modes of a substance,[3] and I am a substance, it seems possible that they are contained in me eminently.

So there remain only the idea of God; and I must consider whether there is anything in the idea which could not have originated in myself. By the word 'God' I understand a substance that is infinite, ⟨eternal, immutable,⟩ independent, supremely intelligent, supremely powerful, and which created both myself and everything else (if anything else there be)

---

1 'And since ideas, being like images, must in each case appear to us to represent something' (French version).
2 '. . . in so far as they represent substances' (French version).
3 '. . . and as it were the garments under which corporeal substance appears to us' (French version).

that exists. All these attributes are such that, the more carefully I concentrate on them, the less possible it seems that they[1] could have originated from me alone. So from what has been said it must be concluded that God necessarily exists.

It is true that I have the idea of substance in me in virtue of the fact that I am a substance; but this would not account for my having the idea of an infinite substance, when I am finite, unless this idea proceeded from some substance which really was infinite.

And I must not think that, just as my conceptions of rest and darkness are arrived at by negating movement and light, so my perception of the infinite is arrived at not by means of a true idea but merely by negating the finite. On the contrary, I clearly understand that there is more reality in an infinite substance than in a finite one, and hence that my perception of the infinite, that is God, is in some way prior to my perception of the finite, that is myself. For how could I understand that I doubted or desired – that is, lacked something – and that I was not wholly perfect, unless there were in me some idea of a more perfect being which enabled me to recognize my own defects by comparison?

Nor can it be said that this idea of God is perhaps materially false and so could have come from nothing,[2] which is what I observed just a moment ago in the case of the ideas of heat and cold, and so on. On the contrary, it is utterly clear and distinct, and contains in itself more objective reality than any other idea; hence there is no idea which is in itself truer or less liable to be suspected of falsehood. This idea of a supremely perfect and infinite being is, I say, true in the highest degree; for although perhaps one may imagine that such a being does not exist, it cannot be supposed that the idea of such a being represents something unreal, as I said with regard to the idea of cold. The idea is, moreover, utterly clear and distinct; for whatever I clearly and distinctly perceive as being real and true, and implying any perfection, is wholly contained in it. It does not matter that I do not grasp the infinite, or that there are countless additional attributes of God which I cannot in any way grasp, and perhaps cannot even reach in my thought; for it is in the nature of the infinite not to be grasped by a finite being like myself. It is enough that I understand[3] the infinite, and that I judge that all the attributes which I clearly perceive and know to imply some perfection – and perhaps countless others of which I am ignorant – are present in God either

46

---

1 '. . . that the idea I have of them' (French version).

2 '. . . i.e. could be in me in virtue of my imperfection' (added in French version).

3 According to Descartes one can know or understand something without fully grasping it 'just as we can touch a mountain but not put our arms around it. To grasp something is to embrace it in one's thought; to know something, it suffices to touch it with one's thought' (letter to Mersenne, 26 May 1630).

formally or eminently. This is enough to make the idea that I have of God the truest and most clear and distinct of all my ideas.

But perhaps I am something greater than I myself understand, and all the perfections which I attribute to God are somehow in me potentially, though not yet emerging or actualized. For I am now experiencing a gradual increase in my knowledge, and I see nothing to prevent its increasing more and more to infinity. Further, I see no reason why I should not be able to use this increased knowledge to acquire all the other perfections of God. And finally, if the potentiality for these perfections is already within me, why should not this be enough to generate the idea of such perfections?   47

But all this is impossible. First, though it is true that there is a gradual increase in my knowledge, and that I have many potentialities which are not yet actual, this is all quite irrelevant to the idea of God, which contains absolutely nothing that is potential;[1] indeed, this gradual increase in knowledge is itself the surest sign of imperfection. What is more, even if my knowledge always increases more and more, I recognize that it will never actually be infinite, since it will never reach the point where it is not capable of a further increase; God, on the other hand, I take to be actually infinite, so that nothing can be added to his perfection. And finally, I perceive that the objective being of an idea cannot be produced merely by potential being, which strictly speaking is nothing, but only by actual or formal being.

If one concentrates carefully, all this is quite evident by the natural light. But when I relax my concentration, and my mental vision is blinded by the images of things perceived by the senses, it is not so easy for me to remember why the idea of a being more perfect than myself must necessarily proceed from some being which is in reality more perfect. I   48 should therefore like to go further and inquire whether I myself, who have this idea, could exist if no such being existed.

From whom, in that case, would I derive my existence? From myself presumably, or from my parents, or from some other beings less perfect than God; for nothing more perfect than God, or even as perfect, can be thought of or imagined.

Yet if I derived my existence from myself,[2] then I should neither doubt nor want, nor lack anything at all; for I should have given myself all the perfections of which I have any idea, and thus I should myself be God. I must not suppose that the items I lack would be more difficult to acquire than those I now have. On the contrary, it is clear that, since I am a thinking thing or substance, it would have been far more difficult for

---

1 '. . . but only what is actual and real' (added in French version).
2 '. . . and were independent of every other being' (added in French version).

me to emerge out of nothing than merely to acquire knowledge of the many things of which I am ignorant – such knowledge being merely an accident of that substance. And if I had derived my existence from myself, which is a greater achievement, I should certainly not have denied myself the knowledge in question, which is something much easier to acquire, or indeed any of the attributes which I perceive to be contained in the idea of God; for none of them seem any harder to achieve. And if any of them were harder to achieve, they would certainly appear so to me, if I had indeed got all my other attributes from myself, since I should experience a limitation of my power in this respect.

I do not escape the force of these arguments by supposing that I have always existed as I do now, as if it followed from this that there was no need to look for any author of my existence. For a lifespan can be divided into countless parts, each completely independent of the others, so that it does not follow from the fact that I existed a little while ago that I must exist now, unless there is some cause which as it were creates me afresh at this moment – that is, which preserves me. For it is quite clear to anyone who attentively considers the nature of time that the same power and action are needed to preserve anything at each individual moment of its duration as would be required to create that thing anew if it were not yet in existence. Hence the distinction between preservation and creation is only a conceptual one,[1] and this is one of the things that are evident by the natural light.

I must therefore now ask myself whether I possess some power enabling me to bring it about that I who now exist will still exist a little while from now. For since I am nothing but a thinking thing – or at least since I am now concerned only and precisely with that part of me which is a thinking thing – if there were such a power in me, I should undoubtedly be aware of it. But I experience no such power, and this very fact makes me recognize most clearly that I depend on some being distinct from myself.

But perhaps this being is not God, and perhaps I was produced either by my parents or by other causes less perfect than God. No; for as I have said before, it is quite clear that there must be at least as much in the cause as in the effect.[2] And therefore whatever kind of cause is eventually proposed, since I am a thinking thing and have within me some idea of God, it must be admitted that what caused me is itself a thinking thing and possesses the idea of all the perfections which I attribute to God. In respect of this cause one may again inquire whether it derives its existence from itself or from another cause. If from itself, then it is clear from what has been said that it is itself God, since if it has the power of

1 Cf. *Principles*, Part 1, art. 62 (p. 181 below).
2 '. . . at least as much reality in the cause as in its effect' (French version).

existing through its own might,[1] then undoubtedly it also has the power of actually possessing all the perfections of which it has an idea – that is, all the perfections which I conceive to be in God. If, on the other hand, it derives its existence from another cause, then the same question may be repeated concerning this further cause, namely whether it derives its existence from itself or from another cause, until eventually the ultimate cause is reached, and this will be God.

It is clear enough that an infinite regress is impossible here, especially since I am dealing not just with the cause that produced me in the past, but also and most importantly with the cause that preserves me at the present moment.

Nor can it be supposed that several partial causes contributed to my creation, or that I received the idea of one of the perfections which I attribute to God from one cause and the idea of another from another – the supposition here being that all the perfections are to be found somewhere in the universe but not joined together in a single being, God. On the contrary, the unity, the simplicity, or the inseparability of all the attributes of God is one of the most important of the perfections which I understand him to have. And surely the idea of the unity of all his perfections could not have been placed in me by any cause which did not also provide me with the ideas of the other perfections; for no cause could have made me understand the interconnection and inseparability of the perfections without at the same time making me recognize what they were.

Lastly, as regards my parents, even if everything I have ever believed about them is true, it is certainly not they who preserve me; and in so far as I am a thinking thing, they did not even make me; they merely placed certain dispositions in the matter which I have always regarded as containing me, or rather my mind, for that is all I now take myself to 51 be. So there can be no difficulty regarding my parents in this context. Altogether then, it must be concluded that the mere fact that I exist and have within me an idea of a most perfect being, that is, God, provides a very clear proof that God indeed exists.

It only remains for me to examine how I received this idea from God. For I did not acquire it from the senses; it has never come to me unexpectedly, as usually happens with the ideas of things that are perceivable by the senses, when these things present themselves to the external sense organs – or seem to do so. And it was not invented by me either; for I am plainly unable either to take away anything from it or to add anything to it. The only remaining alternative is that it is innate in me, just as the idea of myself is innate in me.

1 Lat. *per se*; literally 'through itself'.

And indeed it is no surprise that God, in creating me, should have placed this idea in me to be, as it were, the mark of the craftsman stamped on his work – not that the mark need be anything distinct from the work itself. But the mere fact that God created me is a very strong basis for believing that I am somehow made in his image and likeness, and that I perceive that likeness, which includes the idea of God, by the same faculty which enables me to perceive myself. That is, when I turn my mind's eye upon myself, I understand that I am a thing which is incomplete and dependent on another and which aspires without limit to ever greater and better things; but I also understand at the same time that he on whom I depend has within him all those greater things, not just indefinitely and potentially but actually and infinitely, and hence that he is God. The whole force of the argument lies in this: I recognize that it would be impossible for me to exist with the kind of nature I have – that is, having within me the idea of God – were it not the case that God really existed. By 'God' I mean the very being the idea of whom is within me, that is, the possessor of all the perfections which I cannot grasp, but can somehow reach in my thought, who is subject to no defects whatsoever.[1] It is clear enough from this that he cannot be a deceiver, since it is manifest by the natural light that all fraud and deception depend on some defect.

But before examining this point more carefully and investigating other truths which may be derived from it, I should like to pause here and spend some time in the contemplation of God; to reflect on his attributes, and to gaze with wonder and adoration on the beauty of this immense light, so far as the eye of my darkened intellect can bear it. For just as we believe through faith that the supreme happiness of the next life consists solely in the contemplation of the divine majesty, so experience tells us that this same contemplation, albeit much less perfect, enables us to know the greatest joy of which we are capable in this life.

FOURTH MEDITATION

Truth and falsity

During these past few days I have accustomed myself to leading my mind away from the senses; and I have taken careful note of the fact that there is very little about corporeal things that is truly perceived, whereas much more is known about the human mind, and still more about God. The result is that I now have no difficulty in turning my mind away from

1 '. . . and has not one of the things which indicate some imperfection' (added in French version).

imaginable things[1] and towards things which are objects of the intellect alone and are totally separate from matter. And indeed the idea I have of the human mind, in so far as it is a thinking thing, which is not extended in length, breadth or height and has no other bodily characteristics, is much more distinct than the idea of any corporeal thing. And when I consider the fact that I have doubts, or that I am a thing that is incomplete and dependent, then there arises in me a clear and distinct idea of a being who is independent and complete, that is, an idea of God. And from the mere fact that there is such an idea within me, or that I who possess this idea exist, I clearly infer that God also exists, and that every single moment of my entire existence depends on him. So clear is this conclusion that I am confident that the human intellect cannot know anything that is more evident or more certain. And now, from this contemplation of the true God, in whom all the treasures of wisdom and the sciences lie hidden, I think I can see a way forward to the knowledge of other things.[2]

To begin with, I recognize that it is impossible that God should ever deceive me. For in every case of trickery or deception some imperfection is to be found; and although the ability to deceive appears to be an indication of cleverness or power, the will to deceive is undoubtedly evidence of malice or weakness, and so cannot apply to God.

Next, I know by experience that there is in me a faculty of judgement which, like everything else which is in me, I certainly received from God. And since God does not wish to deceive me, he surely did not give me the kind of faculty which would ever enable me to go wrong while using it correctly.

There would be no further doubt on this issue were it not that what I have just said appears to imply that I am incapable of ever going wrong. For if everything that is in me comes from God, and he did not endow me with a faculty for making mistakes, it appears that I can never go wrong. And certainly, so long as I think only of God, and turn my whole attention to him, I can find no cause of error or falsity. But when I turn back to myself, I know by experience that I am prone to countless errors. On looking for the cause of these errors, I find that I possess not only a real and positive idea of God, or a being who is supremely perfect, but also what may be described as a negative idea of nothingness, or of that which is farthest removed from all perfection. I realize that I am, as it were, something intermediate between God and nothingness, or between supreme being and non-being: my nature is such that in so far as I was created by the supreme being, there is nothing in me to enable me to go

1 '. . . from things which can be perceived by the senses or imagined' (French version).
2 '. . . of the other things in the universe' (French version).

wrong or lead me astray; but in so far as I participate in nothingness or non-being, that is, in so far as I am not myself the supreme being and am lacking in countless respects, it is no wonder that I make mistakes. I understand, then, that error as such is not something real which depends on God, but merely a defect. Hence my going wrong does not require me to have a faculty specially bestowed on me by God; it simply happens as a result of the fact that the faculty of true judgement which I have from God is in my case not infinite.

55   But this is still not entirely satisfactory. For error is not a pure negation,[1] but rather a privation or lack of some knowledge which somehow should be in me. And when I concentrate on the nature of God, it seems impossible that he should have placed in me a faculty which is not perfect of its kind, or which lacks some perfection which it ought to have. The more skilled the craftsman the more perfect the work produced by him; if this is so, how can anything produced by the supreme creator of all things not be complete and perfect in all respects? There is, moreover, no doubt that God could have given me a nature such that I was never mistaken; again, there is no doubt that he always wills what is best. Is it then better that I should make mistakes than that I should not do so?

As I reflect on these matters more attentively, it occurs to me first of all that it is no cause for surprise if I do not understand the reasons for some of God's actions; and there is no call to doubt his existence if I happen to find that there are other instances where I do not grasp why or how certain things were made by him. For since I now know that my own nature is very weak and limited, whereas the nature of God is immense, incomprehensible and infinite, I also know without more ado that he is capable of countless things whose causes are beyond my knowledge. And for this reason alone I consider the customary search for final causes to be totally useless in physics; there is considerable rashness in thinking myself capable of investigating the ⟨impenetrable⟩ purposes of God.

It also occurs to me that whenever we are inquiring whether the works of God are perfect, we ought to look at the whole universe, not just at one created thing on its own. For what would perhaps rightly appear very imperfect if it existed on its own is quite perfect when its function as a part of the universe is considered. It is true that, since my decision to doubt everything, it is so far only myself and God whose existence I have been able to know with certainty; but after considering the immense power of God, I cannot deny that many other things have been made by him, or at least could have been made, and hence that I may have a place in the universal scheme of things.

56

---

1 '. . . i.e. not simply the defect or lack of some perfection to which I have no proper claim' (added in French version).

Next, when I look more closely at myself and inquire into the nature of my errors (for these are the only evidence of some imperfection in me), I notice that they depend on two concurrent causes, namely on the faculty of knowledge which is in me, and on the faculty of choice or freedom of the will; that is, they depend on both the intellect and the will simultaneously. Now all that the intellect does is to enable me to perceive[1] the ideas which are subjects for possible judgements; and when regarded strictly in this light, it turns out to contain no error in the proper sense of that term. For although countless things may exist without there being any corresponding ideas in me, it should not, strictly speaking, be said that I am deprived of these ideas,[2] but merely that I lack them, in a negative sense. This is because I cannot produce any reason to prove that God ought to have given me a greater faculty of knowledge than he did; and no matter how skilled I understand a craftsman to be, this does not make me think he ought to have put into every one of his works all the perfections which he is able to put into some of them. Besides, I cannot complain that the will or freedom of choice which I received from God is not sufficiently extensive or perfect, since I know by experience that it is not restricted in any way. Indeed, I think it is very noteworthy that there is nothing else in me which is so perfect and so great that the possibility of a further increase in its perfection or greatness is beyond my understanding. If, for example, I consider the faculty of understanding, I immediately recognize that in my case it is extremely slight and very finite, and I at once form the idea of an understanding which is much greater – indeed supremely great and infinite; and from the very fact that I can form an idea of it, I perceive that it belongs to the nature of God. Similarly, if I examine the faculties of memory or imagination, or any others, I discover that in my case each one of these faculties is weak and limited, while in the case of God it is immeasurable. It is only the will, or freedom of choice, which I experience within me to be so great that the idea of any greater faculty is beyond my grasp; so much so that it is above all in virtue of the will that I understand myself to bear in some way the image and likeness of God. For although God's will is incomparably greater than mine, both in virtue of the knowledge and power that accompany it and make it more firm and efficacious, and also in virtue of its object, in that it ranges over a greater number of items, nevertheless it does not seem any greater than mine when considered as will in the essential and strict sense. This is because the will simply consists in our ability to do or not do something (that is, to affirm or deny, to pursue

57

1 '... without affirming or denying anything' (added in French version).
2 '... it cannot be said that my understanding is deprived of these ideas, as if they were something to which its nature entitles it' (French version).

or avoid); or rather, it consists simply in the fact that when something is put forward for our consideration by the intellect, we are moved to affirm or deny it, or pursue or avoid it, in such a way that we feel we are not determined by any external force. For in order to be free, there is no need for me to be capable of moving both ways; on the contrary, the more I incline in one direction – either because I clearly understand that reasons of truth and goodness point that way, or because of a divinely produced disposition of my inmost thoughts – the freer is my choice. Neither divine grace nor natural knowledge ever diminishes freedom; on the contrary, they increase and strengthen it. But the indifference I feel when there is no reason pushing me in one direction rather than another is the lowest grade of freedom; it is evidence not of any perfection of freedom, but rather of a defect in knowledge or a kind of negation. For if I always saw clearly what was true and good, I should never have to deliberate about the right judgement or choice; in that case, although I should be wholly free, it would be impossible for me ever to be in a state of indifference.

From these considerations I perceive that the power of willing which I received from God is not, when considered in itself, the cause of my mistakes; for it is both extremely ample and also perfect of its kind. Nor is my power of understanding to blame; for since my understanding comes from God, everything that I understand I undoubtedly understand correctly, and any error here is impossible. So what then is the source of my mistakes? It must be simply this: the scope of the will is wider than that of the intellect; but instead of restricting it within the same limits, I extend its use to matters which I do not understand. Since the will is indifferent in such cases, it easily turns aside from what is true and good, and this is the source of my error and sin.

For example, during these past few days I have been asking whether anything in the world exists, and I have realized that from the very fact of my raising this question it follows quite evidently that I exist. I could not but judge that something which I understood so clearly was true; but this was not because I was compelled so to judge by any external force, but because a great light in the intellect was followed by a great inclination in the will, and thus the spontaneity and freedom of my belief was all the greater in proportion to my lack of indifference. But now, besides the knowledge that I exist, in so far as I am a thinking thing, an idea of corporeal nature comes into my mind; and I happen to be in doubt as to whether the thinking nature which is in me, or rather which I am, is distinct from this corporeal nature or identical with it. I am making the further supposition that my intellect has not yet come upon any persuasive reason in favour of one alternative rather than the other. This obviously implies that I am indifferent as to whether I should assert or deny either alternative, or indeed refrain from making any judgement on the matter.

What is more, this indifference does not merely apply to cases where the intellect is wholly ignorant, but extends in general to every case where the intellect does not have sufficiently clear knowledge at the time when the will deliberates. For although probable conjectures may pull me in one direction, the mere knowledge that they are simply conjectures, and not certain and indubitable reasons, is itself quite enough to push my assent the other way. My experience in the last few days confirms this: the mere fact that I found that all my previous beliefs were in some sense open to doubt was enough to turn my absolutely confident belief in their truth into the supposition that they were wholly false.

If, however, I simply refrain from making a judgement in cases where I do not perceive the truth with sufficient clarity and distinctness, then it is clear that I am behaving correctly and avoiding error. But if in such cases I either affirm or deny, then I am not using my free will correctly. If I go for the alternative which is false, then obviously I shall be in error; if I take the other side, then it is by pure chance that I arrive at the truth, and I shall still be at fault since it is clear by the natural light that the perception of the intellect should always precede the determination of the will. In this incorrect use of free will may be found the privation which constitutes the essence of error. The privation, I say, lies in the operation of the will in so far as it proceeds from me, but not in the faculty of will which I received from God, nor even in its operation, in so far as it depends on him.

And I have no cause for complaint on the grounds that the power of understanding or the natural light which God gave me is no greater than it is; for it is in the nature of a finite intellect to lack understanding of many things, and it is in the nature of a created intellect to be finite. Indeed, I have reason to give thanks to him who has never owed me anything for the great bounty that he has shown me, rather than thinking myself deprived or robbed of any gifts he did not bestow.[1]

Nor do I have any cause for complaint on the grounds that God gave me a will which extends more widely than my intellect. For since the will consists simply of one thing which is, as it were, indivisible, it seems that its nature rules out the possibility of anything being taken away from it. And surely, the more widely my will extends, then the greater thanks I owe to him who gave it to me.

Finally, I must not complain that the forming of those acts of will or judgements in which I go wrong happens with God's concurrence. For in

1 '. . . rather than entertaining so unjust a thought as to imagine that he deprived me of, or unjustly withheld, the other perfections which he did not give me' (French version).

so far as these acts depend on God, they are wholly true and good; and my ability to perform them means that there is in a sense more perfection in me than would be the case if I lacked this ability. As for the privation involved – which is all that the essential definition of falsity and wrong consists in – this does not in any way require the concurrence of God, since it is not a thing; indeed, when it is referred to God as its cause, it should be called not a privation but simply a negation.[1] For it is surely no imperfection in God that he has given me the freedom to assent or not to assent in those cases where he did not endow my intellect with a clear and distinct perception; but it is undoubtedly an imperfection in me to misuse that freedom and make judgements about matters which I do not fully understand. I can see, however, that God could easily have brought it about that without losing my freedom, and despite the limitations in my knowledge, I should nonetheless never make a mistake. He could, for example, have endowed my intellect with a clear and distinct perception of everything about which I was ever likely to deliberate; or he could simply have impressed it unforgettably on my memory that I should never make a judgement about anything which I did not clearly and distinctly understand. Had God made me this way, then I can easily understand that, considered as a totality,[2] I would have been more perfect than I am now. But I cannot therefore deny that there may in some way be more perfection in the universe as a whole because some of its parts are not immune from error, while others are immune, than there would be if all the parts were exactly alike. And I have no right to complain that the role God wished me to undertake in the world is not the principal one or the most perfect of all.

What is more, even if I have no power to avoid error in the first way just mentioned, which requires a clear perception of everything I have to deliberate on, I can avoid error in the second way, which depends merely on my remembering to withhold judgement on any occasion when the truth of the matter is not clear. Admittedly, I am aware of a certain weakness in me, in that I am unable to keep my attention fixed on one and the same item of knowledge at all times; but by attentive and repeated meditation I am nevertheless able to make myself remember it as often as the need arises, and thus get into the habit of avoiding error.

It is here that man's greatest and most important perfection is to be found, and I therefore think that today's meditation, involving an investigation into the cause of error and falsity, has been very profitable. The cause of error must surely be the one I have explained; for if,

1 '... understanding these terms in accordance with scholastic usage' (added in French version).
2 '... as if there were only myself in the world' (added in French version).

whenever I have to make a judgement, I restrain my will so that it extends to what the intellect clearly and distinctly reveals, and no further, then it is quite impossible for me to go wrong. This is because every clear and distinct perception is undoubtedly something,[1] and hence cannot come from nothing, but must necessarily have God for its author. Its author, I say, is God, who is supremely perfect, and who cannot be a deceiver on pain of contradiction; hence the perception is undoubtedly true. So today I have learned not only what precautions to take to avoid ever going wrong, but also what to do to arrive at the truth. For I shall unquestionably reach the truth, if only I give sufficient attention to all the things which I perfectly understand, and separate these from all the other cases where my apprehension is more confused and obscure. And this is just what I shall take good care to do from now on.

FIFTH MEDITATION 63

The essence of material things, and the existence of God considered a second time

There are many matters which remain to be investigated concerning the attributes of God and the nature of myself, or my mind; and perhaps I shall take these up at another time. But now that I have seen what to do and what to avoid in order to reach the truth, the most pressing task seems to be to try to escape from the doubts into which I fell a few days ago, and see whether any certainty can be achieved regarding material objects.

But before I inquire whether any such things exist outside me, I must consider the ideas of these things, in so far as they exist in my thought, and see which of them are distinct, and which confused.

Quantity, for example, or 'continuous' quantity as the philosophers commonly call it, is something I distinctly imagine. That is, I distinctly imagine the extension of the quantity (or rather of the thing which is quantified) in length, breadth and depth. I also enumerate various parts of the thing, and to these parts I assign various sizes, shapes, positions and local motions; and to the motions I assign various durations.

Not only are all these things very well known and transparent to me when regarded in this general way, but in addition there are countless particular features regarding shape, number, motion and so on, which I perceive when I give them my attention. And the truth of these matters is so open and so much in harmony with my nature, that on first 64

1 '... something real and positive' (French version).

discovering them it seems that I am not so much learning something new as remembering what I knew before; or it seems like noticing for the first time things which were long present within me although I had never turned my mental gaze on them before.

But I think the most important consideration at this point is that I find within me countless ideas of things which even though they may not exist anywhere outside me still cannot be called nothing; for although in a sense they can be thought of at will, they are not my invention but have their own true and immutable natures. When, for example, I imagine a triangle, even if perhaps no such figure exists, or has ever existed, anywhere outside my thought, there is still a determinate nature, or essence, or form of the triangle which is immutable and eternal, and not invented by me or dependent on my mind. This is clear from the fact that various properties can be demonstrated of the triangle, for example that its three angles equal two right angles, that its greatest side subtends its greatest angle, and the like; and since these properties are ones which I now clearly recognize whether I want to or not, even if I never thought of them at all when I previously imagined the triangle, it follows that they cannot have been invented by me.

It would be beside the point for me to say that since I have from time to time seen bodies of triangular shape, the idea of the triangle may have come to me from external things by means of the sense organs. For I can think up countless other shapes which there can be no suspicion of my ever having encountered through the senses, and yet I can demonstrate various properties of these shapes, just as I can with the triangle. All these properties are certainly true, since I am clearly aware of them, and therefore they are something, and not merely nothing; for it is obvious that whatever is true is something; and I have already amply demonstrated that everything of which I am clearly aware is true. And even if I had not demonstrated this, the nature of my mind is such that I cannot but assent to these things, at least so long as I clearly perceive them. I also remember that even before, when I was completely preoccupied with the objects of the senses, I always held that the most certain truths of all were the kind which I recognized clearly in connection with shapes, or numbers or other items relating to arithmetic or geometry, or in general to pure and abstract mathematics.

But if the mere fact that I can produce from my thought the idea of something entails that everything which I clearly and distinctly perceive to belong to that thing really does belong to it, is not this a possible basis for another argument to prove the existence of God? Certainly, the idea of God, or a supremely perfect being, is one which I find within me just as surely as the idea of any shape or number. And my understanding that it belongs to his nature that he always exists[1] is no less clear and distinct than is the case when I prove of any shape or number that some property belongs to its nature. Hence, even if it turned out that not everything on which I have meditated in these past days is true, I ought still to regard the existence of God as having at least the same level of certainty as I have hitherto attributed to the truths of mathematics.[2]

At first sight, however, this is not transparently clear, but has some appearance of being a sophism. Since I have been accustomed to distinguish between existence and essence in everything else, I find it easy to persuade myself that existence can also be separated from the essence of God, and hence that God can be thought of as not existing. But when I concentrate more carefully, it is quite evident that existence can no more be separated from the essence of God than the fact that its three angles equal two right angles can be separated from the essence of a triangle, or than the idea of a mountain can be separated from the idea of a valley. Hence it is just as much of a contradiction to think of God (that is, a supremely perfect being) lacking existence (that is, lacking a perfection), as it is to think of a mountain without a valley.

However, even granted that I cannot think of God except as existing, just as I cannot think of a mountain without a valley, it certainly does not follow from the fact that I think of a mountain with a valley that there is any mountain in the world; and similarly, it does not seem to follow from the fact that I think of God as existing that he does exist. For my thought does not impose any necessity on things; and just as I may imagine a winged horse even though no horse has wings, so I may be able to attach existence to God even though no God exists.

But there is a sophism concealed here. From the fact that I cannot think of a mountain without a valley, it does not follow that a mountain and valley exist anywhere, but simply that a mountain and a valley, whether they exist or not, are mutually inseparable. But from the fact that I cannot think of God except as existing, it follows that existence is inseparable from God, and hence that he really exists. It is not that my thought makes it so, or imposes any necessity on any thing; on the contrary, it is the necessity of the thing itself, namely the existence of God, which determines my thinking in this respect. For I am not free to think of God without existence (that is, a supremely perfect being without a supreme perfection) as I am free to imagine a horse with or without wings.

And it must not be objected at this point that while it is indeed necessary for me to suppose God exists, once I have made the supposition

---

1 '. . . that actual and eternal existence belongs to his nature' (French version).
2 '. . . which concern only figures and numbers' (added in French version).

that he has all perfections (since existence is one of the perfections), nevertheless the original supposition was not necessary. Similarly, the objection would run, it is not necessary for me to think that all quadrilaterals can be inscribed in a circle; but given this supposition, it will be necessary for me to admit that a rhombus can be inscribed in a circle – which is patently false. Now admittedly, it is not necessary that I ever light upon any thought of God; but whenever I do choose to think of the first and supreme being, and bring forth the idea of God from the treasure house of my mind as it were, it is necessary that I attribute all perfections to him, even if I do not at that time enumerate them or attend to them individually. And this necessity plainly guarantees that, when I later realize that existence is a perfection, I am correct in inferring that the first and supreme being exists. In the same way, it is not necessary for me ever to imagine a triangle; but whenever I do wish to consider a rectilinear figure having just three angles, it is necessary that I attribute to

68 it the properties which license the inference that its three angles equal no more than two right angles, even if I do not notice this at the time. By contrast, when I examine what figures can be inscribed in a circle, it is in no way necessary for me to think that this class includes all quadrilaterals. Indeed, I cannot even imagine this, so long as I am willing to admit only what I clearly and distinctly understand. So there is a great difference between this kind of false supposition and the true ideas which are innate in me, of which the first and most important is the idea of God. There are many ways in which I understand that this idea is not something fictitious which is dependent on my thought, but is an image of a true and immutable nature. First of all, there is the fact that, apart from God, there is nothing else of which I am capable of thinking such that existence belongs[1] to its essence. Second, I cannot understand how there could be two or more Gods of this kind; and after supposing that one God exists, I plainly see that it is necessary that he has existed from eternity and will abide for eternity. And finally, I perceive many other attributes of God, none of which I can remove or alter.

But whatever method of proof I use, I am always brought back to the fact that it is only what I clearly and distinctly perceive that completely convinces me. Some of the things I clearly and distinctly perceive are obvious to everyone, while others are discovered only by those who look more closely and investigate more carefully; but once they have been discovered, the latter are judged to be just as certain as the former. In the

69 case of a right-angled triangle, for example, the fact that the square on the hypotenuse is equal to the square on the other two sides is not so

1 '. . . necessarily belongs' (French version).

readily apparent as the fact that the hypotenuse subtends the largest angle; but once one has seen it, one believes it just as strongly. But as regards God, if I were not overwhelmed by preconceived opinions, and if the images of things perceived by the senses did not besiege my thought on every side, I would certainly acknowledge him sooner and more easily than anything else. For what is more self-evident than the fact that the supreme being exists, or that God, to whose essence alone existence belongs,[1] exists?

Although it needed close attention for me to perceive this, I am now just as certain of it as I am of everything else which appears most certain. And what is more, I see that the certainty of all other things depends on this, so that without it nothing can ever be perfectly known.

Admittedly my nature is such that so long as[2] I perceive something very clearly and distinctly I cannot but believe it to be true. But my nature is also such that I cannot fix my mental vision continually on the same thing, so as to keep perceiving it clearly; and often the memory of a previously made judgement may come back, when I am no longer attending to the arguments which led me to make it. And so other arguments can now occur to me which might easily undermine my opinion, if I were unaware of God; and I should thus never have true and certain knowledge about anything, but only shifting and changeable opinions. For example, when I consider the nature of a triangle, it appears most evident to me, steeped as I am in the principles of geometry, that its three angles are equal to two right angles; and so long as I attend to the proof, I cannot but believe this to be true. But as soon as I turn my mind's eye away from the proof, then in spite of still remembering that I perceived it very clearly, I can easily fall into doubt about its truth, if I am unaware of God. For I can convince myself that I have a natural disposition to go wrong from time to time in matters which I think I perceive as evidently as can be. This will seem even more likely when I remember that there have been frequent cases where I have regarded things as true and certain, but have later been led by other arguments to judge them to be false.

Now, however, I have perceived that God exists, and at the same time I have understood that everything else depends on him, and that he is no deceiver; and I have drawn the conclusion that everything which I clearly and distinctly perceive is of necessity true. Accordingly, even if I am no longer attending to the arguments which led me to judge that this is true, as long as I remember that I clearly and distinctly perceived it, there are

70

---

1 '... in the idea of whom alone necessary and eternal existence is comprised' (French version).

2 '... as soon as' (French version).

no counter-arguments which can be adduced to make me doubt it, but on the contrary I have true and certain knowledge of it. And I have knowledge not just of this matter, but of all matters which I remember ever having demonstrated, in geometry and so on. For what objections can now be raised?[1] That the way I am made makes me prone to frequent error? But I now know that I am incapable of error in those cases where my understanding is transparently clear. Or can it be objected that I have in the past regarded as true and certain many things which I afterwards recognized to be false? But none of these were things which I clearly and distinctly perceived: I was ignorant of this rule for establishing the truth, and believed these things for other reasons which I later discovered to be less reliable. So what is left to say? Can one raise the objection I put to myself a while ago, that I may be dreaming, or that everything which I am now thinking has as little truth as what comes to the mind of one who 71 is asleep? Yet even this does not change anything. For even though I might be dreaming, if there is anything which is evident to my intellect, then it is wholly true.

Thus I see plainly that the certainty and truth of all knowledge depends uniquely on my awareness of the true God, to such an extent that I was incapable of perfect knowledge about anything else until I became aware of him. And now it is possible for me to achieve full and certain knowledge of countless matters, both concerning God himself and other things whose nature is intellectual, and also concerning the whole of that corporeal nature which is the subject-matter of pure mathematics.[2]

SIXTH MEDITATION

The existence of material things, and the real distinction between mind and body[3]

It remains for me to examine whether material things exist. And at least I now know they are capable of existing, in so far as they are the subject-matter of pure mathematics, since I perceive them clearly and distinctly. For there is no doubt that God is capable of creating everything that I am capable of perceiving in this manner; and I have never judged that something could not be made by him except on the grounds that there would be a contradiction in my perceiving it

---

1 '... to oblige me to call these matters into doubt' (added in French version).
2 '... and also concerning things which belong to corporeal nature in so far as it can serve as the object of geometrical demonstrations which have no concern with whether that object exists' (French version).
3 '... between the soul and body of a man' (French version).

distinctly. The conclusion that material things exist is also suggested by the faculty of imagination, which I am aware of using when I turn my mind to material things. For when I give more attentive consideration to what imagination is, it seems to be nothing else but an application of the cognitive faculty to a body which is intimately present to it, and which therefore exists.

72

To make this clear, I will first examine the difference between imagination and pure understanding. When I imagine a triangle, for example, I do not merely understand that it is a figure bounded by three lines, but at the same time I also see the three lines with my mind's eye as if they were present before me; and this is what I call imagining. But if I want to think of a chiliagon, although I understand that it is a figure consisting of a thousand sides just as well as I understand the triangle to be a three-sided figure, I do not in the same way imagine the thousand sides or see them as if they were present before me. It is true that since I am in the habit of imagining something whenever I think of a corporeal thing, I may construct in my mind a confused representation of some figure; but it is clear that this is not a chiliagon. For it differs in no way from the representation I should form if I were thinking of a myriagon, or any figure with very many sides. Moreover, such a representation is useless for recognizing the properties which distinguish a chiliagon from other polygons. But suppose I am dealing with a pentagon: I can of course understand the figure of a pentagon, just as I can the figure of a chiliagon, without the help of the imagination; but I can also imagine a pentagon, by applying my mind's eye to its five sides and the area contained within them. And in doing this I notice quite clearly that imagination requires a peculiar effort of mind which is not required for understanding; this additional effort of mind clearly shows the difference between imagination and pure understanding.

73

Besides this, I consider that this power of imagining which is in me, differing as it does from the power of understanding, is not a necessary constituent of my own essence, that is, of the essence of my mind. For if I lacked it, I should undoubtedly remain the same individual as I now am; from which it seems to follow that it depends on something distinct from myself. And I can easily understand that, if there does exist some body to which the mind is so joined that it can apply itself to contemplate it, as it were, whenever it pleases, then it may possibly be this very body that enables me to imagine corporeal things. So the difference between this mode of thinking and pure understanding may simply be this: when the mind understands, it in some way turns towards itself and inspects one of the ideas which are within it; but when it imagines, it turns towards the body and looks at something in the body which conforms to an idea understood by the mind or perceived by the senses. I can, as I say, easily understand that this is how imagination comes about, if the body exists; and since there is no other equally suitable way of explaining imagination that comes to mind, I can make a probable conjecture that the body exists. But this is only a probability; and despite a careful and comprehensive investigation, I do not yet see how the distinct idea of corporeal nature which I find in my imagination can provide any basis for a necessary inference that some body exists.

74   But besides that corporeal nature which is the subject-matter of pure mathematics, there is much else that I habitually imagine, such as colours, sounds, tastes, pain and so on – though not so distinctly. Now I perceive these things much better by means of the senses, which is how, with the assistance of memory, they appear to have reached the imagination. So in order to deal with them more fully, I must pay equal attention to the senses, and see whether the things which are perceived by means of that mode of thinking which I call 'sensory perception' provide me with any sure argument for the existence of corporeal things.

To begin with, I will go back over all the things which I previously took to be perceived by the senses, and reckoned to be true; and I will go over my reasons for thinking this. Next, I will set out my reasons for subsequently calling these things into doubt. And finally I will consider what I should now believe about them.

First of all then, I perceived by my senses that I had a head, hands, feet and other limbs making up the body which I regarded as part of myself, or perhaps even as my whole self. I also perceived by my senses that this body was situated among many other bodies which could affect it in various favourable or unfavourable ways; and I gauged the favourable effects by a sensation of pleasure, and the unfavourable ones by a sensation of pain. In addition to pain and pleasure, I also had sensations within me of hunger, thirst, and other such appetites, and also of physical propensities towards cheerfulness, sadness, anger and similar emotions.

75   And outside me, besides the extension, shapes and movements of bodies, I also had sensations of their hardness and heat, and of the other tactile qualities. In addition, I had sensations of light, colours, smells, tastes and sounds, the variety of which enabled me to distinguish the sky, the earth, the seas, and all other bodies, one from another. Considering the ideas of all these qualities which presented themselves to my thought, although the ideas were, strictly speaking, the only immediate objects of my sensory awareness, it was not unreasonable for me to think that the items which I was perceiving through the senses were things quite distinct from my thought, namely bodies which produced the ideas. For my experience was that these ideas came to me quite without my consent, so that I could

not have sensory awareness of any object, even if I wanted to, unless it was present to my sense organs; and I could not avoid having sensory awareness of it when it was present. And since the ideas perceived by the senses were much more lively and vivid and even, in their own way, more distinct than any of those which I deliberately formed through meditating or which I found impressed on my memory, it seemed impossible that they should have come from within me; so the only alternative was that they came from other things. Since the sole source of my knowledge of these things was the ideas themselves, the supposition that the things resembled the ideas was bound to occur to me. In addition, I remembered that the use of my senses had come first, while the use of my reason came only later; and I saw that the ideas which I formed myself were less vivid than those which I perceived with the senses and were, for the most part, made up of elements of sensory ideas. In this way I easily convinced myself that I had nothing at all in the intellect which I had not previously had in sensation. As for the body which by some special right I called   76 'mine', my belief that this body, more than any other, belonged to me had some justification. For I could never be separated from it, as I could from other bodies; and I felt all my appetites and emotions in, and on account of, this body; and finally, I was aware of pain and pleasurable ticklings in parts of this body, but not in other bodies external to it. But why should that curious sensation of pain give rise to a particular distress of mind; or why should a certain kind of delight follow on a tickling sensation? Again, why should that curious tugging in the stomach which I call hunger tell me that I should eat, or a dryness of the throat tell me to drink, and so on? I was not able to give any explanation of all this, except that nature taught me so. For there is absolutely no connection (at least that I can understand) between the tugging sensation and the decision to take food, or between the sensation of something causing pain and the mental apprehension of distress that arises from that sensation. These and other judgements that I made concerning sensory objects, I was apparently taught to make by nature; for I had already made up my mind that this was how things were, before working out any arguments to prove it.

Later on, however, I had many experiences which gradually undermined all the faith I had had in the senses. Sometimes towers which had looked round from a distance appeared square from close up; and enormous statues standing on their pediments did not seem large when observed from the ground. In these and countless other such cases, I found that the judgements of the external senses were mistaken. And this applied not just to the external senses but to the internal senses as well. For what can be more internal than pain? And yet I had heard that those   77 who had had a leg or an arm amputated sometimes still seemed to feel pain intermittently in the missing part of the body. So even in my own case it was apparently not quite certain that a particular limb was hurting, even if I felt pain in it. To these reasons for doubting, I recently added two very general ones.[1] The first was that every sensory experience I have ever thought I was having while awake I can also think of myself as sometimes having while asleep; and since I do not believe that what I seem to perceive in sleep comes from things located outside me, I did not see why I should be any more inclined to believe this of what I think I perceive while awake. The second reason for doubt was that since I did not know the author of my being (or at least was pretending not to), I saw nothing to rule out the possibility that my natural constitution made me prone to error even in matters which seemed to me most true. As for the reasons for my previous confident belief in the truth of the things perceived by the senses, I had no trouble in refuting them. For since I apparently had natural impulses towards many things which reason told me to avoid, I reckoned that a great deal of confidence should not be placed in what I was taught by nature. And despite the fact that the perceptions of the senses were not dependent on my will, I did not think that I should on that account infer that they proceeded from things distinct from myself, since I might perhaps have a faculty not yet known to me which produced them.[2]

But now, when I am beginning to achieve a better knowledge of myself and the author of my being, although I do not think I should heedlessly accept everything I seem to have acquired from the senses, neither do I think that everything should be called into doubt.

78

First, I know that everything which I clearly and distinctly understand is capable of being created by God so as to correspond exactly with my understanding of it. Hence the fact that I can clearly and distinctly understand one thing apart from another is enough to make me certain that the two things are distinct, since they are capable of being separated, at least by God. The question of what kind of power is required to bring about such a separation does not affect the judgement that the two things are distinct. Thus, simply by knowing that I exist and seeing at the same time that absolutely nothing else belongs to my nature or essence except that I am a thinking thing, I can infer correctly that my essence consists solely in the fact that I am a thinking thing. It is true that I may have (or, to anticipate, that I certainly have) a body that is very closely joined to me. But nevertheless, on the one hand I have a clear and distinct idea of myself, in so far as I am simply a thinking, non-extended thing; and on

1 Cf. Med. I, pp. 77ff above.
2 Cf. Med. III, pp. 89f above.

the other hand I have a distinct idea of body,[1] in so far as this is simply an extended, non-thinking thing. And accordingly, it is certain that I[2] am really distinct from my body, and can exist without it.

Besides this, I find in myself faculties for certain special modes of thinking,[3] namely imagination and sensory perception. Now I can clearly and distinctly understand myself as a whole without these faculties; but I cannot, conversely, understand these faculties without me, that is, without an intellectual substance to inhere in. This is because there is an intellectual act included in their essential definition; and hence I perceive that the distinction between them and myself corresponds to the distinction between the modes of a thing and the thing itself.[4] Of course I also recognize that there are other faculties (like those of changing position, of taking on various shapes, and so on) which, like sensory perception and imagination, cannot be understood apart from some substance for them   79 to inhere in, and hence cannot exist without it. But it is clear that these other faculties, if they exist, must be in a corporeal or extended substance and not an intellectual one; for the clear and distinct conception of them includes extension, but does not include any intellectual act whatsoever. Now there is in me a passive faculty of sensory perception, that is, a faculty for receiving and recognizing the ideas of sensible objects; but I could not make use of it unless there was also an active faculty, either in me or in something else, which produced or brought about these ideas. But this faculty cannot be in me, since clearly it presupposes no intellectual act on my part,[5] and the ideas in question are produced without my cooperation and often even against my will. So the only alternative is that it is in another substance distinct from me – a substance which contains either formally or eminently all the reality which exists objectively[6] in the ideas produced by this faculty (as I have just noted). This substance is either a body, that is, a corporeal nature, in which case it will contain formally ⟨and in fact⟩ everything which is to be found objectively ⟨or representatively⟩ in the ideas; or else it is God, or some creature more noble than a body, in which case it will contain eminently whatever is to be found in the ideas. But since God is not a

1 The Latin term *corpus* as used here by Descartes is ambiguous as between 'body' (i.e. corporeal matter in general) and 'the body' (i.e. this particular body of mine). The French version preserves the ambiguity.
2 '... that is, my soul, by which I am what I am' (added in French version).
3 '... certain modes of thinking which are quite special and distinct from me' (French version).
4 '... between the shapes, movements and other modes or accidents of a body and the body which supports them' (French version).
5 '... cannot be in me in so far as I am merely a thinking thing, since it does not presuppose any thought on my part' (French version).
6 For the terms 'formally', 'eminently' and 'objectively', see notes, pp. 90–1 above.

deceiver, it is quite clear that he does not transmit the ideas to me either directly from himself, or indirectly, via some creature which contains the objective reality of the ideas not formally but only eminently. For God has given me no faculty at all for recognizing any such source for these ideas; on the contrary, he has given me a great propensity to believe that they are produced by corporeal things. So I do not see how God could be understood to be anything but a deceiver if the ideas were transmitted from a source other than corporeal things. It follows that corporeal things exist. They may not all exist in a way that exactly corresponds with my sensory grasp of them, for in many cases the grasp of the senses is very obscure and confused. But at least they possess all the properties which I clearly and distinctly understand, that is, all those which, viewed in general terms, are comprised within the subject-matter of pure mathematics.

What of the other aspects of corporeal things which are either particular (for example that the sun is of such and such a size or shape), or less clearly understood, such as light or sound or pain, and so on? Despite the high degree of doubt and uncertainty involved here, the very fact that God is not a deceiver, and the consequent impossibility of there being any falsity in my opinions which cannot be corrected by some other faculty supplied by God, offers me a sure hope that I can attain the truth even in these matters. Indeed, there is no doubt that everything that I am taught by nature contains some truth. For if nature is considered in its general aspect, then I understand by the term nothing other than God himself, or the ordered system of created things established by God. And by my own nature in particular I understand nothing other than the totality of things bestowed on me by God.

There is nothing that my own nature teaches me more vividly than that I have a body, and that when I feel pain there is something wrong with the body, and that when I am hungry or thirsty the body needs food and drink, and so on. So I should not doubt that there is some truth in this.

Nature also teaches me, by these sensations of pain, hunger, thirst and so on, that I am not merely present in my body as a sailor is present in a ship,[1] but that I am very closely joined and, as it were, intermingled with it, so that I and the body form a unit. If this were not so, I, who am nothing but a thinking thing, would not feel pain when the body was hurt, but would perceive the damage purely by the intellect, just as a sailor perceives by sight if anything in his ship is broken. Similarly, when the body needed food or drink, I should have an explicit understanding of the fact, instead of having confused sensations of hunger and thirst. For these sensations of hunger, thirst, pain and so on are nothing but

1 '. . . as a pilot in his ship' (French version).

confused modes of thinking which arise from the union and, as it were, intermingling of the mind with the body.

I am also taught by nature that various other bodies exist in the vicinity of my body, and that some of these are to be sought out and others avoided. And from the fact that I perceive by my senses a great variety of colours, sounds, smells and tastes, as well as differences in heat, hardness and the like, I am correct in inferring that the bodies which are the source of these various sensory perceptions possess differences corresponding to them, though perhaps not resembling them. Also, the fact that some of the perceptions are agreeable to me while others are disagreeable makes it quite certain that my body, or rather my whole self, in so far as I am a combination of body and mind, can be affected by the various beneficial or harmful bodies which surround it.

There are, however, many other things which I may appear to have   82
been taught by nature, but which in reality I acquired not from nature but from a habit of making ill-considered judgements; and it is therefore *in class* quite possible that these are false. Cases in point are the belief that any space in which nothing is occurring to stimulate my senses must be empty; or that the heat in a body is something exactly resembling the idea of heat which is in me; or that when a body is white or green, the selfsame whiteness or greenness which I perceive through my senses is present in the body; or that in a body which is bitter or sweet there is the selfsame taste which I experience, and so on; or, finally, that stars and towers and other distant bodies have the same size and shape which they present to my senses, and other examples of this kind. But to make sure that my perceptions in this matter are sufficiently distinct, I must more accurately define exactly what I mean when I say that I am taught something by nature. In this context I am taking nature to be something more limited than the totality of things bestowed on me by God. For this includes many things that belong to the mind alone – for example my perception that what is done cannot be undone, and all other things that are known by the natural light;[1] but at this stage I am not speaking of these matters. It also includes much that relates to the body alone, like the tendency to move in a downward direction, and so on; but I am not speaking of these matters either. My sole concern here is with what God has bestowed on me as a combination of mind and body. My nature, then, in this limited sense, does indeed teach me to avoid what induces a feeling of pain and to seek out what induces feelings of pleasure, and so on. But it does not appear to teach us to draw any conclusions from these sensory perceptions about things located outside us without waiting until

1 '. . . without any help from the body' (added in French version).

83 the intellect has examined[1] the matter. For knowledge of the truth about such things seems to belong to the mind alone, not to the combination of mind and body. Hence, although a star has no greater effect on my eye than the flame of a small light, that does not mean that there is any real or positive inclination in me to believe that the star is no bigger than the light; I have simply made this judgement from childhood onwards without any rational basis. Similarly, although I feel heat when I go near a fire and feel pain when I go too near, there is no convincing argument for supposing that there is something in the fire which resembles the heat, any more than for supposing that there is something which resembles the pain. There is simply reason to suppose that there is something in the fire, whatever it may eventually turn out to be, which produces in us the feelings of heat or pain. And likewise, even though there is nothing in any given space that stimulates the senses, it does not follow that there is no body there. In these cases and many others I see that I have been in the habit of misusing the order of nature. For the proper purpose of the sensory perceptions given me by nature is simply to inform the mind of what is beneficial or harmful for the composite of which the mind is a part; and to this extent they are sufficiently clear and distinct. But I misuse them by treating them as reliable touchstones for immediate judgements about the essential nature of the bodies located outside us; yet this is an area where they provide only very obscure information.

I have already looked in sufficient detail at how, notwithstanding the goodness of God, it may happen that my judgements are false. But a further problem now comes to mind regarding those very things which nature presents to me as objects which I should seek out or avoid, and also regarding the internal sensations, where I seem to have detected errors[2] – e.g. when someone is tricked by the pleasant taste of some food

84 into eating the poison concealed inside it. Yet in this case, what the man's nature urges him to go for is simply what is responsible for the pleasant taste, and not the poison, which his nature knows nothing about. The only inference that can be drawn from this is that his nature is not omniscient. And this is not surprising, since man is a limited thing, and so it is only fitting that his perfection should be limited.

And yet it is not unusual for us to go wrong even in cases where nature does urge us towards something. Those who are ill, for example, may desire food or drink that will shortly afterwards turn out to be bad for them. Perhaps it may be said that they go wrong because their nature is disordered, but this does not remove the difficulty. A sick man is no less

---

1 '. . . carefully and maturely examined' (French version).
2 '. . . and thus seem to have been directly deceived by my nature' (added in French version).

one of God's creatures than a healthy one, and it seems no less a contradiction to suppose that he has received from God a nature which deceives him. Yet a clock constructed with wheels and weights observes all the laws of its nature just as closely when it is badly made and tells the wrong time as when it completely fulfils the wishes of the clockmaker. In the same way, I might consider the body of a man as a kind of machine equipped with and made up of bones, nerves, muscles, veins, blood and skin in such a way that, even if there were no mind in it, it would still perform all the same movements as it now does in those cases where movement is not under the control of the will or, consequently, of the mind.[1] I can easily see that if such a body suffers from dropsy, for example, and is affected by the dryness of the throat which normally produces in the mind the sensation of thirst, the resulting condition of the nerves and other parts will dispose the body to take a drink, with the result that the disease will be aggravated. Yet this is just as natural as the body's being stimulated by a similar dryness of the throat to take a drink when there is no such illness and the drink is beneficial. Admittedly,   85 when I consider the purpose of the clock, I may say that it is departing from its nature when it does not tell the right time; and similarly when I consider the mechanism of the human body, I may think that, in relation to the movements which normally occur in it, it too is deviating from its nature if the throat is dry at a time when drinking is not beneficial to its continued health. But I am well aware that 'nature' as I have just used it has a very different significance from 'nature' in the other sense. As I have just used it, 'nature' is simply a label which depends on my thought; it is quite extraneous to the things to which it is applied, and depends simply on my comparison between the idea of a sick man and a badly-made clock, and the idea of a healthy man and a well-made clock. But by 'nature' in the other sense I understand something which is really to be found in the things themselves; in this sense, therefore, the term contains something of the truth.

When we say, then, with respect to the body suffering from dropsy, that it has a disordered nature because it has a dry throat and yet does not need drink, the term 'nature' is here used merely as an extraneous label. However, with respect to the composite, that is, the mind united with this body, what is involved is not a mere label, but a true error of nature, namely that it is thirsty at a time when drink is going to cause it harm. It thus remains to inquire how it is that the goodness of God does not prevent nature, in this sense, from deceiving us.

The first observation I make at this point is that there is a great difference between the mind and the body, inasmuch as the body is by its

1 '... but occurs merely as a result of the disposition of the organs' (French version).

86   very nature always divisible, while the mind is utterly indivisible. For
when I consider the mind, or myself in so far as I am merely a thinking
thing, I am unable to distinguish any parts within myself; I understand
myself to be something quite single and complete. Although the whole
mind seems to be united to the whole body, I recognize that if a foot or
arm or any other part of the body is cut off, nothing has thereby been
taken away from the mind. As for the faculties of willing, of understanding, of sensory perception and so on, these cannot be termed parts of the
mind, since it is one and the same mind that wills, and understands and
has sensory perceptions. By contrast, there is no corporeal or extended
thing that I can think of which in my thought I cannot easily divide into
parts; and this very fact makes me understand that it is divisible. This one
argument would be enough to show me that the mind is completely
different from the body, even if I did not already know as much from
other considerations.

My next observation is that the mind is not immediately affected by all
parts of the body, but only by the brain, or perhaps just by one small part
of the brain, namely the part which is said to contain the 'common'
sense.[1] Every time this part of the brain is in a given state, it presents the
same signals to the mind, even though the other parts of the body may be
in a different condition at the time. This is established by countless
observations, which there is no need to review here.

I observe, in addition, that the nature of the body is such that whenever
any part of it is moved by another part which is some distance away, it
can always be moved in the same fashion by any of the parts which lie in
between, even if the more distant part does nothing. For example, in a
87   cord ABCD, if one end D is pulled so that the other end A moves, the
exact same movement could have been brought about if one of the
intermediate points B or C had been pulled, and D had not moved at all.
In similar fashion, when I feel a pain in my foot, physiology tells me that
this happens by means of nerves distributed throughout the foot, and
that these nerves are like cords which go from the foot right up to the
brain. When the nerves are pulled in the foot, they in turn pull on inner
parts of the brain to which they are attached, and produce a certain
motion in them; and nature has laid it down that this motion should
produce in the mind a sensation of pain, as occurring in the foot. But
since these nerves, in passing from the foot to the brain, must pass
through the calf, the thigh, the lumbar region, the back and the neck, it

---

1 The supposed faculty which integrates the data from the five specialized senses (the
notion goes back ultimately to Aristotle). 'The seat of the common sense must be very
mobile, to receive all the impressions coming from the senses, but must be moveable only
by the spirits which transmit these impressions. Only the *conarion* (pineal gland) fits
these conditions' (letter to Mersenne, 21 April 1641).

can happen that, even if it is not the part in the foot but one of the intermediate parts which is being pulled, the same motion will occur in the brain as occurs when the foot is hurt, and so it will necessarily come about that the mind feels the same sensation of pain. And we must suppose the same thing happens with regard to any other sensation.

My final observation is that any given movement occurring in the part of the brain that immediately affects the mind produces just one corresponding sensation; and hence the best system that could be devised is that it should produce the one sensation which, of all possible sensations, is most especially and most frequently conducive to the preservation of the healthy man. And experience shows that the sensations which nature has given us are all of this kind; and so there is absolutely nothing to be found in them that does not bear witness to the power and goodness of God. For example, when the nerves in the foot are set in motion in a violent and unusual manner, this motion, by way of the spinal cord, reaches the inner parts of the brain, and there gives the mind its signal for having a certain sensation, namely the sensation of a pain as occurring in the foot. This stimulates the mind to do its best to get rid of the cause of the pain, which it takes to be harmful to the foot. It is true that God could have made the nature of man such that this particular motion in the brain indicated something else to the mind; it might, for example, have made the mind aware of the actual motion occurring in the brain, or in the foot, or in any of the intermediate regions; or it might have indicated something else entirely. But there is nothing else which would have been so conducive to the continued well-being of the body. In the same way, when we need drink, there arises a certain dryness in the throat; this sets in motion the nerves of the throat, which in turn move the inner parts of the brain. This motion produces in the mind a sensation of thirst, because the most useful thing for us to know about the whole business is that we need drink in order to stay healthy. And so it is in the other cases.

It is quite clear from all this that, notwithstanding the immense goodness of God, the nature of man as a combination of mind and body is such that it is bound to mislead him from time to time. For there may be some occurrence, not in the foot but in one of the other areas through which the nerves travel in their route from the foot to the brain, or even in the brain itself; and if this cause produces the same motion which is generally produced by injury to the foot, then pain will be felt as if it were in the foot. This deception of the senses is natural, because a given motion in the brain must always produce the same sensation in the mind; and the origin of the motion in question is much more often going to be something which is hurting the foot, rather than something existing

89 elsewhere. So it is reasonable that this motion should always indicate to the mind a pain in the foot rather than in any other part of the body. Again, dryness of the throat may sometimes arise not, as it normally does, from the fact that a drink is necessary to the health of the body, but from some quite opposite cause, as happens in the case of the man with dropsy. Yet it is much better that it should mislead on this occasion than that it should always mislead when the body is in good health. And the same goes for the other cases.

This consideration is the greatest help to me, not only for noticing all the errors to which my nature is liable, but also for enabling me to correct or avoid them without difficulty. For I know that in matters regarding the well-being of the body, all my senses report the truth much more frequently than not. Also, I can almost always make use of more than one sense to investigate the same thing; and in addition, I can use both my memory, which connects present experiences with preceding ones, and my intellect, which has by now examined all the causes of error. Accordingly, I should not have any further fears about the falsity of what my senses tell me every day; on the contrary, the exaggerated doubts of the last few days should be dismissed as laughable. This applies especially to the principal reason for doubt, namely my inability to distinguish between being asleep and being awake. For I now notice that there is a vast difference between the two, in that dreams are never linked by memory with all the other actions of life as waking experiences are. If, while I am awake, anyone were suddenly to appear to me and then disappear immediately, as happens in sleep, so that I could not see where he had

90 come from or where he had gone to, it would not be unreasonable for me to judge that he was a ghost, or a vision created in my brain,[1] rather than a real man. But when I distinctly see where things come from and where and when they come to me, and when I can connect my perceptions of them with the whole of the rest of my life without a break, then I am quite certain that when I encounter these things I am not asleep but awake. And I ought not to have even the slightest doubt of their reality if, after calling upon all the senses as well as my memory and my intellect in order to check them, I receive no conflicting reports from any of these sources. For from the fact that God is not a deceiver it follows that in cases like these I am completely free from error. But since the pressure of things to be done does not always allow us to stop and make such a meticulous check, it must be admitted that in this human life we are often liable to make mistakes about particular things, and we must acknowledge the weakness of our nature.

---

1 '. . . like those that are formed in the brain when I sleep' (added in French version).

Objections and Replies [Selections]

[ON MEDITATION ONE]

[The rejection of previous beliefs]

Here I shall employ an everyday example to explain to my critic the 481
rationale for my procedure, so as to prevent him misunderstanding it, or
having the gall to pretend he does not understand it, in future. Suppose he
had a basket full of apples and, being worried that some of the apples were
rotten, wanted to take out the rotten ones to prevent the rot spreading.
How would he proceed? Would he not begin by tipping the whole lot out
of the basket? And would not the next step be to cast his eye over each
apple in turn, and pick up and put back in the basket only those he saw to
be sound, leaving the others? In just the same way, those who have never
philosophized correctly have various opinions in their minds which they
have begun to store up since childhood, and which they therefore have
reason to believe may in many cases be false. They then attempt to separate the false beliefs from the others, so as to prevent their contaminating
the rest and making the whole lot uncertain. Now the best way they can
accomplish this is to reject all their beliefs together in one go, as if they
were all uncertain and false. They can then go over each belief in turn and
re-adopt only those which they recognize to be true and indubitable. Thus
I was right to begin by rejecting all my beliefs.

[Seventh Replies: CSM II 324]

[The reliability of the senses]

Although there is deception or falsity, it is not to be found in the senses; for the (332)
senses are quite passive and report only appearances, which must appear in the way
they do owing to their causes. The error or falsity is in the judgement or the mind,
which is not circumspect enough and does not notice that things at a distance will
for one reason or another appear smaller and more blurred than when they are
nearby, and so on. Nevertheless, when deception occurs, we must not deny that it
exists; the only difficulty is whether it occurs all the time, thus making it impossible
for us ever to be sure of the truth of anything which we perceive by the senses.

[Fifth Objections: CSM II 230–1]

Here you show quite clearly that you are relying entirely on a preconceived opinion which you have never got rid of. You maintain that we never suspect any falsity in situations where we have never detected it, and hence that when we look at a tower from nearby and touch it we are sure that it is square, if it appears square. You also maintain that when we are really awake, we cannot doubt whether we are awake or asleep, and so on. But you have no reason to think that you have previously noticed all the circumstances in which error can occur; moreover, it is easy to prove that you are from time to time mistaken in matters which you accept as certain.   [*Fifth Replies*: CSM II 264]

386

*   *   *

(418) Our *ninth* and most worrying difficulty is your assertion that we ought to mistrust the operations of the senses and that the reliability of the intellect is much greater than that of the senses.[1] But how can the intellect enjoy any certainty unless it has previously derived it from the senses when they are working as they should? How can it correct a mistake made by one of the senses unless some other sense first corrects the mistake? Owing to refraction, a stick which is in fact straight appears bent in water. What corrects the error? The intellect? Not at all; it is the sense of touch. And the same sort of thing must be taken to occur in other cases. Hence if you have recourse to all your senses when they are in good working order, and they all give the same report, you will achieve the greatest certainty of which man is naturally capable. But you will often fail to achieve it if you trust the operations of the mind; for the mind often goes astray in just those areas where it had previously supposed doubt to be impossible.   [*Sixth Objections*: CSM II 281–2]

When people say that a stick in water 'appears bent because of refraction', this is the same as saying that it appears to us in a way which would lead a child to judge that it was bent – and which may even lead us to make the same judgement, following the preconceived opinions which we have become accustomed to accept from our earliest years. But I cannot grant my critics' further comment that this error is corrected 'not by the intellect but by the sense of touch'. As a result of touching it, we may judge that the stick is straight, and the kind of judgement involved may be the kind we have been accustomed to make since childhood, and which is therefore referred to as the 'sense' of touch. But the sense alone does not suffice to correct the visual error: in addition we need to have some degree of reason which tells us that in this case we should believe the judgement based on touch rather than that elicited by vision. And since we did not have this power of reasoning in our infancy, it must be attributed not to the senses but to the intellect. Thus even in the very example my critics produce, it is the intellect alone which corrects the error of the senses; and it is not poss-

439

1 See above, Med. I, p. 76; Med. II, pp. 84f; Med. VI, pp. 117f.

ible to produce any case in which error results from our trusting the operation of the mind more than the senses.   [*Sixth Replies*: CSM II 296]

[*The dreaming argument*]

From what is said in this Meditation it is clear enough that there is no criterion enabling us to distinguish our dreams from the waking state and from veridical sensations. And hence the images we have when we are awake and having sensations are not accidents that inhere in external objects, and are no proof that any such external object exists at all. So if we follow our senses, without exercising our reason in any way, we shall be justified in doubting whether anything exists. I acknowledge the correctness of this Meditation. But since Plato and other ancient philosophers discussed this uncertainty in the objects of the senses, and since the difficulty of distinguishing the waking state from dreams is commonly pointed out, I am sorry that the author, who is so outstanding in the field of original speculations, should be publishing this ancient material.

[*Third Objections*: CSM II 121]

The arguments for doubting, which the philosopher here accepts as valid, are ones that I was presenting as merely plausible. I was not trying to sell them as novelties, but had a threefold aim in mind when I used them. Partly I wanted to prepare my readers' minds for the study of the things   172 which are related to the intellect, and help them to distinguish these things from corporeal things; and such arguments seem to be wholly necessary for this purpose. Partly I introduced the arguments so that I could reply to them in the subsequent Meditations. And partly I wanted to show the firmness of the truths which I propound later on, in the light of the fact that they cannot be shaken by these metaphysical doubts. Thus I was not looking for praise when I set out these arguments; but I think I could not have left them out, any more than a medical writer can leave out the description of a disease when he wants to explain how it can be cured.

[*Third Replies*: CSM II 121]

[*Certainty in dreams*]

Has it never happened to you, as it has to many people, that things seemed clear and certain to you while you were dreaming, but that afterwards you discovered that they were doubtful or false? It is indeed 'prudent never to trust completely those who have deceived you even once'.[1] 'But', you reply, 'matters of the utmost   457 certainty are quite different. They are such that they cannot appear doubtful even to those who are dreaming or mad.' But are you really serious in what you say? Can you pretend that matters of the utmost certainty cannot appear doubtful even to dreamers or madmen? What are these utterly certain matters? If things which are

1 Med. I, p. 76 above.

ridiculous or absurd sometimes appear certain, even utterly certain, to people who are asleep or insane, then why should not things which are certain, even utterly certain, appear false and doubtful? I know a man who once, when falling asleep, heard the clock strike four, and counted the strokes as 'one, one, one, one'. It then seemed to him that there was something absurd about this, and he shouted out: 'That clock must be going mad; it has struck one o'clock four times!' Is there really anything so absurd or irrational that it could not come into the mind of someone who is asleep or raving? There are no limits to what a dreamer may not 'prove' or believe, and indeed congratulate himself on, as if he had managed to invent some splendid thought.　　　　　　　　　　　　[*Seventh Objections*: CSM II 306]

(461) 'But matters of the utmost certainty are quite different. They are such that they cannot appear doubtful even to those who are dreaming or mad.' I do not know what kind of analysis has enabled my supremely subtle critic to deduce this from my writings. Admittedly he might have inferred from what I wrote that everything that anyone clearly and distinctly perceives is true, although the person in question may from time to time doubt whether he is dreaming or awake, and may even, if you like, be dreaming or mad. For no matter who the perceiver is, nothing can be clearly and
462 distinctly perceived without its being just as we perceive it to be, i.e. without being true. But because it requires some care to make a proper distinction between what is clearly and distinctly perceived and what merely seems or appears to be, I am not surprised that my worthy critic should here mistake the one for the other.

　　　　　　　　　　　　[*Seventh Replies*: CSM II 309–10]

[ON MEDITATION TWO]

[*Cogito ergo sum* ('*I am thinking, therefore I exist*')]

You conclude that this proposition, *I am, I exist*, is true whenever it is put forward
259 by you or conceived in your mind.[1] But I do not see that you needed all this apparatus, when on other grounds you were certain, and it was true, that you existed. You could have made the same inference from any one of your other actions, since it is known by the natural light that whatever acts exists.

　　　　　　　　　　　　[*Fifth Objections*: CSM II 180]

(352) When you say that I 'could have made the same inference from any one of my other actions' you are far from the truth, since I am not wholly certain of any of my actions, with the sole exception of thought (in using the word 'certain' I am referring to metaphysical certainty, which is the sole issue at

　　　　　　　　　　　　1 Above, p. 80.

this point). I may not, for example, make the inference 'I am walking, therefore I exist', except in so far as the awareness of walking is a thought. The inference is certain only if applied to this awareness, and not to the movement of the body which sometimes – in the case of dreams – is not occurring at all, despite the fact that I seem to myself to be walking. Hence from the fact that I think I am walking I can very well infer the existence of a mind which has this thought, but not the existence of a body that walks. And the same applies in other cases.   [*Fifth Replies*: CSM II 244]

*   *   *

When someone says 'I am thinking, therefore I am, or I exist', he does not deduce existence from thought by means of a syllogism, but recognizes it as something self-evident by a simple intuition of the mind. This is clear from the fact that if he were deducing it by means of a syllogism, he would have to have had previous knowledge of the major premiss 'Everything which thinks is, or exists'; yet in fact he learns it from experiencing in his own case that it is impossible that he should think without existing. It is in 141 the nature of our mind to construct general propositions on the basis of our knowledge of particular ones.   [*Second Replies*: CSM II 100]

*   *   *

From the fact that we are thinking it does not seem to be entirely certain that we 413 exist. For in order to be certain that you are thinking you must know what thought or thinking is, and what your existence is; but since you do not yet know what these things are, how can you know that you are thinking or that you exist? Thus neither when you say 'I am thinking' nor when you add 'therefore, I exist' do you really know what you are saying. Indeed, you do not even know that you are saying or thinking anything, since this seems to require that you should know that you know what you are saying; and this in turn requires that you be aware of knowing that you know what you are saying, and so on *ad infinitum*. Hence it is clear that you cannot know whether you exist or even whether you are thinking.

[*Sixth Objections*: CSM II 278]

It is true that no one can be certain that he is thinking or that he exists (422) unless he knows what thought is and what existence is. But this does not require reflective knowledge, or the kind of knowledge that is acquired by means of demonstrations; still less does it require knowledge of reflective knowledge, i.e. knowing that we know, and knowing that we know that we know, and so on *ad infinitum*. This kind of knowledge cannot possibly be obtained about anything. It is quite sufficient that we should know it by that internal awareness which always precedes reflective knowledge. This inner awareness of one's thought and existence is so innate in all men that, although we may pretend that we do not have it if we are over-whelmed by preconceived opinions and pay more attention to words than to their meanings, we cannot in fact fail to have it. Thus when anyone notices that he is thinking and that it follows from this that he exists, even though he may never before have asked what thought is or what existence is, he still cannot fail to have sufficient knowledge of them both to satisfy himself in this regard.   [*Sixth Replies*: CSM II 285]

[*Sum res cogitans ('I am a thinking thing')*]

Correct. For from the fact that I think, or have an image (whether I am awake or dreaming), it can be inferred that I am thinking; for 'I think' and 'I am thinking' mean the same thing. And from the fact that I am thinking it follows that I exist, since that which thinks is not nothing. But when the author adds 'that is, I am a mind, or intelligence, or intellect or reason',[1] a doubt arises. It does not seem to be a valid argument to say 'I am thinking, therefore I am thought' or 'I am using my intellect, hence I am an intellect.' I might just as well say 'I am walking, therefore I am a walk.' M. Descartes is identifying the thing which understands with in-tellection, which is an act of that which understands. Or at least he is identifying the thing which understands with the intellect, which is a power of that which understands. Yet all philosophers make a distinction between a subject and its

173   faculties and acts, i.e. between a subject and its properties and its essences: an entity is one thing, its essence is another. Hence it may be that the thing that thinks is the subject to which mind, reason or intellect belong; and this subject may thus be something corporeal. The contrary is assumed, not proved. Yet this inference is the basis of the conclusion which M. Descartes seems to want to establish.
                              [*Third Objections*: CSM II 122]

(174)   When I said 'that is, I am a mind, or intelligence, or intellect or reason', what I meant by these terms was not mere faculties, but things endowed with the faculty of thought. This is what the first two terms are commonly taken to mean by everyone; and the second two are often understood in this sense. I stated this point so explicitly, and in so many places, that it seems to me there was no room for doubt.

There is no comparison here between 'a walk' and 'thought'. 'A walk' is usually taken to refer simply to the act of walking, whereas 'thought' is sometimes taken to refer to the act, sometimes to the faculty, and some-times to the thing which possesses the faculty.

I do not say that the thing which understands is the same as intellection. Nor, indeed, do I identify the thing which understands with the intellect, if 'the intellect' is taken to refer to a faculty; they are identical only if 'the

1 Above, p. 82.

intellect' is taken to refer to the thing which understands. Now I freely admit that I used the most abstract terms I could in order to refer to the thing or substance in question, because I wanted to strip away from it everything that did not belong to it. This philosopher, by contrast, uses absolutely concrete words, namely 'subject', 'matter' and 'body', to refer to this thinking thing, because he wants to prevent its being separated from the body.   [*Third Replies*: CSM II 123]

*   *   *

When you go on to say that you are a *thinking* thing, then we know what you are (276) saying; but we knew it already, and it was not what we were asking you to tell us. Who doubts that you are thinking? What we are unclear about, what we are looking for, is that inner substance of yours whose property is to think. Your conclusion should be related to this inquiry, and should tell us not that you are a thinking thing, but what sort of thing this 'you' who thinks really is. If we are asking about wine, and looking for the kind of knowledge which is superior to common knowledge, it will hardly be enough for you to say 'wine is a liquid thing, which is compressed from grapes, white or red, sweet, intoxicating' and so on. You will have to attempt to investigate and somehow explain its internal substance, showing how it can be seen to be manufactured from spirits, tartar, the distillate, and other ingredients mixed together in such and such quantities and proportions. Similarly, given that you are looking for knowledge of yourself which is superior to common knowledge (that is, the kind of knowledge we have had up till now), you must see that it is certainly not enough for you to announce that you are a thing that 277 thinks and doubts and understands etc. You should carefully scrutinize yourself and conduct a kind of chemical investigation of yourself, if you are to succeed in uncovering and explaining to us your internal substance. If you provide such an explanation, we shall ourselves doubtless be able to investigate whether or not you are better known than the body whose nature we know so much about through anatomy, chemistry, so many other sciences, so many senses and so many experiments.   [*Fifth Objections*: CSM II 192–3]

I am surprised that you should say here ... that I distinctly know that I exist, but not that I know what I am or what my nature is; for one thing cannot be demonstrated without the other. Nor do I see what more you expect here, unless it is to be told what colour or smell or taste the human mind has, or the proportions of salt, sulphur and mercury from which it is compounded. You want us, you say, to conduct 'a kind of chemical investigation' of the mind, as we would of wine. This is indeed worthy of you, O Flesh, and of all those who have only a very confused conception of 360 everything, and so do not know the proper questions to ask about each thing. But as for me, I have never thought that anything more is required to reveal a substance than its various attributes; thus the more attributes of a given substance we know, the more perfectly we understand its nature. Now we can distinguish many different attributes in the wax: one, that it is white; two, that it is hard; three, that it can be melted; and so on. And there are correspondingly many attributes in the mind: one, that it has the power of knowing the whiteness of the wax; two, that it has the power of knowing its hardness; three, that it has the power of knowing that it can lose its hardness (i.e. melt), and so on. (Someone can have knowledge of the hardness without thereby having knowledge of the whiteness, e.g. a man born blind; and so on in other cases.) The clear inference from this is that we know more attributes in the case of our mind than we do in the case of anything else. For no matter how many attributes we recognize in any given thing, we can always list a corresponding number of attributes in the mind which it has in virtue of knowing the attributes of the thing; and hence the nature of the mind is the one we know best of all.   [*Fifth Replies*: CSM II 248–9]

[*The nature of thought*]

(214) Let me add something which I forgot to include earlier. The author lays it down as certain that there can be nothing in him, in so far as he is a thinking thing, of which he is not aware,[1] but it seems to me that this is false. For by 'himself, in so far as he is a thinking thing', he means simply his mind, in so far as it is distinct from the body. But all of us can surely see that there may be many things in our mind of which the mind is not aware. The mind of an infant in its mother's womb has the power of thought, but is not aware of it. And there are countless similar examples, which I will pass over.   [*Fourth Objections*: CSM II 150]

As to the fact that there can be nothing in the mind, in so far as it is a thinking thing, of which it is not aware, this seems to me to be self-evident. For there is nothing that we can understand to be in the mind, regarded in this way, that is not a thought or dependent on a thought. If it were not a thought or dependent on a thought it would not belong to the mind *qua* thinking thing; and we cannot have any thought of which we are not aware at the very moment when it is in us. In view of this I do not doubt that the mind begins to think as soon as it is implanted in the body of an infant, and that it is immediately aware of its thoughts, even though it does not remember this afterwards because the impressions of these thoughts do not remain in the memory.

But it must be noted that, although we are always actually aware of the acts or operations of our minds, we are not always aware of the mind's faculties or powers, except potentially. By this I mean that when we con-

1 Cf. Med III, p 96 above.

centrate on employing one of our faculties, then immediately, if the
faculty in question resides in our mind, we become actually aware of it, 247
and hence we may deny that it is in the mind if we are not capable of
becoming aware of it.   [*Fourth Replies*: CSM II 171–2]

[ON MEDITATION THREE]

[*Innate ideas*]

When we say that an idea is innate in us, we do not mean that is always 189
there before us. This would mean that no idea was innate. We simply mean
that we have within ourselves the faculty of summoning up the idea.
                                         [*Third Replies*: CSM II 132]

*   *   *

As for the forms which you say are innate, there do not seem to be any: whatever (280)
ideas are said to belong to this category also appear to have an external origin...
You should also have raised and answered, amongst other things, the question of
why a man born blind has no idea of colour, or a man born deaf has no idea of (283)
sound. Surely this is because external objects have not been able to transmit any
images of themselves to the minds of such unfortunates, because the doors have
been closed since birth, and there have always been barriers in place which have
prevented these images from entering.   [*Fifth Objections*: CSM II 195, 197]

In addition to the arguments which I put forward against myself and re- (363)
futed, you suggest the following: why is there no idea of colour in a man
born blind, and no idea of sound in a man born deaf? Here you show
plainly that you have no telling arguments to produce. How do you know
that there is no idea of colour in a man born blind? From time to time we
find in our own case that even though we close our eyes, sensations of
light and colour are nevertheless aroused. And even if we grant what you
say, those who deny the existence of material things may just as well attribute the absence of ideas of colour in the man born blind to the fact that
his mind lacks the faculty for forming them; this is just as reasonable as
your claim that he does not have the ideas because he is deprived of sight.
                                         [*Fifth Replies*: CSM II 251]

[*The idea of God*]

We have no idea or image corresponding to the sacred name of God. And this is (180)
why we are forbidden to worship God in the form of an image; for otherwise we
might think, that we were conceiving of him who is incapable of being conceived.
                                         [*Third Objections*: CSM II 127]

181   Here my critic wants the term 'idea' to be taken to refer simply to the images of material things which are depicted in the corporeal imagination; and if this is granted, it is easy for him to prove that there can be no proper idea of an angel or of God. But I make it quite clear in several places throughout the book, and in this passage in particular,[1] that I am taking the word 'idea' to refer to whatever is immediately perceived by the mind. For example, when I want something, or am afraid of something, I simultaneously perceive that I want, or am afraid; and this is why I count volition and fear among my ideas. I used the word 'idea' because it was the standard philosophical term used to refer to the forms of perception belonging to the divine mind, even though we recognize that God does not possess any corporeal imagination. And besides, there was not any more appropriate term at my disposal. I think I did give a full enough explanation to the idea of God to satisfy those who are prepared to attend to my meaning; I cannot possibly satisfy those who prefer to attribute a different sense to my words than the one I intended.

[*Third Replies*: CSM II 127–8]

[*Objective reality*]

(92)   What is 'objective being in the intellect'? According to what I was taught, this is simply the determination of an act of the intellect by means of an object. And this is merely an extraneous label which adds nothing to the thing itself. Just as 'being seen' is nothing other than an act of vision attributable to myself, so 'being thought of', or having objective being in the intellect, is simply a thought of the mind which stops and terminates in the mind. And this can occur without any movement or change in the thing itself, and indeed without the thing in question existing at all. So why should I look for a cause of something which is not actual, and which is simply an empty label, a non-entity?   [*First Objections*: CSM II 66–7]

Now I wrote that an idea is the thing which is thought of in so far as it has objective being in the intellect. But to give me an opportunity of explaining these words more clearly the objector pretends to understand them in quite a different way from that in which I used them. 'Objective being in the intellect', he says, 'is simply the determination of an act of the intellect by means of an object, and this is merely an extraneous label which adds nothing to the thing itself.' Notice here that he is referring to the thing itself as if it were located outside the intellect, and in this sense 'objective being in the intellect' is certainly an extraneous label; but I was speaking of the idea, which is never outside the intellect, and in this sense 'objective

1 Above, p. 88.

being' simply means being in the intellect in the way in which objects are normally there. For example, if anyone asks what happens to the sun through its being objectively in my intellect, the best answer is that nothing happens to it beyond the application of an extraneous label which does indeed 'determine an act of the intellect by means of an object'. But if the question is about what the *idea* of the sun is, and we answer that it is the thing which is thought of, in so far as it has objective being in the intellect, no one will take this to be the sun itself with this extraneous label applied to it. 'Objective being in the intellect' will not here mean 'the determination of an act of the intellect by means of an object', but will signify the object's being in the intellect in the way in which its objects are normally there. By this I mean that the idea of the sun is the sun itself existing in the intellect – not of course formally existing, as it does in the heavens, but objectively existing, i.e. in the way in which objects normally are in the intellect. Now this mode of being is of course much less perfect   103 than that possessed by things which exist outside the intellect; but, as I did explain, it is not therefore simply nothing.[1]

[*First Replies*: CSM II 74–5]

[ON MEDITATION FOUR]

[*The cause of error*]

You say that you recognize your will to be equal to that of God – not, indeed, in   (315) respect of its extent, but essentially.[2] But surely the same could be said of the intellect too, since you have defined the essential notion of the intellect in just the same way as you have defined that of the will. In short, will you please tell us if the will can extend to anything that escapes the intellect?

[*Fifth Objections*: CSM II 219]

You ask me to say briefly whether the will can extend to anything that escapes the intellect. The answer is that this occurs whenever we happen to go wrong. Thus when you judge that the mind is a kind of rarefied body, you can understand that the mind is itself, i.e. a thinking thing, and that a rarefied body is an extended thing; but the proposition that it is one and the same thing that thinks and is extended is one which   377 you certainly do not understand. You simply want to believe it, because you have believed it before and do not want to change your view. It is the same when you judge that an apple, which may in fact be poisoned, is nutritious: you understand that its smell, colour and so on, are pleasant,

---

1 Med. III, p. 91 above.
2 Above, p. 101.

but this does not mean that you understand that this particular apple will be beneficial to eat; you judge that it will because you want to believe it. So, while I do admit that when we direct our will towards something, we always have some sort of understanding of some aspect of it, I deny that our understanding and our will are of equal scope. In the case of any given object, there may be many things about it that we desire but very few things of which we have knowledge. And when we make a bad judgement, it is not that we exercise our will in a bad fashion, but that the object of our will is bad. Again, we never understand anything in a bad fashion; when we are said to 'understand in a bad fashion', all that happens is that we judge that our understanding is more extensive than it in fact is.

[*Fifth Replies*: CSM II 259]

[*The indifference of the will*]

The difficulty arises in connection with the indifference that belongs to our judgement, or liberty. This indifference, you claim, does not belong to the perfection of the will but has to do merely with its imperfection; thus, according to you, indifference is removed whenever the mind clearly perceives what it should believe or do or refrain from doing.[1] But do you not see that by adopting this position you are destroying God's freedom, since you are removing from his will the indifference as to whether he shall create this world rather than another world or no world at all? Yet it is an article of faith that God was from eternity indifferent as to whether he should create one world, or innumerable worlds, or none at all. But who doubts that God has always perceived with the clearest vision what he should do or refrain from doing? Thus, a very clear vision and perception of things does not remove indifference of choice; and if indifference cannot be a proper part of human freedom, neither will it find a place in divine freedom, since the essences of things are, like numbers, indivisible and immutable. Therefore indifference is involved in God's freedom of choice no less than it is in the case of human freedom of choice.

[*Sixth Objections*: CSM II 280–1]

417

As for the freedom of the will, the way in which it exists in God is quite different from the way in which it exists in us. It is self-contradictory to suppose that the will of God was not indifferent from eternity with respect to everything which has happened or will ever happen; for it is impossible to imagine that anything is thought of in the divine intellect as good or true, or worthy of belief or action or omission, prior to the decision of the divine will to make it so. I am not speaking here of temporal priority: I mean that there is not even any priority of order, or nature, or of 'rationally determined reason' as they call it, such that God's idea of the good impelled him to choose one thing rather than another. For example, God

432

1 Med. IV, above p. 102.

did not will the creation of the world in time because he saw that it would be better this way than if he had created it from eternity; nor did he will that the three angles of a triangle should be equal to two right angles because he recognized that it could not be otherwise, and so on. On the contrary, it is because he willed to create the world in time that it is better this way than if he had created it from eternity; and it is because he willed that the three angles of a triangle should necessarily equal two right angles that this is true and cannot be otherwise; and so on in other cases. There is no problem in the fact that the merit of the saints may be said to be the cause of their obtaining eternal life; for it is not the cause of this reward in the sense that it determines God to will anything, but is merely the cause of an effect of which God willed from eternity that it should be the cause. Thus the supreme indifference to be found in God is the supreme indication of his omnipotence. But as for man, since he finds that the nature of all goodness and truth is already determined by God, and his will cannot tend towards anything else, it is evident that he will embrace what is good and true all the more willingly, and hence more freely, in proportion as he sees it more clearly. He is never indifferent except when he does not know which of the two alternatives is the better or truer, or at least when he does 433 not see this clearly enough to rule out any possibility of doubt. Hence the indifference which belongs to human freedom is very different from that which belongs to divine freedom. The fact that the essences of things are said to be indivisible is not relevant here. For, firstly, no essence can belong univocally to both God and his creatures; and, secondly, indifference does not belong to the essence of human freedom, since not only are we free when ignorance of what is right makes us indifferent, but we are also free – indeed at our freest – when a clear perception impels us to pursue some object. [*Sixth Replies*: CSM II 291–2]

[ON MEDITATION FIVE]

[*Whether God's essence implies his existence*]

It is quite all right for you to compare essence with essence, but instead of going on to compare existence with existence or a property with a property, you compare existence with a property. It seems that you should have said that omnipotence can no more be separated from the essence of God than the fact that its angles equal two right angles can be separated from the essence of a triangle. Or, at any rate, you 323 should have said that the existence of God can no more be separated from his essence than the existence of a triangle can be separated from its essence. If you had done this, both your comparisons would have been satisfactory, and I would have granted you not only the first one but the second one as well. But you would not for all that have established that God necessarily exists, since a triangle does not necessarily exist either, even though its essence and existence cannot in actual fact be separated. Real separatión is impossible no matter how much the mind may separate them or think of them apart from each other – as indeed it can even in the case of God's essence and existence.   [*Fifth Objections*: CSM II 224]

Here I do not see what sort of thing you want existence to be, nor why it cannot be said to be a property just like omnipotence – provided, of course, that we take the word 'property' to stand for any attribute, or for whatever can be predicated of a thing; and this is exactly how it should be taken in this context. Moreover, in the case of God necessary existence is in fact a property in the strictest sense of the term, since it applies to him alone and forms a part of his essence as it does of no other thing. Hence the existence of a triangle should not be compared with the existence of God, since the relation between existence and essence is manifestly quite different in the case of God from what it is in the case of the triangle.

383

To list existence among the properties which belong to the nature of God is no more 'begging the question' than listing among the properties of a triangle the fact that its angles are equal to two right angles.

Again, it is not true to say that in the case of God, just as in the case of a triangle, existence and essence can be thought of apart from one another; for God is his own existence, but this is not true of the triangle. I do not, however, deny that possible existence is a perfection in the idea of a triangle, just as necessary existence is a perfection in the idea of God; for this fact makes the idea of a triangle superior to the ideas of chimeras, which cannot possibly be supposed to have existence. Thus at no point have you weakened the force of my argument in the slightest.

                                      [*Fifth Replies*: CSM II 262–3]

                    *   *   *

(99) Even if it is granted that a supremely perfect being carries the implication of existence in virtue of its very title, it still does not follow that the existence in question is anything actual in the real world; all that follows is that the concept of existence is inseparably linked to the concept of a supreme being. So you cannot infer that the existence of God is anything actual unless you suppose that the supreme being actually exists; for then it will actually contain all perfections, including the perfection of real existence.   [*First Objections*: CSM II 72]

My argument however was as follows: 'That which we clearly and distinctly understand to belong to the true and immutable nature, or essence, or form of something, can truly be asserted of that thing. But once we have made a sufficiently careful investigation of what God is, we clearly and

116

distinctly understand that existence belongs to his true and immutable nature. Hence we can now truly assert of God that he does exist.' Here at least the conclusion does follow from the premisses. But, what is more, the major premiss cannot be denied, because it has already been conceded that whatever we clearly and distinctly understand is true. Hence only the minor premiss remains, and here I confess that there is considerable difficulty. In the first place we are so accustomed to distinguishing existence from essence in the case of all other things that we fail to notice how closely existence belongs to essence in the case of God as compared with that of other things. Next, we do not distinguish what belongs to the true and immutable essence of a thing from what is attributed to it merely by a fiction of the intellect. So, even if we observe clearly enough that existence belongs to the essence of God, we do not draw the conclusion that God exists, because we do not know whether his essence is immutable and true, or merely invented by us.

But to remove the first part of the difficulty we must distinguish between possible and necessary existence. It must be noted that possible existence is contained in the concept or idea of everything that we clearly and distinctly understand; but in no case is necessary existence so contained, except in the case of the idea of God. Those who carefully attend to this difference between the idea of God and every other idea will undoubtedly perceive that even though our understanding of other things   117
always involves understanding them as if they were existing things, it does not follow that they do exist, but merely that they are capable of existing. For our understanding does not show us that it is necessary for actual existence to be conjoined with their other properties. But, from the fact that we understand that actual existence is necessarily and always conjoined with the other attributes of God, it certainly does follow that God exists.

To remove the second part of the difficulty, we must notice a point about ideas which do not contain true and immutable natures but merely ones which are invented and put together by the intellect. Such ideas can always be split up by the same intellect, not simply by an abstraction but by a clear and distinct intellectual operation, so that any ideas which the intellect cannot split up in this way were clearly not put together by the intellect. When, for example, I think of a winged horse or an actually existing lion, or a triangle inscribed in a square, I readily understand that I am also able to think of a horse without wings, or a lion which does not exist, or a triangle apart from a square, and so on; hence these things do not have true and immutable natures. But if I think of a triangle or a square (I will not now include the lion or the horse, since their natures are not transparently clear to us), then whatever I apprehend as being contained in the idea of a triangle – for example that its three angles are equal to two right angles – I can with truth assert of the triangle. And the same applies to the square with respect to whatever I apprehend as being contained in the idea of a square. For even if I can understand what a triangle is if I abstract the fact that its three angles are equal to two right angles, I cannot deny that this property applies to the triangle by a clear and distinct intellectual operation – that is, while at the same time understanding what I mean by my denial. Moreover, if I consider a triangle inscribed in a square, with a view not to attributing to the square properties that belong only to the triangle, or attributing to the triangle properties that belong to the square, but with a view to examining only the properties which arise out of the conjunction of the two, then the nature of this composite will be just as true and immutable as the nature of the triangle alone or the square alone. And hence it will be quite in order to maintain that the square is not less than double the area of the triangle inscribed within it, and to affirm other similar properties that belong to the nature of this composite figure.

But if I were to think that the idea of a supremely perfect body contained existence, on the grounds that it is a greater perfection to exist both in reality and in the intellect than it is to exist in the intellect alone, I could not infer from this that the supremely perfect body exists, but only that it is capable of existing. For I can see quite well that this idea has been put together by my own intellect which has linked together all bodily perfections; and existence does not arise out of the other bodily perfections because it can equally well be affirmed or denied of them. Indeed, when I examine the idea of a body, I perceive that a body has no power to create itself or maintain itself in existence; and I rightly conclude that necessary existence—and it is only necessary existence that is at issue here – no more belongs to the nature of a body, however perfect, than it belongs to the nature of a mountain to be without a valley, or to the nature of a triangle to have angles whose sum is greater than two right angles. But instead of a body, let us now take a thing – whatever this thing turns out to be – which possesses all the perfections which can exist together. If we ask whether existence should be included among these perfections, we will admittedly be in some doubt at first. For our mind, which is finite, normally thinks of these perfections only separately, and hence may not immediately notice the necessity of their being joined together. Yet if we attentively examine whether existence belongs to a supremely powerful being, and what sort of existence it is, we shall be able to perceive clearly and distinctly the following facts. First, possible existence, at the very least, belongs to such a being, just as it belongs to all the other things of which we have a distinct idea, even to those which are put together through a fiction of the intellect. Next, when we attend to the immense power of this being, we shall be unable to think of its existence as possible without also recognizing that it can exist by its own power; and we shall infer from this that this being does really exist and has existed from eternity, since it is quite evident by the natural light that what can exist by its own power always exists. So we shall come to understand that necessary existence is contained in the idea of a supremely powerful being, not by any fiction of the intellect, but because it belongs to the true and immutable nature of such a being that it exists. And we shall also easily perceive that this supremely powerful being cannot but possess within it all the other perfections that are contained in the idea of God; and hence these perfections exist in God and are joined together not by any fiction of the intellect but by their very nature.

[*First Replies*: CSM II 83–5]

[*Clear and distinct perception and the 'Cartesian Circle'*]

You are not yet certain of the existence of God, and you say that you are not certain of anything, and cannot know anything clearly and distinctly until you have achieved clear and certain knowledge of the existence of God.[1] It follows from this that you do not yet clearly and distinctly know that you are a thinking thing, since, on your own admission, that knowledge depends on the clear knowledge of an existing God; and this you have not yet proved in the passage where you draw the conclusion that you clearly know what you are.

Moreover, an atheist is clearly and distinctly aware that the three angles of a triangle are equal to two right angles; but so far is he from supposing the existence of God that he completely denies it. According to the atheist, if God existed there would be a supreme being and a supreme good; that is to say, the infinite would exist. But the infinite in every category of perfection excludes everything else whatsoever – every kind of being and goodness, as well as every kind of non-being and evil. Yet in fact there are many kinds of being and goodness, and many kinds of non-being and evil. We think you should deal with this objection, so that the impious have no arguments left to put forward.

[*Second Objections*: CSM II 89]

When I said that we can know nothing for certain until we are aware that (140) God exists, I expressly declared that I was speaking only of knowledge of those conclusions which can be recalled when we are no longer attending to the arguments by means of which we deduced them.[2] Now awareness of first principles is not normally called 'knowledge' by dialecticians...

The fact that an atheist can be 'clearly aware that the three angles of a (141)

1 Cf. Med. III, p. 88 above; Med. v, p. 110 above.
2 Cf. Med. v, p. 109 above.

triangle are equal to two right angles' is something I do not dispute. But I maintain that this awareness of his is not true knowledge, since no act of awareness that can be rendered doubtful seems fit to be called knowledge.[1] Now since we are supposing that this individual is an atheist, he cannot be certain that he is not being deceived on matters which seem to him to be very evident (as I fully explained). And although this doubt may not occur to him, it can still crop up if someone else raises the point or if he looks into the matter himself. So he will never be free of this doubt until he acknowledges that God exists.

It does not matter that the atheist may think he has demonstrations to prove that there is no God. For, since these proofs are quite unsound, it will always be possible to point out their flaws to him, and when this happens he will have to abandon his view.   [*Second Replies*: CSM II 100–101]

*   *   *

(126) How can you establish with certainty that you are not deceived, or capable of being deceived, in matters which you think you know clearly and distinctly? Have we not often seen people turn out to have been deceived in matters where they thought their knowledge was as clear as the sunlight? Your principle of clear and distinct knowledge thus requires a clear and distinct explanation, in such a way as to rule out the possibility that anyone of sound mind may be deceived on matters which he thinks he knows clearly and distinctly. Failing this, we do not see that any degree of certainty can possibly be within your reach or that of mankind in general.
[*Second Objections*: CSM II 90]

In the case of our clearest and most careful judgements ... if such judgements were false they could not be corrected by any clearer judgements or by means of any other natural faculty. In such cases I simply assert that it is impossible for us to be deceived. Since God is the supreme being, he must also be supremely good and true, and it would therefore be a contradiction that anything should be created by him which positively tends towards falsehood. Now everything real which is in us must have been bestowed on us by God (this was proved when his existence was proved); moreover, we have a real faculty for recognizing the truth and distinguishing it from falsehood, as is clear merely from the fact that we have within us ideas of truth and falsehood. Hence this faculty must tend towards the truth, at least when we use it correctly (that is, by assenting only to what we clearly and distinctly perceive, for no other correct method of employing this faculty can be imagined). For if it did not so tend then, since God gave it to us, he would rightly have to be regarded as a deceiver.

144

1 Descartes seems to distinguish here between an isolated cognition or act of awareness (*cognitio*) and systematic, properly grounded knowledge (*scientia*). Compare the remarks in *The Search for Truth* about the need to acquire 'a body of knowledge firm and certain enough to deserve the name "science"': AT x 513; CSM II 408.

Hence you see that once we have become aware that God exists it is necessary for us to imagine that he is a deceiver if we wish to cast doubt on what we clearly and distinctly perceive. And since it is impossible to imagine that he is a deceiver, whatever we clearly and distinctly perceive must be completely accepted as true and certain.

But since I see that you are still stuck fast in the doubts which I put forward in the First Meditation, and which I thought I had very carefully removed in the succeeding Meditations, I shall now expound for a second time the basis on which it seems to me that all human certainty can be founded.

First of all, as soon as we think that we correctly perceive something, we are spontaneously convinced that it is true. Now if this conviction is so firm that it is impossible for us ever to have any reason for doubting what we are convinced of, then there are no further questions for us to ask: we have everything that we could reasonably want. What is it to us that someone may make out that the perception whose truth we are so firmly convinced of may appear false to God or an angel, so that it is, absolutely speaking, false? Why should this alleged 'absolute falsity' bother us, since we neither believe in it nor have even the smallest suspicion of it? For the supposition which we are making here is of a conviction so firm that it is quite incapable of being destroyed; and such a conviction is clearly the same as the most perfect certainty.

But it may be doubted whether any such certainty, or firm and immutable conviction, is in fact to be had.

It is clear that we do not have this kind of certainty in cases where our perception is even the slightest bit obscure or confused, for such obscurity, whatever its degree, is quite sufficient to make us have doubts in such cases. Again, we do not have the required kind of certainty with regard to matters which we perceive solely by means of the senses, however clear such perception may be. For we have often noted that error can be detected in the senses, as when someone with dropsy feels thirsty or when someone with jaundice sees snow as yellow; for when he sees it as yellow he sees it just as clearly and distinctly as we do when we see it as white. Accordingly, if there is any certainty to be had, the only remaining alternative is that it occurs in the clear perceptions of the intellect and nowhere else.

Now some of these perceptions are so transparently clear and at the same time so simple that we cannot ever think of them without believing them to be true. The fact that I exist so long as I am thinking, or that what is done cannot be undone, are examples of truths in respect of which we manifestly possess this kind of certainty. For we cannot doubt them unless we think of them; but we cannot think of them without at the same time 146 believing they are true, as was supposed. Hence we cannot doubt them without at the same time believing they are true; that is, we can never doubt them.

It is no objection to this to say that we have often seen people 'turn out to have been deceived in matters where they thought their knowledge was as clear as the sunlight'. For we have never seen, indeed no one could possibly see, this happening to those who have relied solely on the intellect in their quest for clarity in their perceptions; we have seen it happen only to those who tried to derive such clarity from the senses or from some false preconceived opinion.

It is also no objection for someone to make out that such truths might appear false to God or to an angel. For the evident clarity of our perceptions does not allow us to listen to anyone who makes up this kind of story.

There are other truths which are perceived very clearly by our intellect so long as we attend to the arguments on which our knowledge of them depends; and we are therefore incapable of doubting them during this time. But we may forget the arguments in question and later remember simply the conclusions which were deduced from them. The question will now arise as to whether we possess the same firm and immutable conviction concerning these conclusions, when we simply recollect that they were previously deduced from quite evident principles (our ability to call them 'conclusions' presupposes such a recollection). My reply is that the required certainty is indeed possessed by those whose knowledge of God enables them to understand that the intellectual faculty which he gave them cannot but tend towards the truth; but the required certainty is not possessed by others. This point was explained so clearly at the end of the Fifth Meditation[1] that it does not seem necessary to add anything further here.   [*Second Replies:* CSM II 102–5]

                          *   *   *

(214) I have one further worry, namely how the author avoids reasoning in a circle when he says that we are sure that what we clearly and distinctly perceive is true only because God exists.[2]

But we can be sure that God exists only because we clearly and distinctly perceive this. Hence, before we can be sure that God exists, we ought to be able to be sure that whatever we perceive clearly and evidently is true.

                                           [*Fourth Objections:* CSM II 150]

Lastly, as to the fact that I was not guilty of circularity when I said that the only reason we have for being sure that what we clearly and distinctly per-

---

1 Above, pp. 109f.   2 Cf. Med. v, p. 109 above.

ceive is true is the fact that God exists, but that we are sure that God exists　246
only because we perceive this clearly: I have already given an adequate explanation of this point in my reply to the Second Objections, where I made
a distinction between what we in fact perceive clearly and what we
remember having perceived clearly on a previous occasion.[1] To begin
with, we are sure that God exists because we attend to the arguments
which prove this; but subsequently it is enough for us to remember that
we perceived something clearly in order for us to be certain that it is true.
This would not be sufficient if we did not know that God exists and is not
a deceiver.　　　　　　　　　　　　　[*Fourth Replies*: CSM II 171]

[ON MEDITATION SIX]

[*The real distinction between mind and body*]

How does it follow, from the fact that he is aware of nothing else belonging to his　(199)
essence, that nothing else does in fact belong to it? I must confess that I am
somewhat slow, but I have been unable to find anywhere in the Second Meditation
an answer to this question....

So far as I can see, the only result that follows from this is that I can obtain some　(201)
knowledge of myself without knowledge of the body. But it is not yet transparently
clear to me that this knowledge is complete and adequate, so as to enable me to be
certain that I am not mistaken in excluding body from my essence. I shall explain
the point by means of an example.

Suppose someone knows for certain that the angle in a semi-circle is a right
angle, and hence that the triangle formed by this angle and the diameter of the circle
is right-angled. In spite of this, he may doubt, or not yet have grasped for certain,
that the square on the hypotenuse is equal to the squares on the other two sides;
indeed he may even deny this if he is misled by some fallacy. But now, if he uses the
same argument as that proposed by our illustrious author, he may appear to have
confirmation of his false belief, as follows: 'I clearly and distinctly perceive', he may　202
say, 'that the triangle is right-angled; but I doubt that the square on the hypotenuse
is equal to the squares on the other two sides; therefore it does not belong to the
essence of the triangle that the square on its hypotenuse is equal to the squares on
the other sides.'

Again, even if I deny that the square on the hypotenuse is equal to the square on
the other two sides, I still remain sure that the triangle is right-angled, and my mind
retains the clear and distinct knowledge that one of its angles is a right angle. And
given that this is so, not even God could bring it about that the triangle is not
right-angled.

I might argue from this that the property which I doubt, or which can be
removed while leaving my idea intact, does not belong to the essence of the triangle.

1 See above, pp. 139 and 142.

Moreover, 'I know', says M. Descartes, 'that everything which I clearly and distinctly understand is capable of being created by God as to correspond exactly with my understanding of it. And hence the fact that I can clearly and distinctly understand one thing apart from another is enough to make me certain that the two things are distinct, since they are capable of being separated by God.'[1] Yet I clearly and distinctly understand that this triangle is right-angled, without understanding that the square on the hypotenuse is equal to the squares on the other sides. It follows on this reasoning that God, at least, could create a right-angled triangle with the square on its hypotenuse not equal to the squares on the other sides.

I do not see any possible reply here, except that the person in this example does not clearly and distinctly perceive that the triangle is right-angled. But how is my perception of the nature of my mind any clearer than his perception of the nature of the triangle? He is just as certain that the triangle in the semi-circle has one right angle (which is the criterion of a right-angled triangle) as I am certain that I exist because I am thinking.

Now although the man in the example clearly and distinctly knows that the triangle is right-angled, he is wrong in thinking that the aforesaid relationship between the squares on the sides does not belong to the nature of the triangle. Similarly, although I clearly and distinctly know my nature to be something that thinks, may I, too, not perhaps be wrong in thinking that nothing else belongs to my nature apart from the fact that I am a thinking thing? Perhaps the fact that I am an extended thing may also belong to my nature.

[*Fourth Objections*: CSM II 140–3]

(219)   I will begin by pointing out where it was that I embarked on proving 'how, from the fact that I am aware of nothing else belonging to my essence (that is, the essence of the mind alone) apart from the fact that I am a thinking thing, it follows that nothing else does in fact belong to it'. The relevant passage is the one where I proved that God exists – a God who can bring about everything that I clearly and distinctly recognize as possible.[2]

Now it may be that there is much within me of which I am not yet aware (for example, in this passage I was in fact supposing that I was not yet aware that the mind possessed the power of moving the body, or that it was substantially united to it). Yet since that of which I am aware is sufficient to enable me to subsist with it and it alone, I am certain that I could have been created by God without having these other attributes of which I am unaware, and hence that these other attributes do not belong to the essence of the mind.

For if something can exist without some attribute, then it seems to me that that attribute is not included in its essence. And although mind is part of the essence of man, being united to a human body is not strictly speaking part of the essence of mind....

1 Med. VI, p. 114 above.
2 Cf. above, Med. V, pp. 109f, and Med. VI, p. 114.

My critic argues that although I can obtain some knowledge of myself without knowledge of the body, it does not follow that this knowledge is complete and adequate, so as to enable me to be certain that I am not mistaken in excluding body from my essence. He explains the point by   224 using the example of a triangle inscribed in a semi-circle, which we can clearly and distinctly understand to be right-angled although we do not know, or may even deny, that the square on the hypotenuse is equal to the squares on the other sides. But we cannot infer from this that there could be a right-angled triangle such that the square on the hypotenuse is not equal to the squares on the other sides.

But this example differs in many respects from the case under discussion.

First of all, though a triangle can perhaps be taken concretely as a substance having a triangular shape, it is certain that the property of having the square on the hypotenuse equal to the squares on the other sides is not a substance. So neither the triangle nor the property can be understood as a complete thing in the way in which mind and body can be so understood; nor can either item be called a 'thing' in the sense in which I said 'it is enough that I can understand one thing (that is, a complete thing) apart from another' etc.[1] This is clear from the passage which comes next: 'Besides I find in myself faculties' etc. I did not say that these faculties were *things*, but carefully distinguished them from things or substances.

Secondly, although we can clearly and distinctly understand that a triangle in a semi-circle is right-angled without being aware that the square on the hypotenuse is equal to the squares on the other two sides, we cannot have a clear understanding of a triangle having the square on its hypotenuse equal to the squares on the other sides without at the same   225 time being aware that it is right-angled. And yet we can clearly and distinctly perceive the mind without the body and the body without the mind.

Thirdly, although it is possible to have a concept of a triangle inscribed in a semi-circle which does not include the fact that the square on the hypotenuse is equal to the squares on the other sides, it is not possible to have a concept of the triangle such that no ratio at all is understood to hold between the square on the hypotenuse and the squares on the other sides. Hence, though we may be unaware of what that ratio is, we cannot say that any given ratio does not hold unless we clearly understand that it does not belong to the triangle; and where the ratio is one of equality, this can never be understood. Yet the concept of body includes nothing at all which belongs to the mind, and the concept of mind includes nothing at all which belongs to the body.

   1 Med. VI, p. 114 above.

So although I said 'it is enough that I can clearly and distinctly understand one thing apart from another' etc., one cannot go on to argue 'yet I clearly and distinctly understand that this triangle is right-angled without understanding that the square on the hypotenuse' etc. There are three reasons for this. First, the ratio between the square on the hypotenuse and the squares on the other sides is not a complete thing. Secondly, we do not clearly understand the ratio to be equal except in the case of a right-angled triangle. And thirdly, there is no way in which the triangle can be distinctly understood if the ratio which obtains between the square on the hypotenuse and the squares on the other sides is said not to hold.

226   But now I must explain how the mere fact that I can clearly and distinctly understand one substance apart from another is enough to make me certain that one excludes the other.[1]

The answer is that the notion of a *substance* is just this – that it can exist by itself, that is without the aid of any other substance. And there is no one who has ever perceived two substances by means of two different concepts without judging that they are really distinct.

Hence, had I not been looking for greater than ordinary certainty, I should have been content to have shown in the Second Meditation that the mind can be understood as a subsisting thing despite the fact that nothing belonging to the body is attributed to it, and that, conversely, the body can be understood as a subsisting thing despite the fact that nothing belonging to the mind is attributed to it. I should have added nothing more in order to demonstrate that there is a real distinction between the mind and the body, since we commonly judge that the order in which things are mutually related in our perception of them corresponds to the order in which they are related in actual reality. But one of the exaggerated doubts which I put forward in the First Meditation went so far as to make it impossible for me to be certain of this very point (namely whether things do in reality correspond to our perception of them), so long as I was supposing myself to be ignorant of the author of my being. And this is why everything I wrote on the subject of God and truth in the Third, Fourth and Fifth Meditations contributes to the conclusion that there is a real distinction between the mind and the body, which I finally established in the Sixth Meditation.

227   And yet, says M. Arnauld, 'I have a clear understanding of a triangle inscribed in a semi-circle without knowing that the square on the hypotenuse is equal to the squares on the other sides.' It is true that the triangle is intelligible even though we do not think of the ratio which obtains between the square on the hypotenuse and the squares on the other sides; but it is not intelligible that this ratio should be denied of the triangle. In

1 Cf. Med. VI, above p. 114.

the case of the mind, by contrast, not only do we understand it to exist without the body, but, what is more, all the attributes which belong to a body can be denied of it. For it is of the nature of substances that they should mutually exclude one another.

[*Fourth Replies*: CSM II 154–5, 157–9]

*   *   *

When, on the basis of the arguments set out in these Meditations, I first   440
drew the conclusion that the human mind is really distinct from the body, better known than the body, and so on, I was compelled to accept these results because everything in the reasoning was coherent and was inferred from quite evident principles in accordance with the rules of logic. But I confess that for all that I was not entirely convinced; I was in the same plight as astronomers who have established by argument that the sun is several times larger than the earth, and yet still cannot prevent themselves judging that it is smaller, when they actually look at it. However, I went on from here, and proceeded to apply the same fundamental principles to the consideration of physical things. First I attended to the ideas or notions of each particular thing which I found within myself, and I carefully distinguished them one from the other so that all my judgements should match them. I observed as a result that nothing whatever belongs to the concept of body except the fact that it is something which has length, breadth and depth and is capable of various shapes and motions; moreover, these shapes and motions are merely modes which no power whatever can cause to exist apart from body. But colours, smells, tastes and so on, are, I observed, merely certain sensations which exist in my thought, and are as different from bodies as pain is different from the shape and motion of the weapon which produces it. And lastly, I observed that heaviness and hardness and the power to heat or to attract, or to purge, and all the other qualities which we experience in bodies, consist solely in the motion of bodies, or its absence, and the configuration and situation of their parts.

Since these opinions were completely different from those which I had   441
previously held regarding physical things, I next began to consider what had led me to take a different view before. The principal cause, I discovered, was this. From infancy I had made a variety of judgements about physical things in so far as they contributed to preserving the life which I was embarking on; and subsequently I retained the same opinions I had originally formed of these things. But at that age the mind employed the bodily organs less correctly than it now does, and was more firmly attached to them; hence it had no thoughts apart from them and perceived things only in a confused manner. Although it was aware of its own nature and had within itself an idea of thought as well as an idea of exten-

sion, it never exercised its intellect on anything without at the same time picturing something in the imagination. It therefore took thought and extension to be one and the same thing, and referred to the body all the notions which it had concerning things related to the intellect. Now I had never freed myself from these preconceived opinions in later life, and hence there was nothing that I knew with sufficient distinctness, and there was nothing I did not suppose to be corporeal; however, in the case of those very things that I supposed to be corporeal, the ideas or concepts which I formed were frequently such as to refer to minds rather than bodies.

For example, I conceived of gravity[1] as if it were some sort of real quality, which inhered in solid bodies; and although I called it a 'quality', thereby referring it to the bodies in which it inhered, by adding that it was 'real' I was in fact thinking that it was a substance. In the same way clothing, regarded in itself, is a substance, even though when referred to the 442 man who wears it, it is a quality. Or again, the mind, even though it is in fact a substance, can nonetheless be said to be a quality of the body to which it is joined. And although I imagined gravity to be scattered throughout the whole body that is heavy, I still did not attribute to it the extension which constitutes the nature of a body. For the true extension of a body is such as to exclude any interpenetration of the parts, whereas I thought that there was the same amount of gravity in a ten foot piece of wood as in one foot lump of gold or other metal—indeed I thought that the whole of the gravity could be contracted to a mathematical point. Moreover, I saw that the gravity, while remaining coextensive with the heavy body, could exercise all its force in any one part of the body; for if the body were hung from a rope attached to any part of it, it would still pull the rope down with all its force, just as if all the gravity existed in the part actually touching the rope instead of being scattered through the remaining parts. This is exactly the way in which I now understand the mind to be coextensive with the body—the whole mind in the whole body and the whole mind in any one of its parts. But what makes it especially clear that my idea of gravity was taken largely from the idea I had of the mind is the fact that I thought that gravity carried bodies towards the centre of the earth as if it had some knowledge of the centre within itself. For this surely could not happen without knowledge, and there can be no knowledge except in a mind. Nevertheless I continued to apply to gravity various other attributes which cannot be understood to apply to a mind in this way – for example its being divisible, measurable and so on.

But later on I made the observations which led me to make a careful 443 distinction between the idea of the mind and the ideas of body and corpo-

1 Lat. *gravitas*, literally 'heaviness'.

real motion; and I found that all those other ideas of 'real qualities' or 'substantial forms' which I had previously held were ones which I had put together or constructed from those basic ideas. And thus I very easily freed myself from all the doubts that my critics here put forward. First of all, I did not doubt that I 'had a clear idea of my mind', since I had a close inner awareness of it. Nor did I doubt that 'this idea was quite different from the ideas of other things', and that 'it contained nothing of a corporeal nature'. For I had also looked for true ideas of all these 'other things', and I appeared to have some general acquaintance with all of them; yet everything I found in them was completely different from my idea of the mind. Moreover, I found that the distinction between things such as mind and body, which appeared distinct even though I attentively thought about both of them, is much greater than the distinction between things which are such that when we think of both of them we do not see how one can exist apart from the other (even though we may be able to understand one without thinking of the other). For example, we can understand the immeasurable greatness of God even though we do not attend to his justice; but if we attend to both, it is quite self-contradictory to suppose that he is immeasurably great and yet not just. Again, it is possible to have true knowledge of the existence of God even though we lack knowledge of the Persons of the Holy Trinity, since the latter can be perceived only by a mind which faith has illuminated; yet when we do perceive them, I deny that it is intelligible to suppose that there is a real distinction between them, at least as far as the divine essence is concerned, although such a   444
distinction may be admitted as far as their mutual relationship is concerned.

Finally, I was not afraid of being so preoccupied with my method of analysis that I might have made the mistake suggested by my critics: seeing that there are 'certain bodies which do not think' (or, rather, clearly understanding that certain bodies can exist without thought), I preferred, they claim, to assert that thought does not belong to the nature of the body rather than to notice that there are certain bodies, namely human ones, which do think, and to infer that thought is a mode of the body. In fact I have never seen or perceived that human bodies think; all I have seen is that there are human beings, who possess both thought and a body. This happens as a result of a thinking thing's being combined with a corporeal thing: I perceived this from the fact that when I examined a thinking thing on its own, I discovered nothing in it which belonged to body, and similarly when I considered corporeal nature on its own I discovered no thought in it. On the contrary, when I examined all the modes of body and mind, I did not observe a single mode the concept of which did not depend on the concept of the thing of which it was a mode. Also, the fact

that we often see two things joined together does not license the inference
that they are one and the same; but the fact that we sometimes observe
one of them apart from the other entirely justifies the inference that they
are different. Nor should the power of God deter us from making this
inference. For it is a conceptual contradiction to suppose that two things
which we clearly perceive as different should become one and the same
445   (that is intrinsically one and the same, as opposed to by combination); this
is no less a contradiction than to suppose that two things which are in no
way distinct should be separated. Hence, if God has implanted the power
of thought in certain bodies (as he in fact has done in the case of human
bodies), then he can remove this power from them, and hence it still
remains really distinct from them.

[*Sixth Replies*: CSM II 296–9]

[APPENDIX: ARGUMENTS ARRANGED IN GEOMETRICAL FASHION]

(128)   It would be worthwhile if you set out the entire argument in geometrical fashion,
starting from a number of definitions, postulates and axioms. You are highly
experienced in employing this method, and it would enable you to fill the mind of
each reader so that he could see everything as it were at a single glance, and be
permeated with awareness of the divine power.

[*Second Objections*: CSM II 92]

I now turn to your proposal that I should set out my arguments in
geometrical fashion to enable the reader to perceive them 'as it were at a
single glance'. It is worth explaining here how far I have already followed
this method, and how far I think it should be followed in future. I make a
distinction between two things which are involved in the geometrical
manner of writing, namely, the order, and the method of demonstration.

The order consists simply in this. The items which are put forward first
must be known entirely without the aid of what comes later; and the
remaining items must be arranged in such a way that their demonstration
depends solely on what has gone before. I did try to follow this order very
carefully in my *Meditations*, and my adherence to it was the reason for
my dealing with the distinction between the mind and the body only at
the end, in the Sixth Meditation, rather than in the Second. It also
explains why I deliberately and knowingly omitted many matters
which would have required an explanation of an even larger number of
things.

As for the method of demonstration, this divides into two varieties: the
first proceeds by analysis and the second by synthesis.

Analysis shows the true way by means of which the thing in question was discovered methodically and as it were *a priori*,[1] so that if the reader is willing to follow it and give sufficient attention to all points, he will make the thing his own and understand it just as perfectly as if he had discovered it for himself. But this method contains nothing to compel belief in an argumentative or inattentive reader; for if he fails to attend   156 even to the smallest point, he will not see the necessity of the conclusion. Moreover there are many truths which – although it is vital to be aware of them – this method often scarcely mentions, since they are transparently clear to anyone who gives them his attention.

Synthesis, by contrast, employs a directly opposite method where the search is, as it were, *a posteriori* (though the proof itself is often more *a priori* than it is in the analytic method).[2] It demonstrates the conclusion clearly and employs a long series of definitions, postulates, axioms, theorems and problems, so that if anyone denies one of the conclusions it can be shown at once that it is contained in what has gone before, and hence the reader, however argumentative or stubborn he may be, is compelled to give his assent. However, this method is not as satisfying as the method of analysis, nor does it engage the minds of those who are eager to learn, since it does not show how the thing in question was discovered.

It was synthesis alone that the ancient geometers usually employed in their writings. But in my view this was not because they were utterly ignorant of analysis, but because they had such a high regard for it that they kept it to themselves like a sacred mystery.

Now it is analysis which is the best and truest method of instruction, and it was this method alone which I employed in my *Meditations*. As for synthesis, which is undoubtedly what you are asking me to use here, it is a method which it may be very suitable to deploy in geometry as a follow-up to analysis, but it cannot so conveniently be applied to these metaphysical subjects.

The difference is that the primary notions which are presupposed for the demonstration of geometrical truths are readily accepted by anyone, since they accord with the use of our senses. Hence there is no difficulty

---

1 Descartes' use of the term *a priori* here seems to correspond neither with the modern, post-Leibnizian sense (where *a priori* truths are those which are known independently of experience), nor with the medieval, Thomist sense (where *a priori* reasoning is that which proceeds from cause to effect). What Descartes may mean when he says that analysis proceeds 'as it were *a priori*' (*tanquam a priori*) is that it starts from what is epistemically prior, i.e. from what is prior in the 'order of discovery' followed by the meditator.

2 Descartes may mean that though the proofs involved are *a priori* (*viz.*, in the traditional, Thomist sense), the method of synthesis starts from premisses which are epistemically posterior – i.e. which are arrived at later in the order of discovery. (See previous footnote.)

157 there, except in the proper deduction of the consequences, which can be done even by the less attentive, provided they remember what has gone before. Moreover, the breaking down of propositions to their smallest elements is specifically designed to enable them to be recited with ease so that the student recalls them whether he wants to or not.

In metaphysics by contrast there is nothing which causes so much effort as making our perception of the primary notions clear and distinct. Admittedly, they are by their nature as evident as, or even more evident than, the primary notions which the geometers study; but they conflict with many preconceived opinions derived from the senses which we have got into the habit of holding from our earliest years, and so only those who really concentrate and meditate and withdraw their minds from corporeal things, so far as is possible, will achieve perfect knowledge of them. Indeed, if they were put forward in isolation, they could easily be denied by those who like to contradict just for the sake of it.

This is why I wrote 'Meditations' rather than 'Disputations', as the philosophers have done, or 'Theorems and Problems', as the geometers would have done. In so doing I wanted to make it clear that I would have nothing to do with anyone who was not willing to join me in meditating and giving the subject attentive consideration. For the very fact that someone braces himself to attack the truth makes him less suited to perceive it, since he will be withdrawing his consideration from the convincing arguments which support the truth in order to find counter-arguments against it...

160   *Arguments*
proving the existence of God and the distinction
between the soul and the body
arranged in geometrical fashion

DEFINITIONS

I. *Thought.* I use this term to include everything that is within us in such a way that we are immediately aware of it. Thus all the operations of the will, the intellect, the imagination and the senses are thoughts. I say 'immediately' so as to exclude the consequences of thoughts; a voluntary movement, for example, originates in a thought but is not itself a thought.

II. *Idea.* I understand this term to mean the form of any given thought, immediate perception of which makes me aware of the thought. Hence, whenever I express something in words, and understand what I am saying, this very fact makes it certain that there is within me an idea of what is signified by the words in question. Thus it is not only the images depicted in the imagination which I call 'ideas'. Indeed, in so far as these images are in the corporeal imagination, that is, are depicted in some part   161 of the brain, I do not call them 'ideas' at all; I call them 'ideas' only in so far as they give form to the mind itself, when it is directed towards that part of the brain.

III. *Objective reality of an idea.* By this I mean the being of the thing which is represented by an idea, in so far as this exists in the idea. In the same way we can talk of 'objective perfection', 'objective intricacy' and so on. For whatever we perceive as being in the objects of our ideas exists objectively in the ideas themselves.

IV. Whatever exists in the objects of our ideas in a way which exactly corresponds to our perception of it is said to exist *formally* in those objects. Something is said to exist *eminently* in an object when, although it does not exactly correspond to our perception of it, its greatness is such that it can fill the role of that which does so correspond.[1]

V. *Substance.* This term applies to every thing in which whatever we perceive immediately resides, as in a subject, or to every thing by means of which whatever we perceive exists. By 'whatever we perceive' is meant any property, quality or attribute of which we have a real idea. The only idea we have of a substance itself, in the strict sense, is that it is the thing in which whatever we perceive (or whatever has objective being in one of our ideas) exists, either formally or eminently. For we know by the natural light that a real attribute cannot belong to nothing.

VI. The substance in which thought immediately resides is called *mind*. I use the term 'mind' rather than 'soul' since the word 'soul' is ambiguous and is often applied to something corporeal.[2]

VII. The substance which is the immediate subject of local extension and of the accidents which presuppose extension, such as shape, position, local motion and so on, is called *body*. Whether what we call mind and body are one and the same substance, or two different substances, is a question which will have to be dealt with later on.   162

VIII. The substance which we understand to be supremely perfect, and in which we conceive absolutely nothing that implies any defect or limitation in that perfection, is called *God*.

IX. When we say that something is *contained in the nature or concept* of a thing, this is the same as saying that it is true of that thing, or that it can be asserted of that thing.

X. Two substances are said to be *really distinct* when each of them can exist apart from the other.

---

1 Cf. Med. III, p. 91 above.
2 E.g. a tenuous wind permeating the body. Cf. Med. II, above p. 82.

POSTULATES[1]

The *first* request I make of my readers is that they should realize how feeble are the reasons that have led them to trust their senses up till now, and how uncertain are all the judgements that they have built up on the basis of the senses. I ask them to reflect long and often on this point, till they eventually acquire the habit of no longer placing too much trust in the senses. In my view this is a prerequisite for perceiving the certainty that belongs to metaphysical things.

Secondly, I ask them to reflect on their own mind, and all its attributes. They will find that they cannot be in doubt about these, even though they suppose that everything they have ever acquired from their senses is false. They should continue with this reflection until they have got into the habit of perceiving the mind clearly and of believing that it can be known more easily than any corporeal thing.

Thirdly, I ask them to ponder on those self-evident propositions that they will find within themselves, such as 'The same thing cannot both be and not be at the same time', and 'Nothingness cannot be the efficient cause of anything', and so on. In this way they will be exercising the intellectual vision which nature gave them, in the pure form which it attains when freed from the senses; for sensory appearances generally interfere with it and darken it to a very great extent. And by this means the truth of the following axioms will easily become apparent to them.

Fourthly, I ask them to examine the ideas of those natures which contain a combination of many attributes, such as the nature of a triangle, or of a square, or of any other figure, as well as the nature of mind, the nature of body, and above all the nature of God, or the supremely perfect being. And they should notice that whatever we perceive to be contained in these natures can be truly affirmed of them. For example, the fact that its three angles are equal to two right angles is contained in the nature of a triangle; and divisibility is contained in the nature of body, or of an extended thing (for we cannot conceive of any extended thing which is so small that we cannot divide it, at least in our thought). And because of these facts it can be truly asserted that the three angles of every triangle are equal to two right angles and that every body is divisible.

Fifthly, I ask my readers to spend a great deal of time and effort on contemplating the nature of the supremely perfect being. Above all they should reflect on the fact that the ideas of all other natures contain possible existence, whereas the idea of God contains not only possible

---

1 Lat. *Postulata*. Descartes is here playing on words, since what follows is not a set of postulates in the Euclidian sense, but a number of informal requests.

but wholly necessary existence. This alone, without a formal argument, will make them realize that God exists; and this will eventually be just as self-evident to them as the fact that the number two is even or that three is odd, and so on. For there are certain truths which some people find self-evident, while others come to understand them only by means of a formal argument.

Sixthly, I ask my readers to ponder on all the examples that I went through in my *Meditations*, both of clear and distinct perception, and of obscure and confused perception, and thereby accustom themselves to distinguishing what is clearly known from what is obscure. This is something that it is easier to learn by examples than by rules, and I think that in the *Meditations* I explained, or at least touched on, all the relevant examples.

Seventhly, and lastly, when they notice that they have never detected any falsity in their clear perceptions, while by contrast they have never, except by accident, found any truth in matters which they grasp only obscurely, I ask them to conclude that it is quite irrational to cast doubt on the clear and distinct perceptions of the pure intellect merely because of preconceived opinions based on the senses, or because of mere hypotheses which contain an element of the unknown. And as a result they will readily accept the following axioms as true and free of doubt. Nevertheless, many of these axioms could have been better explained, and indeed they should have been introduced as theorems rather than as axioms, had I wished to be more precise.

AXIOMS OR COMMON NOTIONS

I. Concerning every existing thing it is possible to ask what is the cause of its existence. This question may even be asked concerning God, not because he needs any cause in order to exist, but because the immensity of his nature is the cause or reason why he needs no cause in order to exist.

II. There is no relation of dependence between the present time and the immediately preceding time, and hence no less a cause is required to preserve something than is required to create it in the first place.[1]

III. It is impossible that *nothing*, a non-existing thing, should be the cause of the existence of anything, or of any actual perfection in anything.

IV. Whatever reality or perfection there is in a thing is present either formally or eminently in its first and adequate cause.

V. It follows from this that the objective reality of our ideas needs a

1 'Preserve', here and below, has the technical sense of 'to maintain in existence'.

cause which contains this reality not merely objectively but formally or eminently. It should be noted that this axiom is one which we must necessarily accept, since on it depends our knowledge of all things, whether they are perceivable through the senses or not. How do we know, for example, that the sky exists? Because we see it? But this 'seeing' does not affect the mind except in so far as it is an idea – I mean an idea which resides in the mind itself, not an image depicted in the corporeal imagination. Now the only reason why we can use this idea as a basis for the judgement that the sky exists is that every idea must have a really existing cause of its objective reality; and in this case we judge that the cause is the sky itself. And we make similar judgements in other cases.

VI. There are various degrees of reality or being: a substance has more reality than an accident or a mode; an infinite substance has more reality than a finite substance. Hence there is more objective reality in the idea of a substance than in the idea of an accident; and there is more objective reality in the idea of an infinite substance than in the idea of a finite substance.

VII. The will of a thinking thing is drawn voluntarily and freely (for this is the essence of will), but nevertheless inevitably, towards a clearly known good. Hence, if it knows of perfections which it lacks, it will straightaway give itself these perfections, if they are in its power.

VIII. Whatever can bring about a greater or more difficult thing can also bring about a lesser thing.

IX. It is a greater thing to create or preserve a substance than to create or preserve the attributes or properties of that substance. However, it is not a greater thing to create something than to preserve it, as has already been said.

X. Existence is contained in the idea or concept of every single thing, since we cannot conceive of anything except as existing. Possible or contingent existence is contained in the concept of a limited thing, whereas necessary and perfect existence is contained in the concept of a supremely perfect being.

PROPOSITION I

*The existence of God can be known
merely by considering his nature*

Demonstration
To say that something is contained in the nature or concept of a thing is the same as saying that it is true of that thing (Def. IX). But necessary

existence is contained in the concept of God (Axiom x). Therefore it may   167
be truly affirmed of God that necessary existence belongs to him, or that
he exists.

This is the syllogism which I employed above in replying to ... your
Objections. And its conclusion can be grasped as self-evident by those who
are free of preconceived opinions, as I said above, in the Fifth Postulate.
But since it is not easy to arrive at such clear mental vision, we shall now
endeavour to establish the same result by other methods.

PROPOSITION II

The existence of God can be demonstrated
a posteriori *merely from the fact that we*
have an idea of God within us

Demonstration

The objective reality of any of our ideas requires a cause which contains
the very same reality not merely objectively but formally or eminently
(Axiom v). But we have an idea of God (Def. II and VIII), and the
objective reality of this idea is not contained in us either formally or
eminently (Axiom VI); moreover it cannot be contained in any other
being except God himself (Def. VIII). Therefore this idea of God, which is
in us, must have God as its cause; and hence God exists (Axiom III).

PROPOSITION III   168

God's existence can also be demonstrated from the
fact that we, who possess the idea of God, exist

Demonstration

If I had the power of preserving myself, how much more would I have the
power of giving myself the perfections which I lack (Axioms VIII and IX);
for these perfections are merely attributes of a substance, whereas I am a
substance. But I do not have the power of giving myself these perfections;
if I did, I should already have them (Axiom VII). Therefore I do not have
the power of preserving myself.

Now I could not exist unless I was preserved throughout my existence
either by myself, if I have that power, or by some other being who has it
(Axioms I and II). But I do exist, and yet, as has just been proved, I do not
have the power of preserving myself. Therefore I am preserved by some
other being.

Moreover, he who preserves me has within himself, either formally or eminently, whatever is in me (Axiom IV). But I have within me the perception of many of the perfections which I lack, as well as an idea of God (Defs. II and VIII). Therefore he who preserves me has a perception of the same perfections.

Finally, this being cannot have the perception of any perfections which he lacks, or which he does not have within himself either formally or eminently (Axiom VII). For since he has the power of preserving me, as I have already said, how much more would he have the power of giving himself those perfections if he lacked them (Axioms VIII and IX). But he has the perception of all the perfections which I know I lack and which I conceive to be capable of existing only in God, as has just been proved. Therefore he has the perfections within himself either formally or eminently, and hence he is God.

169

COROLLARY

God created the heavens and the earth and everything in them. Moreover he can bring about everything which we clearly perceive in a way exactly corresponding to our perception of it

Demonstration

All this clearly follows from the preceding proposition. For in that proposition we proved that God exists from the fact that there must exist someone who possesses either formally or eminently all the perfections of which we have any idea. But we have the idea of a power so great that the possessor of this power, and he alone, created the heavens and the earth and is capable of producing everything that I understand to be possible. Therefore in proving God's existence we have also proved these other facts about him.

PROPOSITION IV

There is a real distinction between the mind and the body

Demonstration

God can bring about whatever we clearly perceive in a way exactly corresponding to our perception of it (preceding Corollary). But we clearly perceive the mind, that is, a thinking substance, apart from the body, that is, apart from an extended substance (Second Postulate). And conversely we can clearly perceive the body apart from the mind (as everyone readily admits). Therefore the mind can, at least through the

170

power of God, exist without the body; and similarly the body can exist apart from the mind.

Now if one substance can exist apart from another the two are really distinct (Def. x). But the mind and the body are substances (Defs. v, vi and vii) which can exist apart from each other (as has just been proved). Therefore there is a real distinction between the mind and the body.

Notice that I introduce the power of God as a means to separate mind and body not because any extraordinary power is needed to bring about such a separation but because the preceding arguments have dealt solely with God, and hence there was nothing else I could use to make the separation. Our knowledge that two things are really distinct is not affected by the nature of the power that separates them.

[*Second Replies*: CSM II 110–20]

Principles of Philosophy

PART ONE

The principles of human knowledge

1. *The seeker after truth must, once in the course of his life, doubt everything, as far as is possible.*

Since we began life as infants, and made various judgements concerning the things that can be perceived by the senses before we had the full use of our reason, there are many preconceived opinions that keep us from knowledge of the truth.[1] It seems that the only way of freeing ourselves from these opinions is to make the effort, once in the course of our life, to doubt everything which we find to contain even the smallest suspicion of uncertainty.

2. *What is doubtful should even be considered as false.*

Indeed, it will even prove useful, once we have doubted these things, to consider them as false, so that our discovery of what is most certain and easy to know may be all the clearer.

3. *This doubt should not meanwhile be applied to ordinary life.*

This doubt, while it continues, should be kept in check and employed solely in connection with the contemplation of the truth. As far as ordinary life is concerned, the chance for action would frequently pass us by if we waited until we could free ourselves from our doubts, and so we are often compelled to accept what is merely probable. From time to time we may even have to make a choice between two alternatives, even though it is not apparent that one of the two is more probable than the other.

4. *The reasons for doubt concerning the things that can be perceived by the senses.*

Given, then, that our efforts are directed solely to the search for truth, our initial doubts will be about the existence of the objects of sense-

---

1 Some examples of such preconceived opinions are given in art. 71, pp. 185f below.

perception and imagination. The first reason for such doubts is that from 6
time to time we have caught out the senses when they were in error, and
it is prudent never to place too much trust in those who have deceived us
even once. The second reason is that in our sleep we regularly seem to
have sensory perception of, or to imagine, countless things which do not
exist anywhere; and if our doubts are on the scale just outlined, there
seem to be no marks by means of which we can with certainty distinguish
being asleep from being awake.

5. *The reasons for doubting even mathematical demonstrations.*
Our doubt will also apply to other matters which we previously regarded
as most certain – even the demonstrations of mathematics and even the
principles which we hitherto considered to be self-evident. One reason
for this is that we have sometimes seen people make mistakes in such
matters and accept as most certain and self-evident things which seemed
false to us. Secondly, and most importantly, we have been told that there
is an omnipotent God who created us. Now we do not know whether he
may have wished to make us beings of the sort who are always deceived
even in those matters which seem to us supremely evident; for such
constant deception seems no less a possibility than the occasional
deception which, as we have noticed on previous occasions, does occur.
We may of course suppose that our existence derives not from a
supremely powerful God but either from ourselves or from some other
source; but in that case, the less powerful we make the author of our
coming into being, the more likely it will be that we are so imperfect as to
be deceived all the time.

6. *We have free will, enabling us to withhold our assent in doubtful*
   matters and hence avoid error.
But whoever turns out to have created us, and however powerful and
however deceitful he may be, in the meantime we nonetheless experience
within us the kind of freedom which enables us always to refrain from
believing things which are not completely certain and thoroughly examined. Hence we are able to take precautions against going wrong on
any occasion.

7. *It is not possible for us to doubt that we exist while we are doubting;*
   and this is the first thing we come to know when we philosophize in
   an orderly way.
In rejecting – and even imagining to be false – everything which we can in 7
any way doubt, it is easy for us to suppose that there is no God and no
heaven, and that there are no bodies, and even that we ourselves have no
hands or feet, or indeed any body at all. But we cannot for all that

suppose that we, who are having such thoughts, are nothing. For it is a contradiction to suppose that what thinks does not, at the very time when it is thinking, exist. Accordingly, this piece of knowledge[1] – *I am thinking, therefore I exist* – is the first and most certain of all to occur to anyone who philosophizes in an orderly way.

8. *In this way we discover the distinction between soul and body, or*
   between a thinking thing and a corporeal thing.

This is the best way to discover the nature of the mind and the distinction between the mind and the body. For if we, who are supposing that everything which is distinct from us is false,[2] examine what we are, we see very clearly that neither extension nor shape nor local motion, nor anything of this kind which is attributable to a body, belongs to our nature, but that thought alone belongs to it. So our knowledge of our thought is prior to, and more certain than, our knowledge of any corporeal thing; for we have already perceived it, although we are still in doubt about other things.

9. *What is meant by 'thought'.*

By the term 'thought', I understand everything which we are aware of as happening within us, in so far as we have awareness of it. Hence, *thinking* is to be identified here not merely with understanding, willing and imagining, but also with sensory awareness. For if I say 'I am seeing, or I am walking, therefore I exist', and take this as applying to vision or walking as bodily activities, then the conclusion is not absolutely certain. This is because, as often happens during sleep, it is possible for me to think I am seeing or walking, though my eyes are closed and I am not moving about; such thoughts might even be possible if I had no body at all. But if I take 'seeing' or 'walking' to apply to the actual sense or awareness of seeing or walking, then the conclusion is quite certain, since it relates to the mind, which alone has the sensation or thought that it is seeing or walking.

10. *Matters which are very simple and self-evident are only rendered*
    more obscure by logical definitions, and should not be counted as
    items of knowledge which it takes effort to acquire.

I shall not here explain many of the other terms which I have already used or will use in what follows, because they seem to me to be sufficiently self-evident. I have often noticed that philosophers make the

---

1 '... this inference' (French version).
2 Lat. *falsum*. Descartes uses this term to refer not only to propositions which are false, but also to objects which are unreal, spurious or non-existent. The French version here reads: 'we who are now thinking that there is nothing outside of our thought which truly is or exists . . .'

mistake of employing logical definitions in an attempt to explain what was already very simple and self-evident; the result is that they only make matters more obscure. And when I said that the proposition *I am thinking, therefore I exist* is the first and most certain of all to occur to anyone who philosophizes in an orderly way, I did not in saying that deny that one must first know what thought, existence and certainty are, and that it is impossible that that which thinks should not exist, and so forth. But because these are very simple notions, and ones which on their own provide us with no knowledge of anything that exists, I did not think they needed to be listed.

11. *How our mind is better known than our body.*
In order to realize that the knowledge of our mind is not simply prior to and more certain than the knowledge of our body, but also more evident, we should notice something very well known by the natural light: nothingness possesses no attributes or qualities. It follows that, wherever we find some attributes or qualities, there is necessarily some thing or substance to be found for them to belong to; and the more attributes we discover in the same thing or substance, the clearer is our knowledge of that substance. Now we find more attributes in our mind than in anything else, as is manifest from the fact that whatever enables us to know anything else cannot but lead us to a much surer knowledge of our own mind. For example, if I judge that the earth exists from the fact that I touch it or see it, this very fact undoubtedly gives even greater support for the judgement that my mind exists. For it may perhaps be the case that I judge that I am touching the earth even though the earth does not exist at all; but it cannot be that, when I make this judgement, my mind which is making the judgement does not exist. And the same applies in other cases <regarding all the things that come into our mind, namely that we who think of them exist, even if they are false or have no existence>.

12. *Why this fact does not come to be known to all alike.*
Disagreement on this point has come from those who have not done their philosophizing in an orderly way; and the reason for it is simply that they have never taken sufficient care to distinguish the mind from the body. Although they may have put the certainty of their own existence before that of anything else, they failed to realize that they should have taken 'themselves' in this context to mean their minds alone. They were inclined instead to take 'themselves' to mean only their bodies – the bodies which they saw with their eyes and touched with their hands, and

to which they incorrectly attributed the power of sense-perception; and this is what prevented them from perceiving the nature of the mind.

13. *The sense in which knowledge of all other things depends on the*
     knowledge of God.
The mind, then, knowing itself, but still in doubt about all other things, looks around in all directions in order to extend its knowledge further. First of all, it finds within itself ideas of many things; and so long as it merely contemplates these ideas and does not affirm or deny the existence outside itself of anything resembling them, it cannot be mistaken. Next, it finds certain common notions from which it constructs various proofs; and, for as long as it attends to them, it is completely convinced of their truth. For example, the mind has within itself ideas of numbers and shapes, and it also has such common notions as: *If you add equals to equals the results will be equal*; from these it is easy to demonstrate that the three angles of a triangle equal two right angles, and so on. And so the mind will be convinced of the truth of this and similar conclusions, so long as it attends to the premises from which it deduced them. But it cannot attend to them all the time; and subsequently,[1] recalling that it is still ignorant as to whether it may have been created with the kind of nature that makes it go wrong even in matters which appear most evident, the mind sees that it has just cause to doubt such conclusions, and that the possession of certain knowledge will not be possible until it has come to know the author of its being.

14. *The existence of God is validly inferred from the fact that necessary*
     existence is included in our concept of God.
The mind next considers the various ideas which it has within itself, and finds that there is one idea – the idea of a supremely intelligent, supremely powerful and supremely perfect being – which stands out from all the others. <And it readily judges from what it perceives in this idea, that God, who is the supremely perfect being, is, or exists. For although it has distinct ideas of many other things it does not observe anything in them to guarantee the existence of their object.> In this one idea the mind recognizes existence – not merely the possible and contingent existence which belongs to the ideas of all the other things which it distinctly perceives, but utterly necessary and eternal existence. Now on the basis of its perception that, for example, it is necessarily contained in the idea of a triangle that its three angles should equal two

1 '... when it happens that it remembers a conclusion without attending to the sequence which enables it to be demonstrated' (added in French version).

right angles, the mind is quite convinced that a triangle does have three angles equalling two right angles. In the same way, simply on the basis of its perception that necessary and eternal existence is contained in the idea of a supremely perfect being, the mind must clearly conclude that the supreme being does exist.

15. *Our concepts of other things do not similarly contain necessary existence, but merely contingent existence.*

The mind will be even more inclined to accept this if it considers that it cannot find within itself an idea of any other thing such that necessary existence is seen to be contained in the idea in this way. And from this it understands that the idea of a supremely perfect being is not an idea which was invented by the mind, or which represents some chimera, but that it represents a true and immutable nature which cannot but exist, since necessary existence is contained within it.

16. *Preconceived opinions prevent the necessity of the existence of God from being clearly recognized by everyone.*

Our mind will, as I say, easily accept this, provided that it has first of all completely freed itself from preconceived opinions. But we have got into the habit of distinguishing essence from existence in the case of all other things; and we are also in the habit of making up at will various ideas of things which do not exist anywhere and have never done so. Hence, at times when we are not intent on the contemplation of the supremely perfect being, a doubt may easily arise as to whether the idea of God is not one of those which we made up at will, or at least one of those which do not include existence in their essence.

11

17. *The greater the objective perfection in any of our ideas, the greater its cause must be.*

When we reflect further on the ideas that we have within us, we see that some of them, in so far as they are merely modes of thinking, do not differ much one from another; but in so far as one idea represents one thing and another represents another, they differ widely; and the greater the amount of objective[1] perfection they contain within themselves, the more perfect their cause must be. For example, if someone has within himself the idea of a highly intricate machine, it would be fair to ask what was the cause of his possession of the idea: did he somewhere see such a machine made by someone else; or did he make such a close study of mechanics, or is his own ingenuity so great, that he was able to think it up on his own, although he never saw it anywhere? All the intricacy

1 If an idea represents some object which is F, the idea is said to possess 'objective' F-ness, or to contain F-ness 'objectively'. Cf. Med. III, p. 90 above.

which is contained in the idea merely objectively – as in a picture – must be contained in its cause, whatever kind of cause it turns out to be; and it must be contained not merely objectively or representatively, but in actual reality, either formally or eminently,[1] at least in the case of the first and principal cause.

18. *This gives us a second reason for concluding that God exists.*
Since, then, we have within us the idea of God, or a supreme being, we may rightly inquire into the cause of our possession of this idea. Now we find in the idea such immeasurable greatness that we are quite certain that it could have been placed in us only by something which truly possesses the sum of all perfections, that is, by a God who really exists. For it is very evident by the natural light not only that nothing comes from nothing but also that what is more perfect cannot be produced by – that is, cannot have as its efficient and total cause – what is less perfect. Furthermore, we cannot have within us the idea or image of anything without there being somewhere, either within us or outside us, an original which contains in reality all the perfections belonging to the idea. And since the supreme perfections of which we have an idea are in no way to be found in us, we rightly conclude that they reside in something distinct from ourselves, namely God – or certainly that they once did so, from which it most evidently follows that they are still there.

19. *Even if we do not grasp the nature of God, his perfections are*
     known to us more clearly than any other thing.
This is sufficiently certain and manifest to those who are used to contemplating the idea of God and to considering his supreme perfections. Although we do not fully grasp these perfections, since it is in the nature of an infinite being not to be fully grasped by us, who are finite, nonetheless we are able to understand them more clearly and distinctly than any corporeal things. This is because they permeate our thought to a greater extent, being simpler and unobscured by any limitations. <Furthermore, there is no reflection which can better serve to perfect our understanding, or which is more important than this, in so far as the consideration of an object which has no limits to its perfections fills us with satisfaction and assurance.>

20. *We did not make ourselves, but were made by God; and*
     consequently he exists.
However, this is something that not everyone takes note of. When people have an idea of some intricate machine, they generally know

1 To possess a property *formally* is to possess it strictly as defined; to possess it *eminently* is to possess it in some higher or more perfect form.

where they got the idea from; but we do not in the same way have a recollection of the idea of God being sent to us from God, since we have always possessed it. Accordingly, we should now go on to inquire into the source of our being, given that we have within us an idea of the supreme perfections of God. Now it is certainly very evident by the natural light that a thing which recognizes something more perfect than itself is not the source of its own being; for if so, it would have given itself all the perfections of which it has an idea. Hence, the source of its being can only be something which possesses within itself all these perfections — that is, God.

21. *The fact that our existence has duration is sufficient to demonstrate the existence of God.*   13

It will be impossible for anything to obscure the clarity of this proof, if we attend to the nature of time or of the duration of things. For the nature of time is such that its parts are not mutually dependent, and never coexist. Thus, from the fact that we now exist, it does not follow that we shall exist a moment from now, unless there is some cause — the same cause which originally produced us — which continually reproduces us, as it were, that is to say, which keeps us in existence. For we easily understand that there is no power in us enabling us to keep ourselves in existence. We also understand that he who has so great a power that he can keep us in existence, although we are distinct from him, must be all the more able to keep himself in existence; or rather, he requires no other being to keep him in existence, and hence, in short, is God.

22. *Our method of recognizing the existence of God leads to the simultaneous recognition of all the other attributes of God, in so far as they can be known by the natural power of the mind.*

There is a great advantage in proving the existence of God by this method, that is to say, by means of the idea of God. For the method enables us at the same time to come to know the nature of God, in so far as the feebleness of our nature allows. For when we reflect on the idea of God which we were born with, we see that he is eternal, omniscient, omnipotent, the source of all goodness and truth, the creator of all things, and finally, that he possesses within him everything in which we can clearly recognize some perfection that is infinite or unlimited by any imperfection.

23. *God is not corporeal, and does not perceive through the senses as we do; and he does not will the evil of sin.*

There are many things such that, although we recognize some perfection in them, we also find in them some imperfection or limitation, and these therefore cannot belong to God. For example, the nature of body includes divisibility along with extension in space, and since being divisible is an imperfection, it is certain that God is not a body. Again, the fact that we perceive through the senses is for us a perfection of a kind; but all sense-perception involves being acted upon, and to be acted upon is to be dependent on something else. Hence it cannot in any way be supposed that God perceives by means of the senses, but only that he understands and wills. And even his understanding and willing does not happen, as in our case, by means of operations that are in a certain sense distinct one from another; we must rather suppose that there is always a single identical and perfectly simple act by means of which he simultaneously understands, wills and accomplishes everything. When I say 'everything' I mean all *things*: for God does not will the evil of sin, which is not a thing.

24. We pass from knowledge of God to knowledge of his creatures by remembering that he is infinite and we are finite.

Now since God alone is the true cause of everything which is or can be, it is very clear that the best path to follow when we philosophize will be to start from the knowledge of God himself and try to deduce an explanation of the things created by him. This is the way to acquire the most perfect scientific knowledge, that is, knowledge of effects through their causes. In order to tackle this task with a reasonable degree of safety and without risk of going wrong we must take the precaution of always bearing in mind as carefully as possible both that God, the creator of all things, is infinite, and that we are altogether finite.

25. We must believe everything which God has revealed, even though it may be beyond our grasp.

Hence, if God happens to reveal to us something about himself or others which is beyond the natural reach of our mind – such as the mystery of the Incarnation or of the Trinity – we will not refuse to believe it, despite the fact that we do not clearly understand it. And we will not be at all surprised that there is much, both in the immeasurable nature of God and in the things created by him, which is beyond our mental capacity.

26. We should never enter into arguments about the infinite. Things in which we observe no limits – such as the extension of the world, the division of the parts of matter, the number of the stars, and so on – should instead be regarded as indefinite.

Thus we will never be involved in tiresome arguments about the infinite. For since we are finite, it would be absurd for us to determine anything concerning the infinite; for this would be to attempt to limit it and grasp it. So we shall not bother to reply to those who ask if half an infinite line would itself be infinite, or whether an infinite number is odd or even, and so on. It seems that nobody has any business to think about such matters unless he regards his own mind as infinite. For our part, in the case of anything in which, from some point of view, we are unable to discover a limit, we shall avoid asserting that it is infinite, and instead regard it as indefinite. There is, for example, no imaginable extension which is so great that we cannot understand the possibility of an even greater one; and so we shall describe the size of possible things as indefinite. Again, however many parts a body is divided into, each of the parts can still be understood to be divisible and so we shall hold that quantity is indefinitely divisible. Or again, no matter how great we imagine the number of stars to be, we still think that God could have created even more; and so we will suppose the number of stars to be indefinite. And the same will apply in other cases.

27. *The difference between the indefinite and the infinite.*
Our reason for using the term 'indefinite' rather than 'infinite' in these cases is, in the first place, so as to reserve the term 'infinite' for God alone. For in the case of God alone, not only do we fail to recognize any limits in any respect, but our understanding positively tells us that there are none. Secondly, in the case of other things, our understanding does not in the same way positively tell us that they lack limits in some respect; we merely acknowledge in a negative way that any limits which they may have cannot be discovered by us.

28. *It is not the final but the efficient causes of created things that we must inquire into.*
When dealing with natural things we will, then, never derive any explanations from the purposes which God or nature may have had in view when creating them <and we shall entirely banish from our philosophy the search for final causes>. For we should not be so arrogant as to suppose that we can share in God's plans. We should, instead, consider him as the efficient cause of all things; and starting from the divine attributes which by God's will we have some knowledge of, we shall see, with the aid of our God-given natural light, what conclusions should be drawn concerning those effects which are apparent to our senses.[1] At the same time we should remember, as noted earlier, that the

---

1 '. . . and we shall be assured that what we have once clearly and distinctly perceived to belong to the nature of these things has the perfection of being true' (added in French version, which also omits the last sentence of this article).

natural light is to be trusted only to the extent that it is compatible with divine revelation.

29. God is *not the cause of* our errors.

The first attribute of God that comes under consideration here is that he is supremely truthful and the giver of all light. So it is a complete contradiction to suppose that he might deceive us or be, in the strict and positive sense, the cause of the errors to which we know by experience that we are prone. For although the ability to deceive may perhaps be regarded among us men as a sign of intelligence, the will to deceive must undoubtedly always come from malice, or from fear and weakness, and so cannot belong to God.

30. It follows that everything that we clearly perceive is true; and this removes the doubts mentioned earlier.

It follows from this that the light of nature or faculty of knowledge which God gave us can never encompass any object which is not true in so far as it is indeed encompassed by this faculty, that is, in so far as it is clearly and distinctly perceived. For God would deserve to be called a deceiver if the faculty which he gave us was so distorted that it mistook the false for the true <even when we were using it properly>. This disposes of the most serious doubt, which arose from our ignorance about whether our nature might not be such as to make us go wrong even in matters which seemed to us utterly evident. Indeed, this argument easily demolishes all the other reasons for doubt which were mentioned earlier. Mathematical truths should no longer be suspect, since they are utterly clear to us. And as for our senses, if we notice anything here that is clear and distinct, no matter whether we are awake or asleep, then provided we separate it from what is confused and obscure we will easily recognize – whatever the thing in question – which are the aspects that may be regarded as true. There is no need for me to expand on this point here, since I have already dealt with it in the *Meditations on Metaphysics*;[1] and a more precise explanation of the point requires knowledge of what I shall be saying later on.

31. Our errors, if considered in relation to God, are merely negations; if considered in relation to ourselves they are privations.

Yet although God is no deceiver, it often happens that we fall into error. In order to investigate the origin and cause of our errors and learn to guard against them, we should realize that they do not depend on our

---

1 Cf. Med. VI, pp. 114ff above.

intellect so much as on our will. Moreover, errors are not things, requiring the real concurrence of God for their production. Considered in relation to God they are merely negations,[1] and considered in relation to ourselves they are privations.

32. *We possess only two modes of thinking: the perception of the intellect and the operation of the will.*

All the modes of thinking that we experience within ourselves can be brought under two general headings: perception, or the operation of the intellect, and volition, or the operation of the will. Sensory perception, imagination and pure understanding are simply various modes of perception; desire, aversion, assertion, denial and doubt are various modes of willing.

33. *We fall into error only when we make judgements about things which we have not sufficiently perceived.*

Now when we perceive something, so long as we do not make any assertion or denial about it, we clearly avoid error. And we equally avoid error when we confine our assertions or denials to what we clearly and distinctly perceive should be asserted or denied. Error arises only when, 18 as often happens, we make a judgement about something even though we do not have an accurate perception of it.

34. *Making a judgement requires not only the intellect but also the will.*

In order to make a judgement, the intellect is of course required since, in the case of something which we do not in any way perceive, there is no judgement we can make. But the will is also required so that, once something is perceived in some manner, our assent may then be given. Now a judgement – some kind of judgement at least – can be made without the need for a complete and exhaustive perception of the thing in question; for we can assent to many things which we know only in a very obscure and confused manner.

35. *The scope of the will is wider than that of the intellect, and this is the cause of error.*

Moreover, the perception of the intellect extends only to the few objects presented to it, and is always extremely limited. The will, on the other hand, can in a certain sense be called infinite, since we observe without exception that its scope extends to anything that can possibly be an object of any other will – even the immeasurable will of God. So it is easy

---

1 '... that is, he did not bestow on us everything which he was able to bestow, but which equally we can see he was not obliged to give us' (added in French version).

for us to extend our will beyond what we clearly perceive; and when we do this it is no wonder that we may happen to go wrong.

36. *Our errors cannot be imputed to God.*
But it must not in any way be imagined that, because God did not give us an omniscient intellect, this makes him the author of our errors. For it is of the nature of a created intellect to be finite; and it is of the nature of a finite intellect that its scope should not extend to everything.

37. *The supreme perfection of man is that he acts freely or voluntarily, and it is this which makes him deserve praise or blame.*
The extremely broad scope of the will is part of its very nature. And it is a supreme perfection in man that he acts voluntarily, that is, freely; this makes him in a special way the author of his actions and deserving of praise for what he does. We do not praise automatons for accurately producing all the movements they were designed to perform, because the production of these movements occurs necessarily. It is the designer who is praised for constructing such carefully-made devices; for in constructing them he acted not out of necessity but freely. By the same principle, when we embrace the truth, our doing so voluntarily is much more to our credit than would be the case if we could not do otherwise.

38. *The fact that we fall into error is a defect in the way we act, not a defect in our nature. The faults of subordinates may often be attributed to their masters, but never to God.*
The fact that we fall into error is a defect in the way we act or in the use we make of our freedom, but not a defect in our nature. For our nature remains the same whether we judge correctly or incorrectly. And although God could have endowed our intellect with a discernment so acute as to prevent our ever going wrong, we have no right to demand this of him. Admittedly, when one of us men has the power to prevent some evil, but does not prevent it, we say that he is the cause of the evil; but we must not similarly suppose that because God could have brought it about that we never went wrong, this makes him the cause of our errors. The power which men have over each other was given them so that they might employ it in discouraging others from evil; but the power which God has over all men is both absolute and totally free. So we should give him the utmost thanks for the goods which he has so lavishly bestowed upon us, instead of unjustly complaining that he did not bestow on us all the gifts which it was in his power to bestow.

39. *The freedom of the will is self-evident.*
That there is freedom in our will, and that we have power in many cases to give or withhold our assent at will, is so evident that it must be

counted among the first and most common notions that are innate in us. This was obvious earlier on when, in our attempt to doubt everything, we went so far as to make the supposition of some supremely powerful author of our being who was attempting to deceive us in every possible way. For in spite of that supposition, the freedom which we experienced within us was nonetheless so great as to enable us to abstain from believing whatever was not quite certain or fully examined. And what we saw to be beyond doubt even during the period of that supposition is as self-evident and as transparently clear as anything can be.

20

40. *It is also certain that everything was preordained by God.*

But now that we have come to know God, we perceive in him a power so immeasurable that we regard it as impious to suppose that we could ever do anything which was not already preordained by him. And we can easily get ourselves into great difficulties if we attempt to reconcile this divine preordination with the freedom of our will, or attempt to grasp both these things at once.

41. *How to reconcile the freedom of our will with divine preordination.*

But we shall get out of these difficulties if we remember that our mind is finite, while the power of God is infinite – the power by which he not only knew from eternity whatever is or can be, but also willed it and preordained it. We may attain sufficient knowledge of this power to perceive clearly and distinctly that God possesses it; but we cannot get a sufficient grasp of it to see how it leaves the free actions of men undetermined. Nonetheless, we have such close awareness of the freedom and indifference which is in us, that there is nothing we can grasp more evidently or more perfectly. And it would be absurd, simply because we do not grasp one thing, which we know must by its very nature be beyond our comprehension, to doubt something else of which we have an intimate grasp and which we experience within ourselves.

42. *Although we do not want to go wrong, nevertheless we go wrong by our own will.*

Now that we know that all our errors depend on the will, it may seem surprising that we should ever go wrong, since there is no one who wants to go wrong. But there is a great difference between choosing to go wrong and choosing to give one's assent in matters where, as it happens, error is to be found. And although there is in fact no one who expressly wishes to go wrong, there is scarcely anyone who does not often wish to give his assent to something which, though he does not know it, contains some error. Indeed, precisely because of their eagerness to find the truth,

21

people who do not know the right method of finding it often pass judgement on things of which they lack perception, and this is why they fall into error.

43. *We never go wrong when we assent only to what we clearly and distinctly perceive.*

It is certain, however, that we will never mistake the false for the true provided we give our assent only to what we clearly and distinctly perceive. I say that this is certain, because God is not a deceiver, and so the faculty of perception which he has given us cannot incline to falsehood; and the same goes for the faculty of assent, provided its scope is limited to what is clearly perceived. And even if there were no way of proving this, the minds of all of us have been so moulded by nature that whenever we perceive something clearly, we spontaneously give our assent to it and are quite unable to doubt its truth.

44. *When we give our assent to something which is not clearly perceived, this is always a misuse of our judgement, even if by chance we stumble on the truth. The giving of our assent to something unclear happens because we imagine that we clearly perceived it on some previous occasion.*

It is also certain that when we assent to some piece of reasoning when our perception of it is lacking, then either we go wrong, or, if we do stumble on the truth, it is merely by accident, so that we cannot be sure that we are not in error. Of course it seldom happens that we assent to something when we are aware of not perceiving it, since the light of nature tells us that we should never make a judgement except about things we know. What does very often give rise to error is that there are many things which we think we perceived in the past; once these things are committed to memory, we give our assent to them just as we would if we had fully perceived them, whereas in reality we never perceived them at all.

45. *What is meant by a clear perception, and by a distinct perception.*

Indeed there are very many people who in their entire lives never perceive anything with sufficient accuracy to enable them to make a judgement about it with certainty. A perception which can serve as the basis for a certain and indubitable judgement needs to be not merely clear but also distinct. I call a perception 'clear' when it is present and accessible to the attentive mind – just as we say that we see something clearly when it is present to the eye's gaze and stimulates it with a sufficient degree of strength and accessibility. I call a perception 'distinct' if, as well as being clear, it is so sharply separated from all other perceptions that it contains within itself only what is clear.

46. *The example of pain shows that a perception can be clear without being distinct, but cannot be distinct without being clear.*

For example, when someone feels an intense pain, the perception he has of it is indeed very clear, but is not always distinct. For people commonly confuse this perception with an obscure judgement they make concerning the nature of something which they think exists in the painful spot and which they suppose to resemble the sensation of pain; but in fact it is the sensation alone which they perceive clearly. Hence a perception can be clear without being distinct, but not distinct without being clear.

47. *In order to correct the preconceived opinions of our early childhood we must consider the simple notions and what elements in each of them are clear.*

In our childhood the mind was so immersed in the body that although there was much that it perceived clearly, it never perceived anything distinctly. But in spite of this the mind made judgements about many things, and this is the origin of the many preconceived opinions which most of us never subsequently abandon. To enable us to get rid of these preconceived opinions, I shall here briefly list all the simple notions which are the basic components of our thoughts; and in each case I shall distinguish the clear elements from those which are obscure or liable to lead us into error.

48. *All the objects of our perception may be regarded either as things or affections of things, or as eternal truths. The former are listed here.*

All the objects of our perception we regard either as things, or affections of things, or else as eternal truths which have no existence outside our thought.[1] The most general items which we regard as things are *substance, duration, order, number* and any other items of this kind which extend to all classes of things. But I recognize only two ultimate classes of things: first, intellectual or thinking things, i.e. those which pertain to mind or thinking substance; and secondly, material things, i.e. those which pertain to extended substance or body. Perception, volition and all the modes both of perceiving and of willing are referred to thinking substance; while to extended substance belong size

23

---

1 An 'affection' of a thing is one of its qualities or modes; see art. 56, below. The French version omits this technical term and simply distinguishes between, on the one hand, 'things which have some existence', and, on the other hand, 'truths which are nothing outside our thought'.

(that is, extension in length, breadth and depth), shape, motion, position, divisibility of component parts and the like. But we also experience within ourselves certain other things which must not be referred either to the mind alone or to the body alone. These arise, as will be made clear later on, in the appropriate place,[1] from the close and intimate union of our mind with the body. This list includes, first, appetites like hunger and thirst; secondly, the emotions or passions of the mind which do not consist of thought alone, such as the emotions of anger, joy, sadness and love; and finally, all the sensations, such as those of pain, pleasure, light, colours, sounds, smells, tastes, heat, hardness and the other tactile qualities.

49. *It is not possible – or indeed necessary – to give a similar list of eternal truths.*

Everything in the preceding list we regard either as a thing or as a quality or mode of a thing. But when we recognize that it is impossible for anything to come from nothing, the proposition *Nothing comes from nothing* is regarded not as a really existing thing, or even as a mode of a thing, but as an eternal truth which resides within our mind. Such truths are termed common notions or axioms. The following are examples of this class: *It is impossible for the same thing to be and not to be at the same time; What is done cannot be undone; He who thinks cannot but exist while he thinks*; and countless others. It would not be easy to draw up a list of all of them; but nonetheless we cannot fail to know them when the occasion for thinking about them arises, provided that we are not blinded by preconceived opinions.

50. *Eternal truths are clearly perceived; but, because of preconceived opinions, not all of them are clearly perceived by everyone.*

In the case of these common notions, there is no doubt that they are capable of being clearly and distinctly perceived; for otherwise they would not properly be called common notions. But some of them do not really have an equal claim to be called 'common' among all people, since they are not equally well perceived by everyone. This is not, I think, because one man's faculty of knowledge extends more widely than another's, but because the common notions are in conflict with the preconceived opinions of some people who, as a result, cannot easily grasp them. But the selfsame notions are perceived with the utmost clarity by other people who are free from such preconceived opinions.

1 See Part 4, art. 189–97, pp. 201ff below.

51. *What is meant by 'substance' – a term which does not apply
    univocally to God and his creatures.*

In the case of those items which we regard as things or modes of things, it
is worthwhile examining each of them separately. By *substance* we can
understand nothing other than a thing which exists in such a way as to
depend on no other thing for its existence. And there is only one
substance which can be understood to depend on no other thing whatsoever, namely God. In the case of all other substances, we perceive that
they can exist only with the help of God's concurrence. Hence the term
'substance' does not apply *univocally*, as they say in the Schools, to God
and to other things; that is, there is no distinctly intelligible meaning of
the term which is common to God and his creatures. <In the case of
created things, some are of such a nature that they cannot exist without
other things, while some need only the ordinary concurrence of God in
order to exist. We make this distinction by calling the latter 'substances'
and the former 'qualities' or 'attributes' of those substances.>

52. *The term 'substance' applies univocally to mind and to body. How a
    substance itself is known.*

But as for corporeal substance and mind (or created thinking sub-   25
stance), these can be understood to fall under this common concept:
things that need only the concurrence of God in order to exist. However,
we cannot initially become aware of a substance merely through its being
an existing thing, since this alone does not of itself have any effect on us.
We can, however, easily come to know a substance by one of its
attributes, in virtue of the common notion that nothingness possesses no
attributes, that is to say, no properties or qualities. Thus, if we perceive
the presence of some attribute, we can infer that there must also be
present an existing thing or substance to which it may be attributed.

53. *To each substance there belongs one principal attribute; in the case
    of mind, this is thought, and in the case of body it is extension.*

A substance may indeed be known through any attribute at all; but each
substance has one principal property which constitutes its nature and
essence, and to which all its other properties are referred. Thus extension
in length, breadth and depth constitutes the nature of corporeal substance; and thought constitutes the nature of thinking substance. Everything else which can be attributed to body presupposes extension, and is
merely a mode of an extended thing; and similarly, whatever we find in
the mind is simply one of the various modes of thinking. For example,
shape is unintelligible except in an extended thing; and motion is

unintelligible except as motion in an extended space; while imagination, sensation and will are intelligible only in a thinking thing. By contrast, it is possible to understand extension without shape or movement, and thought without imagination or sensation, and so on; and this is quite clear to anyone who gives the matter his attention.

54. *How we can have clear and distinct notions of thinking substance and of corporeal substance, and also of God.*

Thus we can easily have two clear and distinct notions or ideas, one of created thinking substance, and the other of corporeal substance, provided we are careful to distinguish all the attributes of thought from the attributes of extension. We can also have a clear and distinct idea of uncreated and independent thinking substance, that is of God. Here we must simply avoid supposing that the idea adequately represents everything which is to be found in God; and we must not invent any additional features, but concentrate only on what is really contained in the idea and on what we clearly perceive to belong to the nature of a supremely perfect being. And certainly no one can deny that we possess such an idea of God, unless he reckons that there is absolutely no knowledge of God to be found in the minds of men.

55. *How we can also have a distinct understanding of duration, order and number.*

We shall also have a very distinct understanding of *duration, order* and *number,* provided we do not mistakenly tack on to them any concept of substance. Instead, we should regard the duration of a thing simply as a mode under which we conceive the thing in so far as it continues to exist. And similarly we should not regard order or number as anything separate from the things which are ordered and numbered, but should think of them simply as modes under which we consider the things in question.

56. *What modes, qualities and attributes are.*

By *mode,* as used above, we understand exactly the same as what is elsewhere meant by an *attribute* or *quality.* But we employ the term *mode* when we are thinking of a substance as being affected or modified; when the modification enables the substance to be designated as a substance of such and such a kind, we use the term *quality*; and finally, when we are simply thinking in a more general way of what is in a substance, we use the term *attribute.* Hence we do not, strictly speaking, say that there are modes or qualities in God, but simply attributes, since in the case of God, any variation is unintelligible. And even in the case of created things, that which always remains unmodified – for example existence or duration in a thing which exists and endures – should be called not a quality or a mode but an attribute.

57. *Some attributes are in things and others in thought. What duration and time are.*

Now some attributes or modes are in the very things of which they are   27
said to be attributes or modes, while others are only in our thought. For example, when time is distinguished from duration taken in the general sense and called the measure of movement, it is simply a mode of thought. For the duration which we understand to be involved in movement is certainly no different from the duration involved in things which do not move. This is clear from the fact that if there are two bodies moving for an hour, one slowly and the other quickly, we do not reckon the amount of time to be greater in the latter case than the former, even though the amount of movement may be much greater. But in order to measure the duration of all things, we compare their duration with the duration of the greatest and most regular motions which give rise to years and days, and we call this duration 'time'. Yet nothing is thereby added to duration, taken in its general sense, except for a mode of thought.

58. *Number and all universals are simply modes of thinking.*

In the same way, number, when it is considered simply in the abstract or in general, and not in any created things, is merely a mode of thinking; and the same applies to all the other *universals*, as we call them.

59. *How universals arise. The five common universals: genus, species, differentia, property, accident.*

These universals arise solely from the fact that we make use of one and the same idea for thinking of all individual items which resemble each other: we apply one and the same term to all the things which are represented by the idea in question, and this is the universal term. When we see two stones, for example, and direct our attention not to their nature but merely to the fact that there are two of them, we form the idea of the number which we call 'two'; and when we later see two birds or two trees, and consider not their nature but merely the fact that there are two of them, we go back to the same idea as before. This, then, is the universal idea; and we always designate the number in question by the same universal term 'two'. In the same way, when we see a figure made up of   28
three lines, we form an idea of it which we call the idea of a triangle; and we later make use of it as a universal idea, so as to represent to our mind all the other figures made up of three lines. Moreover, when we notice that some triangles have one right angle, and others do not, we form the

universal idea of a right-angled triangle; since this idea is related to the preceding idea as a special case, it is termed a *species*. And the rectangularity is the universal *differentia* which distinguishes all right-angled triangles from other triangles. And the fact that the square on the hypotenuse is equal to the sum of the squares on the other two sides is a *property* belonging to all and only right-angled triangles. Finally, if we suppose that some right-angled triangles are in motion while others are not, this will be a universal *accident* of such triangles. Hence five universals are commonly listed: *genus, species, differentia, property* and *accident*.

60. *Three sorts of distinction: firstly, what is meant by a 'real distinction'.*

Now number, in things themselves, arises from the distinction between them. But *distinction* can be taken in three ways: as a *real* distinction, a *modal* distinction, or a *conceptual* distinction. Strictly speaking, a *real* distinction exists only between two or more substances; and we can perceive that two substances are really distinct simply from the fact that we can clearly and distinctly understand one apart from the other. For when we come to know God, we are certain that he can bring about anything of which we have a distinct understanding. For example, even though we may not yet know for certain that any extended or corporeal substance exists in reality, the mere fact that we have an idea of such a substance enables us to be certain that it is capable of existing. And we can also be certain that, if it exists, each and every part of it, as delimited by us in our thought, is really distinct from the other parts of the same substance. Similarly, from the mere fact that each of us understands himself to be a thinking thing and is capable, in thought, of excluding from himself every other substance, whether thinking or extended, it is certain that each of us, regarded in this way, is really distinct from every other thinking substance and from every corporeal substance. And even if we suppose that God has joined some corporeal substance to such a thinking substance so closely that they cannot be more closely conjoined, thus compounding them into a unity, they nonetheless remain really distinct. For no matter how closely God may have united them, the power which he previously had of separating them, or keeping one in being without the other, is something he could not lay aside; and things which God has the power to separate, or to keep in being separately, are really distinct.

61. *What is meant by a 'modal distinction'.*

A *modal distinction* can be taken in two ways: firstly, as a distinction between a mode, properly so called, and the substance of which it is a mode; and secondly, as a distinction between two modes of the same substance. The first kind of modal distinction can be recognized from the fact that we can clearly perceive a substance apart from the mode which we say differs from it, whereas we cannot, conversely, understand the mode apart from the substance. Thus there is a modal distinction between shape or motion and the corporeal substance in which they inhere; and similarly, there is a modal distinction between affirmation or recollection and the mind. The second kind of modal distinction is recognized from the fact that we are able to arrive at knowledge of one mode apart from another, and *vice versa*, whereas we cannot know either mode apart from the substance in which they both inhere. For example, if a stone is in motion and is square-shaped, I can understand the square shape without the motion and, conversely, the motion without the square shape; but I can understand neither the motion nor the shape apart from the substance of the stone. A different case, however, is the distinction by which the mode of one substance is distinct from another substance or from the mode of another substance. An example of this is the way in which the motion of one body is distinct from another body, or from the mind; or the way in which motion differs from doubt.[1] It seems more appropriate to call this kind of distinction a real distinction, rather than a modal distinction, since the modes in question cannot be clearly understood apart from the really distinct substances of which they are modes.

62. What is meant by a 'conceptual distinction'.

Finally, a *conceptual distinction* is a distinction between a substance and some attribute of that substance without which the substance is unintelligible; alternatively, it is a distinction between two such attributes of a single substance. Such a distinction is recognized by our inability to form a clear and distinct idea of the substance if we exclude from it the attribute in question, or, alternatively, by our inability to perceive clearly the idea of one of the two attributes if we separate it from the other. For example, since a substance cannot cease to endure without also ceasing to be, the distinction between the substance and its duration is merely a conceptual one. And in the case of all the modes of thought[2] which we consider as being in objects, there is merely a conceptual distinction between the modes and the object which they are thought of as applying to; and the same is true of the distinction between the modes

---

1 In place of *dubitatione* ('doubt') AT read *duratione* ('duration'); the former reading is undoubtedly correct, and is followed in the French version.
2 See above, art. 57 and 58.

themselves when these are in one and the same object.[1] I am aware that elsewhere I did lump this type of distinction with the modal distinction, namely at the end of my Replies to the First Set of Objections to the *Meditations on First Philosophy*; but that was not a suitable place for making a careful distinction between the two types; it was enough for my purposes to distinguish both from the real distinction.

63. *How thought and extension may be distinctly recognized as constituting the nature of mind and of body.*

Thought and extension can be regarded as constituting the natures of intelligent substance and corporeal substance; they must then be considered as nothing else but thinking substance itself and extended substance itself – that is, as mind and body. In this way we will have a very clear and distinct understanding of them. Indeed, it is much easier for us to have an understanding of extended substance or thinking substance than it is for us to understand substance on its own, leaving out the fact that it thinks or is extended. For we have some difficulty in abstracting the notion of substance from the notions of thought and extension, since the distinction between these notions and the notion of substance itself is merely a conceptual distinction. A concept is not any more distinct because we include less in it; its distinctness simply depends on our carefully distinguishing what we do include in it from everything else.

64. *How thought and extension may also be distinctly recognized as modes of a substance.*

Thought and extension may also be taken as modes of a substance, in so far as one and the same mind is capable of having many different thoughts; and one and the same body, with its quantity unchanged, may be extended in many different ways (for example, at one moment it may be greater in length and smaller in breadth or depth, and a little later, by contrast, it may be greater in breadth and smaller in length).[2] The distinction between thought or extension and the substance will then be a modal one; and our understanding of them will be capable of being just as clear and distinct as our understanding of the substance itself, provided they are regarded not as substances (that is, things which are separate from other things) but simply as modes of things. By regarding

---

1 For this sentence the French version substitutes: 'And in general all the attributes which cause us to have different thoughts concerning a single thing, such as the extension of a body and its property of being divided into several parts, do not differ from the body ... or from each other, except in so far as we sometimes think confusedly of one without thinking of the other.'
2 Cf. the example of the wax in Med. II, p. 84 above.

them as being in the substances of which they are modes, we distinguish them from the substances in question and see them for what they really are. If, on the other hand, we attempted to consider them apart from the substances in which they inhere, we would be regarding them as things which subsisted in their own right, and would thus be confusing the ideas of a mode and a substance.

65. *How the modes of thought and extension are to be known.*   32
There are various modes of thought such as understanding, imagination, memory, volition, and so on; and there are various modes of extension, or modes which belong to extension, such as all shapes, the positions of parts and the motions of the parts. And, just as before, we shall arrive at the best perception of all these items if we regard them simply as modes of the things in which they are located. As far as motion is concerned, it will be best if we think simply of local motion, without inquiring into the force which produces it (though I shall attempt to explain this later in the appropriate place[1]).

66. *How sensations, emotions and appetites may be clearly known, despite the fact that we are frequently wrong in our judgements concerning them.*
There remains sensations, emotions and appetites.[2] These may be clearly perceived provided we take great care in our judgements concerning them to include no more than what is strictly contained in our perception – no more than that of which we have inner awareness. But this is a very difficult rule to observe, at least with regard to sensations. For all of us have, from our early childhood, judged that all the objects of our sense-perception are things existing outside our minds and closely resembling our sensations, i.e. the perceptions that we had of them. Thus, on seeing a colour, for example, we supposed we were seeing a thing located outside us which closely resembled the idea of colour that we experienced within us at the time. And this was something that, because of our habit of making such judgements, we thought we saw clearly and distinctly – so much so that we took it for something certain and indubitable.

67. *We frequently make mistakes, even in our judgements concerning pain.*
The same thing happens with regard to everything else of which we have sensory awareness, even to pleasure and pain. For, although we do not

1 In Part 2; see especially art. 43 and 44, AT VIIIA 66–7; CSM I 243–4.
2 These are the items remaining from the objects of perception listed above, art. 48.

suppose that these exist outside us, we generally regard them not as being in the mind alone, or in our perception, but as being in the hand or foot or in some other part of our body. But the fact that we feel a pain as it were in our foot does not make it certain that the pain exists outside our mind, in the foot, any more than the fact that we see light as it were in the sun, makes it certain the light exists outside us, in the sun. Both these beliefs are preconceived opinions of our early childhood, as will become clear below.

68. *How to distinguish what we clearly know in such matters from what can lead us astray.*

In order to distinguish what is clear in this connection from what is obscure, we must be very careful to note that pain and colour and so on are clearly and distinctly perceived when they are regarded merely as sensations or thoughts. But when they are judged to be real things existing outside our mind, there is no way of understanding what sort of things they are. If someone says he sees colour in a body or feels pain in a limb, this amounts to saying that he sees or feels something there of which he is wholly ignorant, or, in other words, that he does not know what he is seeing or feeling. Admittedly, if he fails to pay sufficient attention, he may easily convince himself that he has some knowledge of what he sees or feels, because he may suppose that it is something similar to the sensation of colour or pain which he experiences within himself. But if he examines the nature of what is represented by the sensation of colour or pain – what is represented as existing in the coloured body or the painful part – he will realize that he is wholly ignorant of it.

69. *We know size, shape and so forth in quite a different way from the way in which we know colours, pains and the like.*

This will be especially clear if we consider the wide gap between our knowledge of those features of bodies which we clearly perceive, as stated earlier,[1] and our knowledge of those features which must be referred to the senses, as I have just pointed out. To the former class belong the size of the bodies we see, their shape, motion, position, duration, number and so on (by 'motion' I mean local motion: philosophers have imagined that there are other kinds of motion distinct from local motion, thereby only making the nature of motion less intelligible to themselves).[2] To the latter class belong the colour in a body, as well as

---

1 See above, art. 48.
2 By 'local motion' is meant, roughly, movement from place to place. Scholastic philosophers, following Aristotle, sometimes classified any alteration (e.g. a quantitative or a qualitative change) as a type of motion; various other distinctions, e.g. that between 'natural' and 'violent' motion, were also commonplace.

pain, smell, taste and so on. It is true that when we see a body we are just as certain of its existence in virtue of its having a visible colour as we are in virtue of its having a visible shape; but our knowledge of what it is for the body to have a shape is much clearer than our knowledge of what it is for it to be coloured.

70. *There are two ways of making judgements concerning the things that can be perceived by the senses: the first enables us to avoid error, while the second allows us to fall into error.*

It is clear, then, that when we say that we perceive colours in objects, this is really just the same as saying that we perceive something in the objects whose nature we do not know, but which produces in us a certain very clear and vivid sensation which we call the sensation of colour. But the way in which we make our judgement can vary very widely. As long as we merely judge that there is in the objects (that is, in the things, whatever they may turn out to be, which are the source of our sensations) something whose nature we do not know, then we avoid error; indeed, we are actually guarding against error, since the recognition that we are ignorant of something makes us less liable to make any rash judgement about it. But it is quite different when we suppose that we perceive colours in objects. Of course, we do not really know what it is that we are calling a colour; and we cannot find any intelligible resemblance between the colour which we suppose to be in objects and that which we experience in our sensation. But this is something we do not take account of; and, what is more, there are many other features, such as size, shape and number which we clearly perceive to be actually or at least possibly present in objects in a way exactly corresponding to our sensory perception or understanding. And so we easily fall into the error of judging that what is called colour in objects is something exactly like the colour of which we have sensory awareness; and we make the mistake of thinking that we clearly perceive what we do not perceive at all. 35

71. *The chief cause of error arises from the preconceived opinions of childhood.*

It is here that the first and main cause of all our errors may be recognized. In our early childhood the mind was so closely tied to the body that it had no leisure for any thoughts except those by means of which it had sensory awareness of what was happening to the body. It did not refer these thoughts to anything outside itself, but merely felt pain when something harmful was happening to the body and felt pleasure when something beneficial occurred. And when nothing very beneficial or harmful was happening to the body, the mind had various sensations corresponding to the different areas where, and ways in which, the body was being stimulated, namely what we call the sensations of tastes, smells, sounds, heat, cold, light, colours and so on – sensations which do not represent anything located outside our thought.[1] At the same time the mind perceived sizes, shapes, motions and so on, which were presented to it not as sensations but as things, or modes of things, existing (or at least capable of existing) outside thought, although it was not yet aware of the difference between things and sensations. The next stage arose when the mechanism of the body, which is so constructed by nature that it has the ability to move in various ways by its own power, twisted around aimlessly in all directions in its random attempts to pursue the beneficial and avoid the harmful; at this point the mind that was attached to the body began to notice that the objects of this pursuit or avoidance had an existence outside itself. And it attributed to them not only sizes, shapes, motions and the like, which it perceived as things or modes of things, but also tastes, smells and so on, the sensations of which were, it realized, produced by the objects in question. Moreover, since the mind judged everything in terms of its utility to the body in which it was immersed, it assessed the amount of reality in each object by the extent to which it was affected by it. As a result, it supposed that there was more substance or corporeality in rocks and metals than in water or air, since it felt more hardness and heaviness in them. Indeed, it regarded the air as a mere nothing, so long as it felt no wind or cold or heat in it. And because the light coming from the stars appeared no brighter than that produced by the meagre glow of an oil lamp, it did not imagine any star as being any bigger than this. And because it did not observe that the earth turns on its axis or that its surface is curved to form a globe, it was rather inclined to suppose that the earth was immobile and its surface flat. Right from infancy our mind was swamped with a thousand such preconceived opinions; and in later childhood, forgetting that they were adopted without sufficient examination, it regarded them as known by the senses or implanted by nature, and accepted them as utterly true and evident.

72. *The second cause of error is that we cannot forget our preconceived opinions.*

In later years the mind is no longer a total slave to the body, and does not refer everything to it. Indeed, it inquires into the truth of things considered in themselves, and discovers very many of its previous judgements to be false. But despite this, it is not easy for the mind to erase

---

1 '... but which vary according to the different movements which pass from all parts of our body to the part of the brain to which our mind is closely joined and united' (added in French version).

these false judgements from its memory; and as long as they stick there, they can cause a variety of errors. For example, in our early childhood we imagined the stars as being very small; and although astronomical 37 arguments now clearly show us that they are very large indeed, our preconceived opinion is still strong enough to make it very hard for us to imagine them differently from the way we did before.

73. *The third cause of error is that we become tired if we have to attend to things which are not present to the senses; as a result, our judgements on these things are habitually based not on present perception but on preconceived opinion.*

What is more, our mind is unable to keep its attention on things without some degree of difficulty and fatigue; and it is hardest of all for it to attend to what is not present to the senses or even to the imagination. This may be due to the very nature that the mind has as a result of being joined to the body; or it may be because it was exclusively occupied with the objects of sense and imagination in its earliest years, and has thus acquired more practice and a greater aptitude for thinking about them than it has for thinking about other things. The result of this is that many people's understanding of substance is still limited to that which is imaginable and corporeal, or even to that which is capable of being perceived by the senses. Such people do not know that the objects of the imagination are restricted to those which have extension, motion and shape, whereas there are many other things that are objects of the understanding. Also, they suppose that nothing can subsist unless it is a body, and that no body can subsist unless it can be perceived by the senses. Now since, as will be clearly shown below, there is nothing whose true nature we perceive by the senses alone, it turns out that most people have nothing but confused perceptions throughout their entire lives.

74. *The fourth cause of error is that we attach our concepts to words which do not precisely correspond to real things.*

Finally, because of the use of language, we tie all our concepts to the words used to express them; and when we store the concepts in our memory we always simultaneously store the corresponding words. Later on we find the words easier to recall than the things; and because of this it is very seldom that our concept of a thing is so distinct that we can separate it totally from our concept of the words involved. The thoughts of almost all people are more concerned with words than with things; and as a result people very often give their assent to words they do not understand, thinking they once understood them, or that they got them 38 from others who did understand them correctly. This is not the place to give a precise account of all these matters, since the nature of the human body has not yet been dealt with – indeed the existence of any body has not yet been proved. Nonetheless, what has been said appears to be sufficiently intelligible to help us distinguish those of our concepts which are clear and distinct from those which are obscure and confused.

75. *Summary of the rules to be observed in order to philosophize correctly.*

In order to philosophize seriously and search out the truth about all the things that are capable of being known, we must first of all lay aside all our preconceived opinions, or at least we must take the greatest care not to put our trust in any of the opinions accepted by us in the past until we have first scrutinized them afresh and confirmed their truth. Next, we must give our attention in an orderly way to the notions that we have within us, and we must judge to be true all and only those whose truth we clearly and distinctly recognize when we attend to them in this way. When we do this we shall realize, first of all, that we exist in so far as our nature consists in thinking; and we shall simultaneously realize both that there is a God, and that we depend on him, and also that a consideration of his attributes enables us to investigate the truth of other things, since he is their cause. Finally, we will see that besides the notions of God and of our mind, we have within us knowledge of many propositions which are eternally true, such as 'Nothing comes from nothing'. We shall also find that we have knowledge both of a corporeal or extended nature which is divisible, moveable, and so on, and also of certain sensations which affect us, such as the sensations of pain, colours, tastes and so on (though we do not yet know the cause of our being affected in this way). When we contrast all this knowledge with the confused thoughts we had before, we will acquire the habit of forming clear and distinct concepts of all the things that can be known. These few instructions seem to me to contain the most important principles of human knowledge.

39

76. *Divine authority must be put before our own perception; but, that aside, the philosopher should give his assent only to what he has perceived.*

But above all else we must impress on our memory the overriding rule that whatever God has revealed to us must be accepted as more certain than anything else. And although the light of reason may, with the utmost clarity and evidence, appear to suggest something different, we must still put our entire faith in divine authority rather than in our own judgement. But on matters where we are not instructed by divine faith, it is quite unworthy of a philosopher to accept anything as true if he has never established its truth by thorough scrutiny; and he should never rely on the senses, that is, on the ill-considered judgements of his childhood, in preference to his mature powers of reason.

PART TWO

The principles of material things

40

1. *The arguments that lead to the certain knowledge of the existence of material things.*

Everyone is quite convinced of the existence of material things. But earlier on we cast doubt on this belief and counted it as one of the preconceived opinions of our childhood.[1] So it is necessary for us to investigate next the arguments by which the existence of material things may be known with certainty. Now, all our sensations undoubtedly come to us from something that is distinct from our mind. For it is not in our power to make ourselves have one sensation rather than another; this is obviously dependent on the thing that is acting on our senses. Admittedly one can raise the question of whether this thing is God or something different from God. But we have sensory awareness of, or rather as a result of sensory stimulation we have a clear and distinct perception of, some kind of matter, which is extended in length, breadth and depth, and has various differently shaped and variously moving parts which give rise to our various sensations of colours, smells, pain and so on. And if God were himself immediately producing in our mind the idea of such extended matter, or even if he were causing the idea to be produced by 41 something which lacked extension, shape and motion, there would be no way of avoiding the conclusion that he should be regarded as a deceiver. For we have a clear understanding of this matter as something that is quite different from God and from ourselves or our mind; and we appear to see clearly that the idea of it comes to us from things located outside ourselves, which it wholly resembles. And we have already noted that it is quite inconsistent with the nature of God that he should be a deceiver.[2] The unavoidable conclusion, then, is that there exists something extended in length, breadth and depth and possessing all the properties which we clearly perceive to belong to an extended thing. And it is this extended thing that we call 'body' or 'matter'.

1 See Part 1, art. 4, p. 160 above.   2 See Part 1, art. 29, p. 170 above.

2. *The basis for our knowledge that the human body is closely conjoined with the mind.*

By the same token, the conclusion that there is a particular body that is more closely conjoined with our mind than any other body follows from our clear awareness that pain and other sensations come to us quite unexpectedly. The mind is aware that these sensations do not come from itself alone, and that they cannot belong to it simply in virtue of its being a thinking thing; instead, they can belong to it only in virtue of its being joined to something other than itself which is extended and moveable – namely what we call the human body. But this is not the place for a detailed explanation of its nature.

3. *Sensory perception does not show us what really exists in things, but merely shows us what is beneficial or harmful to man's composite nature.*

It will be enough, for the present, to note that sensory perceptions are related exclusively to this combination of the human body and mind. They normally tell us of the benefit or harm that external bodies may do to this combination, and do not, except occasionally and accidentally, show us what external bodies are like in themselves. If we bear this in mind we will easily lay aside the preconceived opinions acquired from the senses, and in this connection make use of the intellect alone, carefully attending to the ideas implanted in it by nature.

4. *The nature of body consists not in weight, hardness, colour, or the like, but simply in extension.*

If we do this, we shall perceive that the nature of matter, or body considered in general, consists not in its being something which is hard or heavy or coloured, or which affects the senses in any way, but simply in its being something which is extended in length, breadth and depth. For as regards hardness, our sensation tells us no more than that the parts of a hard body resist the motion of our hands when they come into contact with them. If, whenever our hands moved in a given direction, all the bodies in that area were to move away at the same speed as that of our approaching hands, we should never have any sensation of hardness. And since it is quite unintelligible to suppose that, if bodies did move away in this fashion, they would thereby lose their bodily nature, it follows that this nature cannot consist in hardness. By the same reasoning it can be shown that weight, colour, and all other such qualities that are perceived by the senses as being in corporeal matter, can be removed from it, while the matter itself remains intact; it thus follows that its nature does not depend on any of these qualities.

5. *This truth about the nature of body is obscured by preconceived*
opinions concerning rarefaction and empty space.

But there are still two possible reasons for doubting that the true nature
of body consists solely in extension. The first is the widespread belief that
many bodies can be rarefied and condensed in such a way that when
rarefied they possess more extension than when condensed. Indeed, the
subtlety of some people goes so far that they distinguish the substance of
a body from its quantity, and even its quantity from its extension. The
second reason is that if we understand there to be nothing in a given place 43
but extension in length, breadth and depth, we generally say not that
there is a body there, but simply that there is a space, or even an empty
space; and almost everyone is convinced that this amounts to nothing at
all.

6. *How rarefaction occurs.*

But with regard to rarefaction and condensation, anyone who attends to
his own thoughts, and is willing to admit only what he clearly perceives,
will not suppose that anything happens in these processes beyond a
change of shape. Rarefied bodies, that is to say, are those which have
many gaps between their parts – gaps which are occupied by other
bodies; and they become denser simply in virtue of the parts coming
together and reducing or completely closing the gaps. In this last
eventuality a body becomes so dense that it would be a contradiction to
suppose that it could be made any denser. Now in this condition, the
extension of a body is no less than when it occupies more space in virtue
of the mutual separation of its parts; for whatever extension is comprised
in the pores or gaps left between the parts must be attributed not to the
body itself but to the various other bodies which fill the gaps. In just the
same way, when we see a sponge filled with water or some other liquid,
we do not suppose that in terms of its own individual parts it has a
greater extension than when it is squeezed dry; we simply suppose that its
pores are open wider, so that it spreads over a greater space.

7. *This is the only intelligible way of explaining rarefaction.*

I really do not see what has prompted others to say that rarefaction
occurs through an increase of quantity, in preference to explaining it by
means of this example of the sponge.[1] It is true that when air or water is
rarefied, we do not see any pores being made larger, or any new body 44

---

1 Scholastic philosophers explained rarefaction in terms of a given amount of matter
occupying a larger quantity or volume of space: for Descartes, however, this is
unintelligible, since there is no real distinction between the notions of 'quantity', 'matter'
and 'space'. See below, art. 8–12.

coming to fill them up. But to invent something unintelligible so as to provide a purely verbal explanation of rarefaction is surely less rational than inferring the existence of pores or gaps which are made larger, and supposing that some new body comes and fills them. Admittedly, we do not perceive this new body with any of our senses; but there is no compelling reason to believe that all the bodies which exist must affect our senses. Moreover, it is very easy for us to see how rarefaction can occur in this way, but we cannot see how it could occur in any other way. Finally, it is a complete contradiction to suppose that something should be augmented by new quantity or new extension without new extended substance, i.e. a new body, being added to it at the same time. For any addition of extension or quantity is unintelligible without the addition of substance which has quantity and extension. This will become clearer from what follows.

8. The distinction between quantity or number and the thing that has quantity or number is merely a conceptual distinction.

There is no real difference between quantity and the extended substance; the difference is merely a conceptual one, like that between number and the thing which is numbered. We can, for example, consider the entire nature of the corporeal substance which occupies a space of ten feet without attending to the specific measurement; for we understand this nature to be exactly the same in any part of the space as in the whole space. And, conversely, we can think of the number ten, or the continuous quantity *ten feet*, without attending to this determinate substance. For the concept of the number ten is exactly the same irrespective of whether it is referred to this measurement of ten feet or to anything else; and as for the continuous quantity *ten feet*, although this is unintelligible without some extended substance of which it is the quantity, it can be understood apart from this determinate substance. In reality, however, it is impossible to take even the smallest fraction from the quantity or extension without also removing just as much from the substance; and conversely, it is impossible to remove the smallest amount from the substance without taking away just as much from the quantity or extension.

9. If corporeal substance is distinguished from its quantity, it is conceived in a confused manner as something incorporeal.

Others may disagree, but I do not think they have any alternative perception of the matter. When they make a distinction between substance and extension or quantity, either they do not understand anything by the term 'substance', or else they simply have a confused idea of incorporeal substance, which they falsely attach to corporeal substance; and they relegate the true idea of corporeal substance to the category of extension, which, however, they term an accident. There is thus no correspondence between their verbal expressions and what they grasp in their minds.

10. *What is meant by 'space', or 'internal place'.*
There is no real distinction between space, or internal place,[1] and the corporeal substance contained in it; the only difference lies in the way in which we are accustomed to conceive of them. For in reality the extension in length, breadth and depth which constitutes a space is exactly the same as that which constitutes a body. The difference arises as follows: in the case of a body, we regard the extension as something particular, and thus think of it as changing whenever there is a new body; but in the case of a space, we attribute to the extension only a generic unity, so that when a new body comes to occupy the space, the extension of the space is reckoned not to change but to remain one and the same, so long as it retains the same size and shape and keeps the same position relative to certain external bodies which we use to determine the space in question.

11. *There is no real difference between space and corporeal substance.*   46
It is easy for us to recognize that the extension constituting the nature of a body is exactly the same as that constituting the nature of a space. There is no more difference between them than there is between the nature of a genus or species and the nature of an individual. Suppose we attend to the idea we have of some body, for example a stone, and leave out everything we know to be non-essential to the nature of body: we will first of all exclude hardness, since if the stone is melted or pulverized it will lose its hardness without thereby ceasing to be a body; next we will exclude colour, since we have often seen stones so transparent as to lack colour; next we will exclude heaviness, since although fire is extremely light it is still thought of as being corporeal; and finally we will exclude cold and heat and all other such qualities, either because they are not thought of as being in the stone, or because if they change, the stone is not on that account reckoned to have lost its bodily nature. After all this, we will see that nothing remains in the idea of the stone except that it is something extended in length, breadth and depth. Yet this is just what is

---

1 The scholastics distinguished between *locus internus*, or 'internal place' (the space occupied by a body), and *locus externus*, or 'external space' (the external surface containing a body). Descartes employs the traditional terminology here and at art. 13 below, but puts it to his own use.

comprised in the idea of a space – not merely a space which is full of bodies, but even a space which is called 'empty'.[1]

12. The difference between space and corporeal substance lies in our way of conceiving them.

There is, however, a difference in the way in which we conceive of space and corporeal substance. For if a stone is removed from the space or place where it is, we think that its extension has also been removed from that place, since we regard the extension as something particular and inseparable from the stone. But at the same time we think that the extension of the place where the stone used to be remains, and is the same as before, although the place is now occupied by wood or water or air or some other body, or is even supposed to be empty. For we are now considering extension as something general, which is thought of as being the same, whether it is the extension of a stone or of wood, or of water or of air or of any other body – or even of a vacuum, if there is such a thing – provided only that it has the same size and shape, and keeps the same position relative to the external bodies that determine the space in question.

13. What is meant by 'external place'.

The terms 'place' and 'space', then, do not signify anything different from the body which is said to be in a place; they merely refer to its size, shape and position relative to other bodies. To determine the position, we have to look at various other bodies which we regard as immobile; and in relation to different bodies we may say that the same thing is both changing and not changing its place at the same time. For example, when a ship is under way, a man sitting on the stern remains in one place relative to the other parts of the ship with respect to which his position is unchanged; but he is constantly changing his place relative to the neighbouring shores, since he is constantly receding from one shore and approaching another. Then again, if we believe the earth moves,[2] and suppose that it advances the same distance from west to east as the ship travels from east to west in the corresponding period of time, we shall again say that the man sitting on the stern is not changing his place; for we are now determining the place by means of certain fixed points in the heavens. Finally, if we suppose that there are no such genuinely fixed points to be found in the universe (a supposition which will be shown below to be probable[3]) we shall conclude that nothing has a permanent place, except as determined by our thought.

1 Lat. *vacuum*. See below, art. 16.   2 '. . . turns on its axis' (French version).
3 The French version has 'demonstrable' instead of 'probable'.

14. *The difference between place and space.*

The difference between the terms 'place' and 'space' is that the former designates more explicitly the position, as opposed to the size or shape, while it is the size and shape that we are concentrating on when we talk of space. For we often say that one thing leaves a given place and another thing arrives there, even though the second thing is not strictly of the same size and shape; but in this case we do not say it occupies the same space. By contrast, when something alters its position, we always say the place is changed, despite the fact that the size and shape remain unaltered. When we say that a thing is in a given place, all we mean is that it occupies such and such a position relative to other things; but when we go on to say that it fills up a given space or place, we mean in addition that it has precisely the size and shape of the space in question.

15. *How external place is rightly taken to be the surface of the surrounding body.*

Thus we always take a space to be an extension in length, breadth and depth. But with regard to place, we sometimes consider it as internal to the thing which is in the place in question, and sometimes as external to it. Now internal place is exactly the same as space; but external place may be taken as being the surface immediately surrounding what is in the place. It should be noted that 'surface' here does not mean any part of the surrounding body but merely the boundary between the surrounding and surrounded bodies, which is no more than a mode. Or rather what is meant is simply the common surface, which is not a part of one body rather than the other but is always reckoned to be the same, provided it keeps the same size and shape. For if there are two bodies, one surrounding the other, and the entire surrounding body changes, surface and all, the surrounded body is not therefore thought of as changing its place, provided that during this time it keeps the same position relative to the external bodies which are regarded as immobile. If, for example, we suppose that a ship on a river is being pulled equally in one direction by the current and in the opposite direction by the wind, so that it does not change its position relative to the banks, we will all readily admit that it stays in the same place, despite the complete change in the surrounding surface.

16. *It is a contradiction to suppose there is such a thing as a vacuum, i.e. that in which there is nothing whatsoever.*

The impossibility of a vacuum, in the philosophical sense of that in which there is no substance whatsoever, is clear from the fact that there is no difference between the extension of a space, or internal place, and the extension of a body. For a body's being extended in length, breadth and depth in itself warrants the conclusion that it is a substance, since it is a complete contradiction that a particular extension should belong to nothing; and the same conclusion must be drawn with respect to a space that is supposed to be a vacuum, namely that since there is extension in it, there must necessarily be substance in it as well.

17. *The ordinary use of the term 'empty' does not imply the total
     absence of bodies.*

In its ordinary use the term 'empty'[1] usually refers not to a place or space in which there is absolutely nothing at all, but simply to a place in which there is none of the things that we think ought to be there. Thus a pitcher made to hold water is called 'empty' when it is simply full of air; a fishpond is called 'empty', despite all the water in it, if it contains no fish; and a merchant ship is called 'empty' if it is loaded only with sand ballast. And similarly a space is called 'empty' if it contains nothing perceivable by the senses, despite the fact that it is full of created, self-subsistent matter; for normally the only things we give any thought to are those which are detected by our senses. But if we subsequently fail to keep in mind what ought to be understood by the terms 'empty' and 'nothing', we may suppose that a space we call empty contains not just nothing perceivable by the senses but nothing whatsoever; that would be just as mistaken as thinking that the air in a jug is not a subsistent thing on the grounds that a jug is usually said to be empty when it contains nothing but air.

18. *How to correct our preconceived opinion regarding an absolute
     vacuum.*

Almost all of us fell into this error in our early childhood. Seeing no necessary connection between a vessel and the body contained in it, we reckoned there was nothing to stop God, at least, removing the body which filled the vessel, and preventing any other body from taking its place. But to correct this error we should consider that, although there is no connection between a vessel and this or that particular body contained in it, there is a very strong and wholly necessary connection between the concave shape of the vessel and the extension, taken in its general sense, which must be contained in the concave shape. Indeed, it is no less contradictory for us to conceive of a mountain without a valley than it is for us to think of the concavity apart from the extension contained within it, or the extension apart from the substance which is

---

1 Lat. *vacuum*, from *vacuus*, 'void', 'unoccupied'; cf. art. 18.

extended; for, as I have often said, nothingness cannot possess any extension. Hence, if someone asks what would happen if God were to take away every single body contained in a vessel, without allowing any other body to take the place of what had been removed, the answer must be that the sides of the vessel would, in that case, have to be in contact. For when there is nothing between two bodies they must necessarily touch each other. And it is a manifest contradiction for them to be apart, or to have a distance between them, when the distance in question is nothing; for every distance is a mode of extension, and therefore cannot exist without an extended substance.

19. *The preceding conclusion confirms what we said regarding rarefaction.*

We have thus seen that the nature of corporeal substance consists simply in its being something extended; and its extension is no different from what is normally attributed to space, however 'empty'. From this we readily see that no one part of it can possibly occupy more space at one time than at another, and hence that rarefaction cannot occur except in the way explained earlier on.[1] Similarly, there cannot be more matter or corporeal substance in a vessel filled with lead or gold or any other body, no matter how heavy and hard, than there is when it contains only air and is thought of as empty. This is because the quantity of the parts of matter does not depend on their heaviness or hardness, but solely on their extension, which is always the same for a given vessel.

51

20. *The foregoing results also demonstrate the impossibility of atoms.*

We also know that it is impossible that there should exist atoms, that is, pieces of matter that are by their very nature indivisible <as some philosophers have imagined>. For if there were any atoms, then no matter how small we imagined them to be, they would necessarily have to be extended; and hence we could in our thought divide each of them into two or more smaller parts, and hence recognize their divisibility. For anything we can divide in our thought must, for that very reason, be known to be divisible; so if we were to judge it to be indivisible, our judgement would conflict with our knowledge. Even if we imagine that God has chosen to bring it about that some particle of matter is incapable of being divided into smaller particles, it will still not be correct, strictly speaking, to call this particle indivisible. For, by making it indivisible by any of his creatures, God certainly could not thereby take away his own power of dividing it, since it is quite impossible for him to diminish his

1 See above, art. 6, p. 191.

52   own power, as has been noted above.[1] Hence, strictly speaking, the
particle will remain divisible, since it is divisible by its very nature.

21. *Similarly, the extension of the world is indefinite.*

What is more we recognize that this world, that is, the whole universe of
corporeal substance, has no limits to its extension. For no matter where
we imagine the boundaries to be, there are always some indefinitely
extended spaces beyond them, which we not only imagine but also
perceive to be imaginable in a true fashion, that is, real. And it follows
that these spaces contain corporeal substance which is indefinitely
extended. For, as has already been shown very fully, the idea of the
extension which we conceive to be in a given space is exactly the same as
the idea of corporeal substance.

22. *Similarly, the earth and the heavens are composed of one and the same matter; and there cannot be a plurality of worlds.*

It can also easily be gathered from this that celestial matter is no different
from terrestrial matter.[2] And even if there were an infinite number of
worlds, the matter of which they were composed would have to be
identical; hence, there cannot in fact be a plurality of worlds, but only
one. For we very clearly understand that the matter whose nature
consists simply in its being an extended substance already occupies
absolutely all the imaginable space in which the alleged additional worlds
would have to be located; and we cannot find within us an idea of any
other sort of matter.

23. *All the variety in matter, all the diversity of its forms, depends on motion.*

The matter existing in the entire universe is thus one and the same, and it
is always recognized as matter simply in virtue of its being extended. All
the properties which we clearly perceive in it are reducible to its
divisibility and consequent mobility in respect of its parts, and its
resulting capacity to be affected in all the ways which we perceive as
being derivable from the movement of the parts. If the division into parts
occurs simply in our thought, there is no resulting change; any variation
53   in matter or diversity in its many forms depends on motion. This seems to
have been widely recognized by the philosophers, since they have stated
that nature is the principle of motion and rest. And what they meant by

---

1 Cf. Part I, art. 60, p. 180 above.
2 Descartes here rejects the scholastic doctrine of a radical difference in kind between
'sublunary' or terrestrial phenomena and the incorruptible world of the heavens.

'nature' in this context is what causes all corporeal things to take on the characteristics of which we are aware in experience.

*   *   *

64. *The only principles which I accept, or require, in physics are those of* (78) *geometry and pure mathematics; these principles explain all natural phenomena, and enable us to provide quite certain demonstrations regarding them.*

I will not here add anything about shapes or about the countless different kinds of motions that can be derived from the infinite variety of different shapes. These matters will be quite clear in themselves when the time comes for me to deal with them. I am assuming that my readers know the basic elements of geometry already, or have sufficient mental aptitude to understand mathematical demonstrations. For I freely acknowledge that I recognize no matter in corporeal things apart from that which the geometers call quantity, and take as the object of their demonstrations, 79 i.e. that to which every kind of division, shape and motion is applicable. Moreoever, my consideration of such matter involves absolutely nothing apart from these divisions, shapes and motions; and even with regard to these, I will admit as true only what has been deduced from indubitable common notions so evidently that it is fit to be considered as a mathematical demonstration. And since all natural phenomena can be explained in this way, as will become clear in what follows, I do not think that any other principles are either admissible or desirable in physics.[1]

PART FOUR

The Earth

(314) 187. *From what has been said we can understand the possible causes of all the other remarkable effects which are usually attributed to occult qualities.*

. . . Consider how amazing are the properties of magnets and of fire, and how different they are from the properties we commonly observe in other bodies: how a huge flame can be kindled from a tiny spark in a moment

1 Part Three ('The Visible Universe') and the first 186 articles of Part Four are omitted.

<when it falls on a large quantity of powder>, and how great its power is; or how the fixed stars radiate their light <instantly> in every direction over such an enormous distance. In this book I have deduced the causes – which I believe to be quite evident – of these and many other phenomena from principles which are known to all and admitted by all, namely the shape, size, position and motion of particles of matter. And anyone who considers all this will readily be convinced that there are no powers in stones and plants that are so mysterious, and no marvels attributed to sympathetic and antipathetic influences that are so astonishing, that they cannot be explained in this way. In short, there is nothing in the whole of nature (nothing, that is, which should be referred to purely corporeal causes, i.e. those devoid of thought and mind) which is incapable of being deductively explained on the basis of these selfsame principles; and hence it is quite unnecessary to add any further principles to the list.

315

188. *What must be borrowed from [my proposed] treatises on animals and on man in order to complete our knowledge of material things.*
I would not add anything further to this fourth part of the *Principles of Philosophy* if, as I originally planned, I was going on to write two further parts – a fifth part on living things, i.e. animals and plants, and a sixth part on man. But I am not yet completely clear about all the matters which I would like to deal with there, and I do not know whether I shall ever have enough free time to complete these sections. So, to avoid delaying the publication of the first four parts any longer, and to make sure there are no gaps caused by my keeping material back for the two final parts, I shall here add a few observations concerning the objects of the senses. Up till now I have described this earth and indeed the whole visible universe as if it were a machine: I have considered only the various shapes and movements of its parts. But our senses show us much else besides – namely colours, smells, sounds and such-like; and if I were to say nothing about these it might be thought that I had left out the most important part of the explanation of the things in nature.

189. *What sensation is and how it operates.*
It must be realized that the human soul, while informing[1] the entire body, nevertheless has its principal seat in the brain; it is here alone that the soul not only understands and imagines but also has sensory awareness. Sensory awareness comes about by means of nerves, which stretch like threads from the brain to all the limbs, and are joined together in such a

---

1 Lat. *informare*. Descartes occasionally employs this standard scholastic term, though of course he rejects the Aristotelian account of the soul as the 'form' of the body. The French version has simply 'while being united to the entire body'.

way that hardly any part of the human body can be touched without 　316
producing movement in several of the nerve-ends that are scattered around
in that area. This movement is then transmitted to the other ends of the
nerves which are all grouped together in the brain around the seat of the
soul, as I explained very fully in Discourse Four of the *Optics*.[1] The result
of these movements being set up in the brain by the nerves is that the soul
or mind that is closely joined to the brain is affected in various ways,
corresponding to the various different sorts of movements. And the
various different states of mind, or thoughts, which are the immediate
result of these movements are called sensory perceptions, or in ordinary
speech, sensations.

190. *Various kinds of sensation. First, internal sensations, i.e. emotional
　　states of the mind and natural appetites.*
The wide variety in sensations is a result, firstly, of differences in the
nerves themselves, and secondly of differences in the sorts of motion
which occur in particular nerves. It is not that each individual nerve
produces a particular kind of sensation; indeed, there are only seven
principal groups of nerves, of which two have to do with internal
sensations and five with external sensations. The nerves which go to the
stomach, oesophagus, throat, and other internal parts whose function is
to keep our natural wants supplied, produce one kind of internal
sensation, which is called 'natural appetite' <e.g. hunger and thirst>.
The nerves which go to the heart and the surrounding area <including
the diaphragm>, despite their very small size, produce another kind of
internal sensation which comprises all the disturbances or passions and
emotions of the mind such as joy, sorrow, love, hate and so on. For
example, when the blood has the right consistency so that it expands in
the heart more readily than usual, it relaxes the nerves scattered around
the openings, and sets up a movement which leads to a subsequent 　317
movement in the brain producing a natural feeling of joy in the mind;
and other causes produce the same sort of movement in these tiny nerves,
thereby giving the same feeling of joy. Thus, if we imagine ourselves
enjoying some good, the act of imagination does not itself contain the
feelings of joy, but it causes the spirits[2] to travel from the brain to the
muscles in which these nerves are embedded. This causes the openings of
the heart to expand, and this in turn produces the movement in the tiny
nerves of the heart which must result in the feeling of joy. In the same
way, when we hear good news, it is first of all the mind which makes a
judgement about it and rejoices with that intellectual joy which occurs

1 *Optics*, pp. 62ff above; cf. *Passions*, pp. 22ff below.
2 I.e. the so-called 'animal spirits'; cf. *Passions*, pp. 221ff below.

without any bodily disturbance and which, for that reason, the Stoics allowed that the man of wisdom could experience <although they required him to be free of all passion>. But later on, when the good news is pictured in the imagination, the spirits flow from the brain to the muscles around the heart and move the tiny nerves there, thereby causing a movement in the brain which produces in the mind a feeling of animal joy. Or again, if the blood is too thick and flows sluggishly into the ventricles of the heart and does not expand enough inside it, it produces a different movement in the same small nerves around the heart; when this movement is transmitted to the brain it produces a feeling of sadness in the mind, although the mind itself may perhaps not know of any reason why it should be sad. And there are several other causes capable of producing the same feeling <by setting up the same kind of movement in these nerves.> Other movements in these tiny nerves produce different emotions such as love, hatred, fear, anger and so on; I am here thinking of these simply as emotions or passions of the soul, that is, as confused thoughts, which the mind does not derive from itself alone but experiences as a result of something happening to the body with which it is closely conjoined. These emotions are quite different in kind from the distinct thoughts which we have concerning what is to be embraced or desired or shunned. The same applies to the natural appetites such as hunger and thirst which depend on the nerves of the stomach, throat and so forth: they are completely different from the volition to eat, drink and so on. But, because they are frequently accompanied by such volition or appetition, they are called appetites.

318

191. *The external senses. First, the sense of touch.*

As far as the external senses are concerned, five are commonly listed corresponding to the five kinds of objects stimulating the sensory nerves, and the five kinds of confused thoughts which the resulting motions produce in the soul. First of all there are the nerves terminating in the skin all over the body.[1] These nerves may be touched, via the skin, by various external bodies; and these bodies, though remaining intact, stimulate the nerves in various different ways – in one way by their hardness, in another way by their heaviness, in another way by their heat, in another way by their humidity, and so on. Corresponding to the different ways in which the nerves are moved, or have their normal motion checked, various different sensations are produced in the mind; and this is how the various tactile qualities get their names. <We call these

---

1 'First there is the sense of touch, which has as its object all the bodies which can move some part of the flesh or skin of our body, and has as its organ all the nerves which are found in this part of the body and move with it' (French version).

qualities hardness, heaviness, heat, humidity and so on, but all that is meant by these terms is that the external bodies possess what is required to bring it about that our nerves excite in the soul the sensations of hardness, heaviness, heat etc.>. Moreover, when the nerves are stimulated with unusual force, but without any damage being occasioned to the body, a pleasurable sensation arises <which is a confused thought in the soul and> which is naturally agreeable to the mind because it is a sign of robust health in the body with which it is closely conjoined <in so far as it can undergo the action causing the pleasure without being damaged>. But if there is some bodily damage, there is a sensation of pain <in the soul, even though the action causing the pain may be only marginally more forceful>. This explains why bodily pleasure and pain arise from such very similar objects, although the sensations are completely opposite.

192. *Taste.*
Then there <is the least subtle sense after that of touch, namely taste. Its organs> are other nerves scattered through the tongue and neighbouring areas. The same external bodies, this time split up into particles and floating in the saliva from the mouth, stimulate these nerves in various ways corresponding to their many different shapes <sizes or movements>, and thus produce the sensations of various tastes.

193. *Smell.*
Thirdly, there <is the sense of smell. Its organs> are two other nerves (or appendages to the brain, since they do not go outside the skull) which are stimulated by separate particles of the same bodies that float in the air. The particles in question cannot be of any kind whatsoever: they must be sufficiently light and energetic to be drawn into the nostrils and through the pores of the so-called spongy bone, thus reaching the two nerves. The various movements of the nerves produce the sensations of various smells.

319

194. *Hearing.*
Fourthly, there <is hearing, whose object is simply various vibrations in the ear. For there> are two other nerves, found in the inmost chambers of the ears, which receive tremors and vibrations from the whole body of surrounding air. When the air strikes the tympanic membrane it produces a disturbance in the little chain of three small bones attached to it; and the sensations of different sounds arise from the various different movements in these bones.

195. *Sight*
Finally, there are the optic nerves <which are the organs of the most subtle

of all the senses, that of sight>. The extremities of these nerves, which make up the coating inside the eye called the retina, are moved not by air or any external bodies entering the eye, but simply by globules of the second element <which pass through the pores and all the fluids and transparent membranes of the eye>. This is the origin of the sensations of light and colours, as I have already explained adequately in the *Optics* and *Meteorology*.[1]

196. *The soul has sensory awareness only in so far as it is in the brain.*

There is clear proof that the soul's sensory awareness, via the nerves, of what happens to the individual limbs of the body does not come about in virtue of the soul's presence in the individual limbs, but simply in virtue of its presence in the brain <or because the nerves by their motions transmit to it the actions of external objects which touch the parts of the body where the nerves are embedded>. Firstly, there are various diseases which affect only the brain but remove or interfere with all sensation. Again, sleep occurs only in the brain, yet every day it deprives us of a great part of our sensory faculties, though these are afterwards restored on waking. Next, when the brain is undamaged, if there is an obstruction in the paths by which the nerves reach the brain from the external limbs, this alone is enough to destroy sensation in those limbs. Lastly, we sometimes feel pain in certain limbs even though there is nothing to cause pain in the limbs themselves; the cause of the pain lies in the other areas through which the nerves travel in their journey from the limbs to the brain. This last point can be proved by countless observations, but it will suffice to mention one here. A girl with a seriously infected hand used to have her eyes bandaged whenever the surgeon visited her, to prevent her being upset by the surgical instruments. After a few days her arm was amputated at the elbow because of a creeping gangrene, and wads of bandages were put in its place so that she was quite unaware that she had lost her arm. However she continued to complain of pains, now in one then in another finger of the amputated hand. The only possible reason for this is that the nerves which used to go from the brain down to the hand now terminated in the arm near the elbow, and were being agitated by the same sorts of motion as must previously have been set up in the hand, so as to produce in the soul, residing in the brain, the sensation of pain in this or that finger. <And this shows clearly that pain in the hand is felt by the soul not because it is present in the hand but because it is present in the brain.>

1 Cf. *Optics*, pp. 64ff above.

197. *The nature of the mind is such that various sensations can be*
produced in it simply by motions in the body.

It can also be proved that the nature of our mind is such that the mere
occurrence of certain motions in the body can stimulate it to have all
manner of thoughts which have no likeness to the movements in
question. This is especially true of the confused thoughts we call
sensations or feelings. For we see that spoken or written words excite all
sorts of thoughts and emotions in our minds. With the same paper, pen
and ink, if the tip of the pen is pushed across the paper in a certain way it   321
will form letters which excite in the mind of the reader thoughts of
battles, storms and violence, and emotions of indignation and sorrow;
but if the movements of the pen are just slightly different they will
produce quite different thoughts of tranquillity, peace and pleasure, and
quite opposite emotions of love and joy. It may be objected that speech or
writing does not immediately excite in the mind any emotions, or images
of things apart from the words themselves; it merely occasions various
acts of understanding which afterwards result in the soul's constructing
within itself the images of various things. But what then will be said of
the sensations of pain and pleasure? A sword strikes our body and cuts it;
but the ensuing pain is completely different from the local motion of the
sword or of the body that is cut – as different as colour or sound or smell
or taste. We clearly see, then, that the sensation of pain is excited in us
merely by the local motion of some parts of our body in contact with
another body; so we may conclude that the nature of our mind is such
that it can be subject to all the other sensations merely as a result of other
local motions.

198. *By means of our senses we apprehend nothing in external objects*
beyond their shapes, sizes and motions.

Moreover, we observe no differences between the various nerves which
would support the view that different nerves allow different things to be
transmitted to the brain from the external sense organs; indeed, we are
not entitled to say that anything reaches the brain except for the local
motion of the nerves themselves. And we see that this local motion
produces not only sensations of pain and pleasure but also those of light
and sound. If someone is struck in the eye, so that the vibration of the
blow reaches the retina, this will cause him to see many sparks of flashing   322
light, yet the light is not outside his eye. And if someone puts a finger in
his ear he will hear a throbbing hum which comes simply from the
movement of air trapped in the ear. Finally, let us consider heat and other
qualities perceived by the senses, in so far as those qualities are in objects,
as well as the forms of purely material things, for example the form of

fire: we often see these arising from the local motion of certain bodies and producing in turn other local motions in other bodies. Now we understand very well how the different size, shape and motion of the particles of one body can produce various local motions in another body. But there is no way of understanding how these same attributes (size, shape and motion) can produce something else whose nature is quite different from their own – like the substantial forms and real qualities which <philosophers> suppose to inhere in things; and we cannot understand how these qualities or forms could have the power subsequently to produce local motions in other bodies. Not only is all this unintelligible, but we know that the nature of our soul is such that different local motions are quite sufficient to produce all the sensations in the soul. What is more, we actually experience the various sensations as they are produced in the soul, and we do not find that anything reaches the brain from the external sense organs except for motions of this kind. In view of all this we have every reason to conclude that the properties in external objects to which we apply the terms light, colour, smell, taste, sound, heat and cold – as well as the other tactile qualities and even what are called 'substantial forms' – are, so far as we can see, simply various dispositions in those objects[1] which make them able to set up various kinds of motions in our nerves <which are required to produce all the various sensations in our soul>.

323

199. *There is no phenomenon of nature which has been overlooked in this treatise.*

A simple enumeration will make it clear that there is no phenomenon of nature which I have omitted to consider in this treatise. For a list of natural phenomena cannot include anything which is not apprehended by the senses. Now I have given an account of the various sizes, shapes and motions which are to be found in all bodies; and apart from these the only things which we perceive by our senses as being located outside us are light, colour, smell, taste, sound and tactile qualities. And I have just demonstrated that these are nothing else in the objects – or at least we cannot apprehend them as being anything else – but certain dispositions depending on size, shape and motion. <So the entire visible world, in so far as it is simply visible or perceivable by the senses, contains nothing apart from the things I have given an account of here.>

200. *I have used no principles in this treatise which are not accepted by everyone; this philosophy is nothing new but is extremely old and very common.*

I should also like it to be noted that in attempting to explain the general

---

1 '... in the shapes, sizes, positions and movements of their parts' (French version).

nature of material things I have not employed any principle which was not accepted by Aristotle and all other philosophers of every age. So this philosophy is not new, but the oldest and most common of all. I have considered the shapes, motions and sizes of bodies and examined the necessary results of their mutual interaction in accordance with the laws of mechanics, which are confirmed by reliable everyday experience. And who has ever doubted that bodies move and have various sizes and shapes, and that their various different motions correspond to these differences in size and shape; or who doubts that when bodies collide bigger bodies are divided into many smaller ones and change their shapes? We detect these facts not just with one sense but several – sight, touch and hearing; and they can also be distinctly imagined and understood by us. But the same cannot be said of the other characteristics like colour, sound and the rest, each of which is perceived not by several senses but by one alone; for the images of them which we have in our thought are always confused, and we do not know what they really are.

201. *There are corporeal particles which cannot be perceived by the senses.*

I do consider, however, that there are many particles in each body which are <so small that they are> not perceived with any of our senses; and this may not meet with the approval of those who take their own senses as the measure of what can be known. <But to desire that our human reasoning should go no further than what we can see is, I think, to do it a great injustice.> Yet who can doubt that there are many bodies so minute that we do not detect them by any of our senses? One simply has to consider something which is slowly growing or shrinking and ask what it is that is being added or taken away hour by hour. A tree grows day by day; and it is unintelligible to suppose that it gets bigger than it was before unless we understand there to be some body which is added to it. But who has ever detected with the senses the minute bodies that are added to a growing tree in one day? It must be admitted, at least by those <philosophers> who accept that quantity is indefinitely divisible, that its parts could be made so tiny as to be imperceptible by any of the senses. And it certainly should not be surprising that we are unable to perceive very minute bodies through our senses. For our nerves, which must be set in motion by objects in order to produce a sensation, are not themselves very minute, but are like small cords made up of many smaller particles; hence they cannot be set in motion by very minute bodies. No one who uses his reason will, I think, deny the advantage of using what happens in large bodies, as perceived by our senses, as a model for our ideas about what happens in tiny bodies which elude our senses merely because of their small size. This is much better than explaining matters by inventing all

325   sorts of strange objects which have no resemblance to what is perceived
by the senses <such as 'prime matter', 'substantial forms' and the whole
range of qualities that people habitually introduce, all of which are
harder to understand than the things they are supposed to explain>.

202. *The philosophy of Democritus differs from my own just as much as it does from the standard view <of Aristotle and others>.*

It is true that Democritus also imagined certain small bodies having
various sizes, shapes and motions, and supposed that all bodies that can
be perceived by the senses arose from the conglomeration and mutual
interaction of these corpuscles; and yet his method of philosophizing
generally meets with total rejection. This rejection, however, has never
been based on the fact that his philosophy deals with certain particles so
minute as to elude the senses, and assigns various sizes, shapes and
motions to them; for no one can doubt that there are in fact many such
particles, as I have just shown. The reasons for the rejection are the
following. First, Democritus supposed his corpuscles to be indivisible – a
notion which leads me to join those who reject his philosophy. Secondly,
he imagined there to be a vacuum around the corpuscles, whereas I
demonstrate the impossibility of a vacuum. Thirdly, he attributed gravity
to these corpuscles, whereas my understanding is that there is no such
thing as gravity in any body taken on its own, but that it exists only as a
function of, and in relation to, the position and motion of other bodies.[1]
And lastly, Democritus did not show how particular things arose merely
from the interaction of corpuscles; or, if he did show this in some cases,
his explanations were not entirely consistent, if we may judge from those
of his opinions which have survived. I leave others to judge whether my
own writings on philosophy have up to now been reasonably consistent
<and sufficiently fertile in the results that can be deduced from them. As
for the consideration of shapes, sizes and motions, this is something that
has been adopted not only by Democritus but also by Aristotle and all the
other philosophers. Now I reject all of Democritus' suppositions, with
this one exception, and I also reject practically all the suppositions of
the other philosophers. Hence it is clear that my method of philosophizing has no more affinity with the Democritean method than with any of
the other particular sects>.

203. *How we may arrive at knowledge of the shapes <sizes> and motions of particles that cannot be perceived by the senses.*

In view of the fact that I assign determinate shapes, sizes, and motions to

---

1 See above, Part 2, art. 20, p. 197.

the imperceptible particles of bodies just as if I had seen them, but
nonetheless maintain that they cannot be perceived, some people may be
led to ask how I know what these particles are like. My reply is this. First
of all <I considered in general all the clear and distinct notions which our
understanding can contain with regard to material things. And I found
no others except for the notions we have of shapes, sizes and motions,
and the rules in accordance with which these three things can be modified
by each other – rules which are the principles of geometry and mechanics. And I judged as a result that all the knowledge which men have of
the natural world must necessarily be derived from these notions; for all
the other notions we have of things that can be perceived by the senses
are confused and obscure, and so cannot serve to give us knowledge of
anything outside ourselves, but may even stand in the way of such
knowledge. Next> I took the simplest and best known principles,
knowledge of which is naturally implanted in our minds; and working
from these I considered, in general terms, firstly, what are the principal
differences which can exist between the sizes, shapes and positions of
bodies which are imperceptible by the senses merely because of their
small size, and, secondly, what observable effects would result from their
various interactions. Later on, when I observed just such effects in objects
that can be perceived by the senses, I judged that they in fact arose from
just such an interaction of bodies that cannot be perceived – especially
since it seemed impossible to think up any other explanation for them. In
this matter I was greatly helped by considering artefacts. For I do not
recognize any difference between artefacts and natural bodies except that
the operations of artefacts are for the most part performed by mechan-
isms which are large enough to be easily perceivable by the senses – as
indeed must be the case if they are to be capable of being manufactured
by human beings. The effects produced in nature, by contrast, almost
always depend on structures which are so minute that they completely
elude our senses. Moreover, mechanics is a division or special case
of physics, and all the explanations belonging to the former also
belong to the latter; so it is no less natural for a clock constructed with
this or that set of wheels to tell the time than it is for a tree which grew
from this or that seed to produce the appropriate fruit. Men who are
experienced in dealing with machinery can take a particular machine
whose function they know and, by looking at some of its parts, easily
form a conjecture about the design of the other parts, which they cannot
see. In the same way I have attempted to consider the observable effects
and parts of natural bodies and track down the imperceptible causes and
particles which produce them.

327   204. *With regard to the things which cannot be perceived by the senses, it is enough to explain their possible nature, even though their actual nature may be different* <*and this is all that Aristotle tried to do*>. However, although this method may enable us to understand how all the things in nature could have arisen, it should not therefore be inferred that they were in fact made in this way. Just as the same craftsman could make two clocks which tell the time equally well and look completely alike from the outside but have completely different assemblies of wheels inside, so the supreme craftsman of the real world could have produced all that we see in several different ways. I am very happy to admit this; and I shall think I have achieved enough provided only that what I have written is such as to correspond accurately with all the phenomena of nature. This will indeed be sufficient for application in ordinary life, since medicine and mechanics, and all the other arts which can be fully developed with the help of physics, are directed only towards items that can be perceived by the senses and are therefore to be counted among the phenomena of nature.[1] And in case anyone happens to be convinced that Aristotle achieved – or wanted to achieve – any more than this, he himself expressly asserts in the first book of the *Meteorologica*, at the beginning of Chapter Seven, that when dealing with things not manifest to the senses, he reckons he has provided adequate reasons and demonstrations if he can simply show that such things are capable of occurring in accordance with his explanations.

205. *Nevertheless my explanations appear to be at least morally certain*[2]. It would be disingenuous, however, not to point out that some things are considered as morally certain, that is, as having sufficient certainty for application to ordinary life, even though they may be uncertain in relation to the absolute power of God. <Thus those who have never been in Rome have no doubt that it is a town in Italy, even though it could be the case that everyone who has told them this has been deceiving them.> Suppose for example that someone wants to read a letter written in Latin but encoded so that the letters of the alphabet do not have their proper

---

1   '. . . are directed simply towards applying certain observable bodies to each other in such a way that certain observable effects are produced as a result of natural causes. And by imagining what the various causes are, and considering their results, we shall achieve our aim irrespective of whether these imagined causes are true or false, since the result is taken to be no different, as far as the observable effects are concerned' (French version).
2   By 'moral certainty' is meant certainty sufficient for ordinary practical purposes. See first sentence of this article, where the French version runs: '. . . moral certainty is certainty which is sufficient to regulate our behaviour, or which measures up to the certainty we have on matters relating to the conduct of life which we never normally doubt, though we know that it is possible, absolutely speaking, that they may be false'.

value, and he guesses that the letter B should be read whenever A   328
appears, and C when B appears, i.e. that each letter should be replaced by
the one immediately following it. If, by using this key, he can make up
Latin words from the letters, he will be in no doubt that the true meaning
of the letter is contained in these words. It is true that his knowledge is
based merely on a conjecture, and it is conceivable that the writer did not
replace the original letters with their immediate successors in the
alphabet, but with others, thus encoding quite a different message; but
this possibility is so unlikely <especially if the message contains many
words> that it does not seem credible. Now if people look at all the many
properties relating to magnetism, fire and the fabric of the entire world,
which I have deduced in this book from just a few principles, then, even if
they think that my assumption of these principles was arbitrary and
groundless, they will still perhaps acknowledge that it would hardly have
been possible for so many items to fit into a coherent pattern if the
original principles had been false.

206. *Indeed, my explanations possess more than moral certainty.*
Besides, there are some matters, even in relation to the things in nature,
which we regard as absolutely, and more than just morally, certain.
<Absolute certainty arises when we believe that it is wholly impossible
that something should be otherwise than we judge it to be.> This certainty
is based on a metaphysical foundation, namely that God is supremely
good and in no way a deceiver, and hence that the faculty which he gave
us for distinguishing truth from falsehood cannot lead us into error, so
long as we are using it properly and are thereby perceiving something
distinctly. Mathematical demonstrations have this kind of certainty,[1] as
does the knowledge that material things exist; and the same goes for all
evident reasoning about material things. And perhaps even these results
of mine will be allowed into the class of absolute certainties, if people
consider how they have been deduced in an unbroken chain from the first
and simplest principles of human knowledge. Their certainty will be
especially appreciated if it is properly understood that we can have no
sensory awareness of external objects unless these objects produce some
local motion in our nerves; and that the fixed stars, owing to their
enormous distance from us, cannot produce such motion unless there is
also some motion occurring both in them and also throughout the entire

329

---

1 '... for we see clearly that it is impossible that two and three added together should
make more or less than five; or that a square should have only three sides, and so on'
(added in French version).

intervening part of the heavens.[1] Once this is accepted, then it seems that all the other phenomena, or at least the general features of the universe and the earth which I have described, can hardly be intelligibly explained except in the way I have suggested.

207. I submit all my views to the authority of the Church.

Nevertheless, mindful of my own weakness, I make no firm pronouncements, but submit all these opinions to the authority of the Catholic Church and the judgement of those wiser than myself. And I would not wish anyone to believe anything except what he is convinced of by evident and irrefutable reasoning.

THE END

1 '. . . from which it follows very evidently that the heavens must be fluid, i.e. composed of small particles which move separately from each other, or at least that they must contain such particles. For whatever I can be said to have assumed in Part 3, art. 46 can be reduced to the sole assertion that the heavens are fluid' (added in French version).

Comments on a Certain Broadsheet

published in Belgium towards the end of 1647, entitled 'An account of the human mind, or rational soul, which explains what it is and what it can be'

[In the *second* article of the *Broadsheet* the author states that the attributes (349) of extension and thought] 'are not opposites, but merely different'. There is a contradiction in this statement. For, when the question concerns attributes which constitute the essence of some substances, there can be no greater opposition between them than the fact that they are different; and when he acknowledges that the one attribute is different from the other, this is tantamount to saying that the one attribute is not the other; but 'is' and 'is not' are contraries. He says 'since they are not opposites but merely different, there is no reason why the mind should not be a sort of attribute co-existing with extension in the same subject, though the one attribute is not included in the concept of the other'.[1] There is a manifest contradiction in this statement, for the author is taking something which can hold strictly speaking only for modes and inferring that it holds for any attribute whatsoever; but he nowhere proves that the mind, or the internal principle of thought, is such a mode. On the contrary, I shall presently show that it is not, on the basis of what he actually says in article five. As for the attributes which constitute the natures of things, it cannot be said that those which 350 are different, and such that the concept of the one is not contained in the concept of the other, are present together in one and the same subject; for that would be equivalent to saying that one and the same subject has two different natures – a statement that implies a contradiction, at least when it is a question of a simple subject (as in the present case) rather than a composite one.

Three points should be borne in mind here. If the author had properly understood them, he would never have fallen into such manifest errors.

First, it is part of the nature of a mode that, although we can readily understand a substance apart from a mode, we cannot *vice versa* clearly understand a mode unless at the same time we have a conception of the substance of which it is a mode (as I explained in the *Principles of Philosophy*, Part 1, article 61). All philosophers are agreed on this point.

1 Article 2 of Regius' *Broadsheet*.

But it is clear from his fifth article that our author has paid no attention to this rule, for he admits there that we can have doubts about the existence of the body, whereas we have no doubts about the existence of the mind. It follows from this that we can understand the mind apart from the body; hence it is not a mode of the body.

Second, I wish at this point to stress the difference between simple entities and composite entities. A composite entity is one which is found to have two or more attributes, each one of which can be distinctly understood apart from the other. For, in virtue of the fact that one of these attributes can be distinctly understood apart from the other, we know that the one is not a mode of the other, but is a thing, or attribute of a thing, which can subsist without the other. A simple entity, on the other hand, is one in which no such attributes are to be found. It is clear from this that a subject which we understand to possess solely extension and the various modes of extension is a simple entity; so too is a subject which we recognize as having thought and the various modes of thought as its sole attribute. But that which we regard as having at the same time both extension and thought is a composite entity, namely a man — an entity consisting of a soul and a body. Our author seems here to have taken a man to be simply a body, of which the man's mind is a mode.

Lastly, we should note that in subjects which are composed of several substances, one such substance often stands out; and we view this substance in such a way that any of the other substances which we associate with it are nothing but modes of it. Thus a man who is dressed can be regarded as a compound of a man and clothes. But with respect to the man, his being dressed is merely a mode, although clothes are substances. In the same way, in the case of a man, who is composed of a soul and a body, our author might be regarding the body as the principal element, in relation to which having a soul or the possession of thought is nothing but a mode. But it is absurd to infer from this that the soul itself, or that in virtue of which the body thinks, is not a substance distinct from the body.

He endeavours to support his contention by means of the following syllogism: 'Whatever we can conceive of can exist. Now it is conceivable that the mind is some such item (*viz.* a substance or a mode of a corporeal substance); for none of these implies a contradiction. Therefore it is possible that the mind is some such item'. We should note that even though the rule, 'Whatever we can conceive of can exist',[1] is my own, it is true only so long as we are dealing with a conception which is clear and distinct, a conception which embraces the possibility of the thing in

1 Cf. Med. VI, p. 110 above.

question, since God can bring about whatever we clearly perceive to be possible. But we ought not to use this rule heedlessly, because it is easy for someone to imagine that he properly understands something when in fact he is blinded by some preconception and does not understand it at all. This is just what happens when the author maintains that there is no contradiction involved in saying that one and the same thing possesses one or the other of two totally different natures, i.e. that it is a substance or a mode. If he had said merely that he could see no reason for regarding the human mind as an incorporeal substance, rather than a mode of a corporeal substance, we could have excused his ignorance. Moreover, if he had said that human intelligence could find no reasons which might decisively settle the question one way or the other, his arrogance would indeed be blameworthy, but his statement would involve no obvious contradiction. But when he says that the nature of things leaves open the possibility that the same thing is either a substance or a mode,[1] what he says is quite self-contradictory, and shows how irrational his mind is....

In article *twelve* the author's disagreement with me seems to be merely (357) verbal. When he says that the mind has no need of ideas, or notions, or axioms which are innate, while admitting that the mind has the power of thinking (presumably natural or innate), he is plainly saying the same thing as I, though verbally denying it. I have never written or taken the view that the mind requires innate ideas which are something distinct from its own faculty of thinking. I did, however, observe that there were 358 certain thoughts within me which neither came to me from external objects nor were determined by my will, but which came solely from the power of thinking within me; so I applied the term 'innate' to the ideas or notions which are the forms of these thoughts in order to distinguish them from others, which I called 'adventitious' and 'invented'.[2] This is the same sense as that in which we say that generosity is 'innate' in certain families, or that certain diseases such as gout or stones are innate in others: it is not so much that the babies of such families suffer from these diseases in their mother's womb, but simply that they are born with a certain 'faculty' or tendency to contract them.

In article *thirteen* he draws an extraordinary conclusion from the preceding article. Because the mind has no need of innate ideas, its power of thinking being sufficient, he says, 'all common notions which are engraved in the mind have their origin in observation of things or in verbal instruction' – as if the power of thinking could achieve nothing on its own, could never perceive or think anything except what it receives

---

1 Article 2 of the *Broadsheet*.
2 Cf. Med. III, p. 89 above.

through observation of things or through verbal instruction, i.e. from the senses. But this is so far from being true that, on the contrary, if we bear well in mind the scope of our senses and what it is exactly that reaches our faculty of thinking by way of them, we must admit that in no case are the ideas of things presented to us by the senses just as we form them in our thinking. So much so that there is nothing in our ideas which is not innate to the mind or the faculty of thinking, with the sole exception of those circumstances which relate to experience, such as the fact that we judge that this or that idea which we now have immediately before our mind refers to a certain thing situated outside us. We make such a judgement not because these things transmit the ideas to our mind through the sense organs, but because they transmit something which, at exactly that moment, gives the mind occasion to form these ideas by means of the faculty innate to it. Nothing reaches our mind from external objects through the sense organs except certain corporeal motions, as our author himself asserts in article nineteen, in accordance with my own principles. But neither the motions themselves nor the figures arising from them are conceived of by us exactly as they occur in the sense organs, as I have explained at length in my *Optics*.[1] Hence it follows that the very ideas of the motions themselves and of the figures are innate in us. The ideas of pain, colours, sounds and the like must be all the more innate if, on the occasion of certain corporeal motions, our mind is to be capable of representing them to itself, for there is no similarity between these ideas and the corporeal motions. Is it possible to imagine anything more absurd than that all the common notions within our mind arise from such motions and cannot exist without them? I would like our author to tell me what the corporeal motion is that is capable of forming some common notion to the effect that 'things which are equal to a third thing are equal to each other', or any other he cares to take. For all such motions are particular, whereas the common notions are universal and bear no affinity with, or relation to, the motions.

In article *fourteen* he goes on to assert that even the idea of God which is within us derives its being not from our faculty of thinking, in which the idea is innate, 'but from divine revelation, or verbal instruction, or observation of things'. It is easier to recognize the error in this assertion if we consider that something can be said to derive its being from something else for two different reasons: either the other thing is its proximate and primary cause, without which it cannot exist, or it is a remote and merely accidental cause, which gives the primary cause occasion to produce its effect at one moment rather than another. Thus workers are the primary and proximate causes of their work, whereas

1 See *Optics*, pp. 64f above.

those who give them orders to do the work, or promise to pay for it, are accidental and remote causes, for the workers might not do the work without instructions. There is, however, no doubt that verbal instruction or observation of things is often a remote cause which induces us to give some attention to the idea which we can have of God, and to bring it directly before our mind. But no one can say that this is the proximate and efficient cause of the idea, except someone who thinks that all we can ever understand about God is what he is called, namely 'God', or what corporeal form painters use to represent him. If the observation is visual, all it can, by its own unaided power, present to the mind are pictures, and indeed pictures which are composed of nothing more than a variety of corporeal motions, as the author himself tells us. If the observation is auditory, all it presents are words and utterances. If the observation is by means of the other senses, it cannot have any reference to God. It is surely obvious to everyone that, strictly speaking, sight in itself presents nothing but pictures, and hearing nothing but utterances and sounds. So everything over and above these utterances and pictures which we think of as being signified by them is represented to us by means of ideas which come 361 to us from no other source than our own faculty of thinking. Consequently these ideas, along with that faculty, are innate in us, i.e. they always exist within us potentially, for to exist in some faculty is not to exist actually, but merely potentially, since the term 'faculty' denotes nothing but a potentiality. But no one can assert that we can know nothing of God other than his name or the corporeal image which artists give him, unless he is prepared openly to admit that he is an atheist and indeed totally lacking in intellect.[1]

---

1 The rest of Descartes' comments are omitted.

The Passions of the Soul

PART ONE

The passions in general

and incidentally the whole nature of man

1. What is a passion with regard to one subject is always an action in some other regard

The defects of the sciences we have from the ancients are nowhere more apparent than in their writings on the passions. This topic, about which knowledge has always been keenly sought, does not seem to be one of the more difficult to investigate since everyone feels passions in himself and so has no need to look elsewhere for observations to establish their nature. And yet the teachings of the ancients about the passions are so meagre and for the most part so implausible that I cannot hope to approach the truth except by departing from the paths they have followed. That is why I shall be obliged to write just as if I were considering a topic that no one had dealt with before me. In the first place, I note that whatever takes place or occurs is generally called by philosophers a 'passion' with regard to the subject to which it happens and an 'action' with regard to that which makes it happen. Thus, although an agent and patient are often quite different, an action and passion must always be a single thing which has these two names on account of the two different subjects to which it may be related.

2. To understand the passions of the soul we must distinguish its functions from those of the body

Next I note that we are not aware of any subject which acts more directly upon our soul than the body to which it is joined. Consequently we should recognize that what is a passion in the soul is usually an action in the body. Hence there is no better way of coming to know about our passions than by examining the difference between the soul and the body, in order to learn to which of the two we should attribute each of the functions present in us.

3. *The rule we must follow in order to do this*

329

We shall not find this very difficult if we bear in mind that anything we experience as being in us, and which we see can also exist in wholly inanimate bodies, must be attributed only to our body. On the other hand, anything in us which we cannot conceive in any way as capable of belonging to a body must be attributed to our soul.

4. *The heat and the movement of the limbs proceed from the body, and thoughts from the soul*

Thus, because we have no conception of the body as thinking in any way at all, we have reason to believe that every kind of thought present in us belongs to the soul. And since we do not doubt that there are inanimate bodies which can move in as many different ways as our bodies, if not more, and which have as much heat or more (as experience shows in the case of a flame, which has in itself much more heat and movement than any of our limbs), we must believe that all the heat and all the movements present in us, in so far as they do not depend on thought, belong solely to the body.

5. *It is an error to believe that the soul gives movement and heat to the body*

330

In this way we shall avoid a very serious error which many have fallen into, and which I regard as the primary cause of our failure up to now to give a satisfactory explanation of the passions and of everything else belonging to the soul. The error consists in supposing that since dead bodies are devoid of heat and movement, it is the absence of the soul which causes this cessation of movement and heat. Thus it has been believed, without justification, that our natural heat and all the movements of our bodies depend on the soul; whereas we ought to hold, on the contrary, that the soul takes its leave when we die only because this heat ceases and the organs which bring about bodily movement decay.

6. *The difference between a living body and a dead body*

So as to avoid this error, let us note that death never occurs through the absence of the soul, but only because one of the principal parts of the body decays. And let us recognize that the difference between the body of a living man and that of a dead man is just like the difference 331 between, on the one hand, a watch or other automaton (that is, a self-moving machine) when it is wound up and contains in itself the corporeal principle of the movements for which it is designed, together with everything else required for its operation; and, on the other hand, the same watch or machine when it is broken and the principle of its movement ceases to be active.

7. *A brief account of the parts of the body and of some of their functions*

To make this more intelligible I shall explain in a few words the way in which the mechanism of our body is composed. Everyone knows that within us there is a heart, brain, stomach, muscles, nerves, arteries, veins, and similar things. We know too that the food we eat goes down to the stomach and bowels, and that its juice then flows into the liver and all the veins, where it mixes with the blood they contain, thus increasing its quantity. Those who have heard anything at all about medicine know in addition how the heart is constructed and how the blood in the veins can flow easily from the vena cava into its right-hand side, pass from there into the lungs through the vessel called the arterial vein, then return from the lungs into the left-hand side of the heart through the vessel called the venous artery, and finally pass from there into the great artery, whose branches spread through the whole body. Likewise all those not completely blinded by the authority of the ancients, and willing to open their eyes to examine the opinion of Harvey regarding the circulation of the blood, do not doubt that the veins and arteries of the body are like streams through which the blood flows constantly and with great rapidity. It makes its way from the right-hand cavity of the heart through the arterial vein, whose branches are spread throughout the lungs and connected with those of the venous artery; and via this artery it passes from the lungs into the left-hand side of the heart. From there it goes into the great artery, whose branches are spread through the rest of the body and connected with the branches of the vena cava, which carries the same blood once again into the right-hand cavity of the heart. These two cavities are thus like sluices through which all the blood passes upon each complete circuit it makes through the body. It is known, moreover, that every movement of the limbs depends on the muscles, which are opposed to each other in such a way that when one of them becomes shorter it draws towards itself the part of the body to which it is attached, which simultaneously causes the muscle opposed to it to lengthen. Then, if the latter happens to shorten at some other time, it makes the former lengthen again, and draws towards itself the part to which they are attached. Finally, it is known that all these movements of the muscles, and likewise all sensations, depend on the nerves, which are like little threads or tubes coming from the brain and containing, like the brain itself, a certain very fine air or wind which is called the 'animal spirits'.

8. *The principle underlying all these functions*   333
But it is not commonly known how these animal spirits and nerves help to
produce movements and sensations, or what corporeal principle makes
them act. That is why, although I have already touched upon this
question in other writings, I intend to speak briefly about it here. While
we are alive there is a continual heat in our hearts, which is a kind of fire
that the blood of the veins maintains there. This fire is the corporeal
principle underlying all the movements of our limbs.

9. *How the movement of the heart takes place*
Its first effect is that it makes the blood which fills the cavities of the
heart expand. This causes the blood, now needing to occupy a larger
space, to rush from the right-hand cavity into the arterial vein and from
the left-hand cavity into the great artery. Then, when this expansion
ceases, fresh blood immediately enters the right-hand cavity of the heart
from the vena cava, and the left-hand cavity from the venous artery. For
there are tiny membranes at the entrances to these four vessels which are
so arranged that the blood can enter the heart only through the latter two   334
and leave it only through the former two. When the new blood has
entered the heart it is immediately rarefied in the same way as before.
This and this alone is what the pulse or beating of the heart and arteries
consists in, and it explains why the beating is repeated each time new
blood enters the heart. It is also the sole cause of the movement of the
blood, making it flow constantly and very rapidly in all the arteries and
veins, so that it carries the heat it acquires in the heart to all the other
parts of the body, and provides them with nourishment.

10. *How the animal spirits are produced in the brain*
What is, however, more worthy of consideration here is that all the most
lively and finest parts of the blood, which have been rarefied by the
heat in the heart, constantly enter the cavities of the brain in large
numbers. What makes them go there rather than elsewhere is that all the
blood leaving the heart through the great artery follows a direct route
towards this place, and since not all this blood can enter there because
the passages are too narrow, only the most active and finest parts pass
into it while the rest spread out into the other regions of the body. Now
these very fine parts of the blood make up the animal spirits. For them to   335
do this the only change they need to undergo in the brain is to be
separated from the other less fine parts of the blood. For what I am
calling 'spirits' here are merely bodies: they have no property other than

that of being extremely small bodies which move very quickly, like the jets of flame that come from a torch. They never stop in any place, and as some of them enter the brain's cavities, others leave it through the pores in its substance. These pores conduct them into the nerves, and then to the muscles. In this way the animal spirits move the body in all the various ways it can be moved.

11. *How the movements of the muscles take place*

For, as already mentioned, the sole cause of all the movements of the limbs is the shortening of certain muscles and the lengthening of the opposed muscles. What causes one muscle to become shorter rather than its opposite is simply that fractionally more spirits from the brain come to it than to the other. Not that the spirits which come directly from the brain are sufficient by themselves to move the muscles; but they cause the other spirits already in the two muscles to leave one of them very suddenly and pass into the other. In this way the one they leave becomes 336 longer and more relaxed, and the one they enter, being suddenly swollen by them, becomes shorter and pulls the limb to which it is attached. This is easy to understand, provided one knows that very few animal spirits come continually from the brain to each muscle, and that any muscle always contains a quantity of its own spirits. These move very quickly, sometimes merely eddying in the place where they are located (that is, when they find no passages open for them to leave from), and sometimes flowing into the opposed muscle. In each of the muscles there are small openings through which the spirits may flow from one into the other, and which are so arranged that when the spirits coming from the brain to one of the muscles are slightly more forceful than those going to the other, they open all the passages through which the spirits in the latter can pass into the former, and at the same time they close all the passages through which the spirits in the former can pass into the latter. In this way all the spirits previously contained in the two muscles are gathered very rapidly in one of them, thus making it swell and become shorter, while the other lengthens and relaxes.

12. *How external objects act upon the sense organs*

We still have to know what causes the spirits not to flow always in the 337 same way from the brain to the muscles, but to come sometimes more to some muscles than to others. In our case, indeed, one of these causes is the activity of the soul (as I shall explain further on). But in addition we must note two other causes, which depend solely on the body. The first consists in differences in the movements produced in the sense organs by their objects. I have already explained this quite fully in the *Optics*.[1] But in order that readers of this work should not need to consult any other, I shall say once again that there are three things to consider in the nerves. First, there is the marrow, or internal substance, which extends in the form of tiny fibres from the brain, where they originate, to the extremities of the parts of the body to which they are attached. Next, there are the membranes surrounding the fibres, which are continuous with those surrounding the brain and form little tubes in which the fibres are enclosed. Finally, there are the animal spirits which, being carried by these tubes from the brain to the muscles, cause the fibres to remain so completely free and extended that if anything causes the slightest motion in the part of the body where one of the fibres terminates, it thereby causes a movement in the part of the brain where the fibre originates, just as we make one end of a cord move by pulling the other end.

13. *This action of external objects may direct the spirits into the muscles* 338
   in various different ways
I explained in the *Optics* how the objects of sight make themselves known to us simply by producing, through the medium of the intervening transparent bodies, local motions in the optic nerve-fibres at the back of our eyes, and then in the regions of the brain where these nerves originate.[2] I explained too that the objects produce as much variety in these motions as they cause us to see in the things, and that it is not the motions occurring in the eye, but those occurring in the brain, which directly represent these objects to the soul. By this example, it is easy to conceive how sounds, smells, tastes, heat, pain, hunger, thirst and, in general, all the objects both of our external senses and of our internal appetites, also produce some movement in our nerves, which passes through them into the brain. Besides causing our soul to have various different sensations, these various movements in the brain can also act without the soul, causing the spirits to make their way to certain muscles rather than others, and so causing them to move our limbs. I shall prove this here by one example only. If someone suddenly thrusts his hand in front of our eyes as if to strike us, then even if we know that he is our 339 friend, that he is doing this only in fun, and that he will take care not to harm us, we still find it difficult to prevent ourselves from closing our eyes. This shows that it is not through the mediation of our soul that they close, since this action is contrary to our volition, which is the only, or at least the principal, activity of the soul. They close rather because the mechanism of our body is so composed that the movement of the hand

1 See *Optics*, p. 62 above.
2 See *Optics*, p. 64 above.

towards our eyes produces another movement in our brain, which directs the animal spirits into the muscles that make our eyelids drop.

14. *Differences among the spirits may also cause them to take various different courses*

The other cause which serves to direct the animal spirits to the muscles in various different ways is the unequal agitation of the spirits and differences in their parts. For when some of their parts are coarser and more agitated than others, they penetrate more deeply in a straight line into the cavities and pores of the brain, and in this way they are directed to muscles other than those to which they would go if they had less force.

340　15. *The causes of these differences*

And this inequality may arise from the different materials of which the spirits are composed. One sees this in the case of those who have drunk a lot of wine: the vapours of the wine enter the blood rapidly and rise from the heart to the brain, where they turn into spirits which, being stronger and more abundant than those normally present there, are capable of moving the body in many strange ways. Such an inequality of the spirits may also arise from various conditions of the heart, liver, stomach, spleen and all the other organs that help to produce them. In this connection we must first note certain small nerves embedded in the base of the heart, which serve to enlarge and contract the openings to its cavities, thus causing the blood, according to the strength of its expansion, to produce spirits having various different dispositions. It must also be observed that even though the blood entering the heart comes there from every other place in the body, it often happens nevertheless that it is driven there more from some parts than from others, because the nerves and muscles responsible for these parts exert more pressure on it or make it more agitated. And differences in these parts are matched by corresponding differences in the expansion of the blood in the heart, which results in the production of spirits having different qualities. Thus, for 341　example, the blood coming from the lower part of the liver, where the gall is located, expands in the heart in a different manner from the blood coming from the spleen; the latter expands differently from the blood coming from the veins of the arms or legs; and this expands differently again from the alimentary juices when, just after leaving the stomach and bowels, they pass rapidly to the heart through the liver.

16. *How all the limbs can be moved by the objects of the senses and by the spirits without the help of the soul*

Finally it must be observed that the mechanism of our body is so composed that all the changes occurring in the movement of the spirits may cause them to open some pores in the brain more than others. Conversely, when one of the pores is opened somewhat more or less than usual by an action of the sensory nerves, this brings about a change in the movement of the spirits and directs them to the muscles which serve to move the body in the way it is usually moved on the occasion of such an action. Thus every movement we make without any contribution from our will – as often happens when we breathe, walk, eat and, indeed, when we perform any action which is common to us and the beasts – depends solely on the arrangement of our limbs and on the route which 342 the spirits, produced by the heat of the heart, follow naturally in the brain, nerves and muscles. This occurs in the same way that the movement of a watch is produced merely by the strength of its spring and the configuration of its wheels.

17. *The functions of the soul*
Having thus considered all the functions belonging solely to the body, it is easy to recognize that there is nothing in us which we must attribute to our soul except our thoughts. These are of two principal kinds, some being actions of the soul and others its passions. Those I call its actions are all our volitions, for we experience them as proceeding directly from our soul and as seeming to depend on it alone. On the other hand, the various perceptions or modes of knowledge present in us may be called its passions, in a general sense, for it is often not our soul which makes them such as they are, and the soul always receives them from the things that are represented by them.

18. *The will*
Our volitions, in turn, are of two sorts. One consists of the actions of the 343 soul which terminate in the soul itself, as when we will to love God or, generally speaking, to apply our mind to some object which is not material. The other consists of actions which terminate in our body, as when our merely willing to walk has the consequence that our legs move and we walk.

19. *Perception*
Our perceptions are likewise of two sorts: some have the soul as their cause, others the body. Those having the soul as their cause are the perceptions of our volitions and of all the imaginings or other thoughts which depend on them. For it is certain that we cannot will anything without thereby perceiving that we are willing it. And although willing

something is an action with respect to our soul, the perception of such willing may be said to be a passion in the soul. But because this perception is really one and the same thing as the volition, and names are always determined by whatever is most noble, we do not normally call it a 'passion', but solely an 'action'.

344   20. *Imaginings and other thoughts formed by the soul*
When our soul applies itself to imagine something non-existent – as in thinking about an enchanted palace or a chimera – and also when it applies itself to consider something that is purely intelligible and not imaginable – for example, in considering its own nature – the perceptions it has of these things depend chiefly on the volition which makes it aware of them. That is why we usually regard these perceptions as actions rather than passions.

21. *Imaginings which are caused solely by the body*
Among the perceptions caused by the body, most of them depend on the nerves. But there are some which do not and which, like those I have just described, are called 'imaginings'. These differ from the others, however, in that our will is not used in forming them. Accordingly they cannot be numbered among the actions of the soul, for they arise simply from the fact that the spirits, being agitated in various different ways and coming upon the traces of various impressions which have preceded them in the
345   brain, make their way by chance through certain pores rather than others. Such are the illusions of our dreams and also the day-dreams we often have when we are awake and our mind wanders idly without applying itself to anything of its own accord. Now some of these imaginings are passions of the soul, taking the word 'passion' in its proper and more exact sense, and all may be regarded as such if the word is understood in a more general sense. Nonetheless, their cause is not so conspicuous and determinate as that of the perceptions which the soul receives by means of the nerves, and they seem to be mere shadows and pictures of these perceptions. So before we can characterize them satisfactorily we must consider how these other perceptions differ from one another.

22. *How these other perceptions differ from one another*
All the perceptions which I have not yet explained come to the soul by means of the nerves. They differ from one another in so far as we refer

some to external objects which strike our senses, others to our body or to certain of its parts, and still others to our soul.

23. *The perceptions we refer to objects outside us* 346

The perceptions we refer to things outside us, namely to the objects of our senses, are caused by these objects, at least when our judgements are not false. For in that case the objects produce certain movements in the organs of the external senses and, by means of the nerves, produce other movements in the brain, which cause the soul to have sensory awareness of the objects. Thus, when we see the light of a torch and hear the sound of a bell, the sound and the light are two different actions which, simply by producing two different movements in some of our nerves, and through them in our brain, give to the soul two different sensations. And we refer these sensations to the subjects we suppose to be their causes in such a way that we think that we see the torch itself and hear the bell, and not that we have sensory awareness merely of movements that come from these objects.

24. *The perceptions we refer to our body*

The perceptions we refer to our body or to certain of its parts are those of hunger, thirst and other natural appetites. To these we may add pain, heat and the other states we feel as being in our limbs, and not as being in 347 objects outside us. Thus, at the same time and by means of the same nerves we can feel the cold of our hand and the heat of a nearby flame or, on the other hand, the heat of our hand and the cold of the air to which it is exposed. This happens without there being any difference between the actions which make us feel the heat or cold in our hand and those which make us feel the heat or cold outside us, except that since one of these actions succeeds the other, we judge that the first is already in us, and that its successor is not yet there but in the object which causes it.

25. *The perceptions we refer to our soul*

The perceptions we refer only to the soul are those whose effects we feel as being in the soul itself, and for which we do not normally know any proximate cause to which we can refer them. Such are the feelings of joy, anger and the like, which are aroused in us sometimes by the objects which stimulate our nerves and sometimes also by other causes. Now all our perceptions, both those we refer to objects outside us and those we refer to the various states of our body, are indeed passions with respect to our soul, so long as we use the term 'passion' in its most general sense; 348 nevertheless we usually restrict the term to signify only perceptions which refer to the soul itself. And it is only the latter that I have undertaken to explain here under the title 'passions of the soul'.[1]

26. *The imaginings which depend solely on the fortuitous movement of the spirits may be passions just as truly as the perceptions which depend on the nerves*

It remains to be noted that everything the soul perceives by means of the nerves may also be represented to it through the fortuitous course of the spirits. The sole difference is that the impressions which come into the brain through the nerves are normally more lively and more definite than those produced there by the spirits – a fact that led me to say in article 21 that the latter are, as it were, a shadow or picture of the former. We must also note that this picture is sometimes so similar to the thing it represents that it may mislead us regarding the perceptions which refer to objects outside us, or even regarding those which refer to certain parts of our body. But we cannot be misled in the same way regarding the passions, in that they are so close and so internal to our soul that it cannot possibly feel them unless they are truly as it feels them to be. Thus often when we sleep, and sometimes even when we are awake, we imagine certain things so vividly that we think we see them before us, or feel them in our body, although they are not there at all. But even if we are asleep and dreaming, we cannot feel sad, or moved by any other passion, unless the soul truly has this passion within it.

349

27. *Definition of the passions of the soul*

After having considered in what respects the passions of the soul differ from all its other thoughts, it seems to me that we may define them generally as those perceptions, sensations or emotions of the soul which

---

1 The classification given in articles 17–25 may be represented schematically as follows:

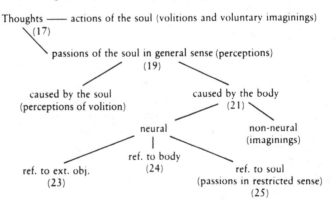

we refer particularly to it, and which are caused, maintained and strengthened by some movement of the spirits.

28. *Explanation of the first part of this definition*
We may call them 'perceptions' if we use this term generally to signify all the thoughts which are not actions of the soul or volitions, but not if we use it to signify only evident knowledge. For experience shows that those who are the most strongly agitated by their passions are not those who know them best, and that the passions are to be numbered among the 350 perceptions which the close alliance between the soul and the body renders confused and obscure. We may also call them 'sensations', because they are received into the soul in the same way as the objects of the external senses, and they are not known by the soul any differently. But it is even better to call them 'emotions' of the soul, not only because this term may be applied to all the changes which occur in the soul – that is, to all the various thoughts which come to it – but more particularly because, of all the kinds of thought which the soul may have, there are none that agitate and disturb it so strongly as the passions.

29. *Explanation of the other part of the definition*
I add that they refer particularly to the soul, in order to distinguish them from other sensations, some referred to external objects (e.g. smells, sounds and colours) and others to our body (e.g. hunger, thirst and pain). I also add that they are caused, maintained and strengthened by some movement of the spirits, both in order to distinguish them from our volitions (for these too may be called 'emotions of the soul which refer to it', but they are caused by the soul itself), and also in order to explain their ultimate and most proximate cause, which distinguishes them once again from other sensations.

30. *The soul is united to all the parts of the body conjointly*   351
But in order to understand all these things more perfectly, we need to recognize that the soul is really joined to the whole body, and that we cannot properly say that it exists in any one part of the body to the exclusion of the others. For the body is a unity which is in a sense indivisible because of the arrangement of its organs, these being so related to one another that the removal of any one of them renders the whole body defective. And the soul is of such a nature that it has no relation to extension, or to the dimensions or other properties of the matter of which the body is composed: it is related solely to the whole assemblage of the body's organs. This is obvious from our inability to conceive of a half or a third of a soul, or of the extension which a soul

occupies. Nor does the soul become any smaller if we cut off some part of the body, but it becomes completely separate from the body when we break up the assemblage of the body's organs.

31. *There is a little gland*[1] *in the brain where the soul exercises its functions more particularly than in the other parts of the body*

352 We need to recognize also that although the soul is joined to the whole body, nevertheless there is a certain part of the body where it exercises its functions more particularly than in all the others. It is commonly held that this part is the brain, or perhaps the heart – the brain because the sense organs are related to it, and the heart because we feel the passions as if they were in it. But on carefully examining the matter I think I have clearly established that the part of the body in which the soul directly exercises its functions is not the heart at all, or the whole of the brain. It is rather the innermost part of the brain, which is a certain very small gland situated in the middle of the brain's substance and suspended above the passage through which the spirits in the brain's anterior cavities communicate with those in its posterior cavities. The slightest movements on the part of this gland may alter very greatly the course of these spirits, and conversely any change, however slight, taking place in the course of the spirits may do much to change the movements of the gland.

32. *How we know that this gland is the principal seat of the soul*

Apart from this gland, there cannot be any other place in the whole body where the soul directly exercises its functions. I am convinced of this by
353 the observation that all the other parts of our brain are double, as also are all the organs of our external senses – eyes, hands, ears and so on. But in so far as we have only one simple thought about a given object at any one time, there must necessarily be some place where the two images coming through the two eyes, or the two impressions coming from a single object through the double organs of any other sense, can come together in a single image or impression before reaching the soul, so that they do not present to it two objects instead of one. We can easily understand that these images or other impressions are unified in this gland by means of the spirits which fill the cavities of the brain. But they cannot exist united in this way in any other place in the body except as a result of their being united in this gland.

33. *The seat of the passions is not in the heart*

As for the opinion of those who think that the soul receives its passions in the heart, this is not worth serious consideration, since it is based solely on the fact that the passions make us feel some change in the heart. It is

1 The pineal gland, which Descartes had identified as the seat of the imagination and the 'common' sense in the *Treatise on Man* (CSM I 106).

easy to see that the only reason why this change is felt as occurring in the heart is that there is a small nerve which descends to it from the brain – just as pain is felt as in the foot by means of the nerves in the foot, and the stars are perceived as in the sky by means of their light and the optic nerves. Thus it is no more necessary that our soul should exercise its functions directly in the heart in order to feel its passions there, than that it should be in the sky in order to see the stars there. 354

34. *How the soul and the body act on each other*
Let us therefore take it that the soul has its principal seat in the small gland located in the middle of the brain. From there it radiates through the rest of the body by means of the animal spirits, the nerves, and even the blood, which can take on the impressions of the spirits and carry them through the arteries to all the limbs. Let us recall what we said previously about the mechanism of our body. The nerve-fibres are so distributed in all the parts of the body that when the objects of the senses produce various different movements in these parts, the fibres are occasioned to open the pores of the brain in various different ways. This, in turn, causes the animal spirits contained in these cavities to enter the muscles in various different ways. In this manner the spirits can move the limbs in all the different ways they are capable of being moved. And all the other causes that can move the spirits in different ways are sufficient to direct them into different muscles. To this we may now add that the small gland which is the principal seat of the soul is suspended within the cavities containing these spirits, so that it can be moved by them in as many different ways as there are perceptible differences in the objects. 355
But it can also be moved in various different ways by the soul, whose nature is such that it receives as many different impressions – that is, it has as many different perceptions as there occur different movements in this gland. And conversely, the mechanism of our body is so constructed that simply by this gland's being moved in any way by the soul or by any other cause, it drives the surrounding spirits towards the pores of the brain, which direct them through the nerves to the muscles; and in this way the gland makes the spirits move the limbs.

35. *Example of the way in which the impressions of objects are united in the gland in the middle of the brain*
Thus, for example, if we see some animal approaching us, the light reflected from its body forms two images, one in each of our eyes; and these images form two others, by means of the optic nerves, on the internal surface of the brain facing its cavities. Then, by means of the spirits that fill these cavities, the images radiate towards the little gland which the spirits surround: the movement forming each point of one of

356   the images tends towards the same point on the gland as the movement
forming the corresponding point of the other image, which represents the
same part of the animal. In this way, the two images in the brain form
only one image on the gland, which acts directly upon the soul and makes
it see the shape of the animal.

36. *Example of the way in which the passions are aroused in the soul*
If, in addition, this shape is very strange and terrifying – that is, if it has a
close relation to things which have previously been harmful to the body –
this arouses the passion of anxiety in the soul, and then that of courage or
perhaps fear and terror, depending upon the particular temperament of
the body or the strength of the soul, and upon whether we have protected
ourselves previously by defence or by flight against the harmful things to
which the present impression is related. Thus in certain persons these
factors dispose their brain in such a way that some of the spirits reflected
from the image formed on the gland proceed from there to the nerves
which serve to turn the back and move the legs in order to flee. The rest
of the spirits go to nerves which expand or constrict the orifices of the
heart, or else to nerves which agitate other parts of the body from which
blood is sent to the heart, so that the blood is rarefied in a different
357   manner from usual and spirits are sent to the brain which are adapted for
maintaining and strengthening the passion of fear – that is, for holding
open or re-opening the pores of the brain which direct the spirits into
these same nerves. For merely by entering into these pores they produce
in the gland a particular movement which is ordained by nature to make
the soul feel this passion. And since these pores are related mainly to the
little nerves which serve to contract or expand the orifices of the heart,
this makes the soul feel the passion chiefly as if it were in the heart.

37. *How all the passions appear to be caused by some movement of the
spirits*
Something similar happens with all the other passions. That is, they are
caused chiefly by the spirits contained in the cavities of the brain making
their way to nerves which serve to expand or constrict the orifices of the
heart, or to drive blood towards the heart in a distinctive way from other
parts of the body, or to maintain the passion in some other way. This
makes it clear why I included in my definition of the passions that they
are caused by some particular movement of the spirits.

358   38. *Example of movements of the body which accompany the passions
and do not depend on the soul*
Moreover, just as the course which the spirits take to the nerves of the
heart suffices to induce a movement in the gland through which fear

enters the soul, so too the mere fact that some spirits at the same time proceed to the nerves which serve to move the legs in flight causes another movement in the gland through which the soul feels and perceives this action. In this way, then, the body may be moved to take flight by the mere disposition of the organs, without any contribution from the soul.

39. *How one and the same cause may excite different passions in different people*

The same impression which the presence of a terrifying object forms on the gland, and which causes fear in some people, may excite courage and boldness in others. The reason for this is that brains are not all constituted in the same way. Thus the very same movement of the gland which in some excites fear, in others causes the spirits to enter the pores of the brain which direct them partly into nerves which serve to move the hands in self-defence and partly into those which agitate the blood and drive it towards the heart in the manner required to produce spirits appropriate for continuing this defence and for maintaining the will to do so.

359

40. *The principal effect of the passions*

For it must be observed that the principal effect of all the human passions is that they move and dispose the soul to want the things for which they prepare the body. Thus the feeling of fear moves the soul to want to flee, that of courage to want to fight, and similarly with the others.

41. *The power of the soul with respect to the body*

But the will is by its nature so free that it can never be constrained. Of the two kinds of thought I have distinguished in the soul – the first its actions, i.e. its volitions, and the second its passions, taking this word in its most general sense to include every kind of perception – the former are absolutely within its power and can be changed only indirectly by the body, whereas the latter are absolutely dependent on the actions which produce them, and can be changed by the soul only indirectly, except when it is itself their cause. And the activity of the soul consists entirely in the fact that simply by willing something it brings it about that the little gland to which it is closely joined moves in the manner required to produce the effect corresponding to this volition.

360

42. *How we find in our memory the things we want to remember*

Thus, when the soul wants to remember something, this volition makes the gland lean first to one side and then to another, thus driving the spirits towards different regions of the brain until they come upon the one containing traces left by the object we want to remember. These traces consist simply in the fact that the pores of the brain through which the spirits previously made their way owing to the presence of this object have thereby become more apt than the others to be opened in the same way when the spirits again flow towards them. And so the spirits enter into these pores more easily when they come upon them, thereby producing in the gland that special movement which represents the same object to the soul, and makes it recognize the object as the one it wanted to remember.

361   43. *How the soul can imagine, be attentive, and move the body*
When we want to imagine something we have never seen, this volition has the power to make the gland move in the way required for driving the spirits towards the pores of the brain whose opening enables the thing to be represented. Again, when we want to fix our attention for some time on some particular object, this volition keeps the gland leaning in one particular direction during that time. And finally, when we want to walk or move our body in some other way, this volition makes the gland drive the spirits to the muscles which serve to bring about this effect.

       44. *Each volition is naturally joined to some movement of the gland, but through effort or habit we may join it to others*
Yet our volition to produce some particular movement or other effect does not always result in our producing it; for that depends on the various ways in which nature or habit has joined certain movements of the gland to certain thoughts. For example, if we want to adjust our eyes
362 to look at a far-distant object, this volition causes the pupils to grow larger; and if we want to adjust them to look at a very near object, this volition makes the pupils contract. But if we think only of enlarging the pupils, we may indeed have such a volition, but we do not thereby enlarge them. For the movement of the gland, whereby the spirits are driven to the optic nerve in the way required for enlarging or contracting the pupils, has been joined by nature with the volition to look at distant or nearby objects, rather than with the volition to enlarge or contract the pupils. Again, when we speak, we think only of the meaning of what we want to say, and this makes us move our tongue and lips much more readily and effectively than if we thought of moving them in all the ways required for uttering the same words. For the habits acquired in learning to speak have made us join the action of the soul (which, by means of the gland, can move the tongue and lips) with the meaning of

the words which follow upon these movements, rather than with the movements themselves.

45. *The power of the soul with respect to its passions*

Our passions, too, cannot be directly aroused or suppressed by the action of our will, but only indirectly through the representation of things which are usually joined with the passions we wish to have and opposed to the passions we wish to reject. For example, in order to arouse boldness and suppress fear in ourselves, it is not sufficient to have the volition to do so. We must apply ourselves to consider the reasons, objects, or precedents which persuade us that the danger is not great; that there is always more security in defence than in flight; that we shall gain glory and joy if we conquer, whereas we can expect nothing but regret and shame if we flee; and so on. 363

46. *What prevents the soul from having full control over its passions*

There is one special reason why the soul cannot readily change or suspend its passions, which is what led me to say in my definition that the passions are not only caused but also maintained and strengthened by some particular movement of the spirits. The reason is that they are nearly all accompanied by some disturbance which takes place in the heart and consequently also throughout the blood and the animal spirits. Until this disturbance ceases they remain present to our mind in the same way as the objects of the senses are present to it while they are acting upon our sense organs. The soul can prevent itself from hearing a slight noise or feeling a slight pain by attending very closely to some other 364 thing, but it cannot in the same way prevent itself from hearing thunder or feeling a fire that burns the hand. Likewise it can easily overcome the lesser passions, but not the stronger and more violent ones, except after the disturbance of the blood and spirits has died down. The most the will can do while this disturbance is at its full strength is not to yield to its effects and to inhibit many of the movements to which it disposes the body. For example, if anger causes the hand to rise to strike a blow, the will can usually restrain it; if fear moves the legs in flight, the will can stop them; and similarly in other cases.

47. *The conflicts that are usually supposed to occur between the lower part and the higher part of the soul*

All the conflicts usually supposed to occur between the lower part of the soul, which we call 'sensitive', and the higher or 'rational' part of the soul – or between the natural appetites and the will – consist simply in the opposition between the movements which the body (by means of its spirits) and the soul (by means of its will) tend to produce at the same time in the gland. For there is within us but one soul, and this soul has within it no diversity of parts: it is at once sensitive and rational too, and all its appetites are volitions. It is an error to identify the different functions of the soul with persons who play different, usually mutually

365 opposed roles – an error which arises simply from our failure to distinguish properly the functions of the soul from those of the body. It is to the body alone that we should attribute everything that can be observed in us to oppose our reason. So there is no conflict here except in so far as the little gland in the middle of the brain can be pushed to one side by the soul and to the other side by the animal spirits (which, as I said above, are nothing but bodies), and these two impulses often happen to be opposed, the stronger cancelling the effect of the weaker. Now we may distinguish two kinds of movement produced in the gland by the spirits. Movements of the first kind represent to the soul the objects which stimulate the senses, or the impressions occurring in the brain; and these have no influence on the will. Movements of the second kind, which do have an influence on the will, cause the passions or the bodily movements which accompany the passions. As to the first, although they often hinder the actions of the soul, or are hindered by them, yet since they are not directly opposed to these actions, we observe no conflict between them. We observe conflict only between movements of the second kind and the volitions which oppose them – for example, between the force with which the spirits push the gland so as to cause the soul to desire something, and the force with which the soul, by its volition to avoid this thing, pushes the gland in a contrary direction. Such a conflict is revealed chiefly through the fact that the will, lacking the power to

366 produce the passions directly (as I have already said), is compelled to make an effort to consider a series of different things, and if one of them happens to have the power to change for a moment the course of the spirits, the next one may happen to lack this power, whereupon the spirits will immediately revert to the same course because no change has occurred in the state of the nerves, heart and blood. This makes the soul feel itself impelled, almost at one and the same time, to desire and not to desire one and the same thing; and that is why it has been thought that the soul has within it two conflicting powers. We may, however, acknowledge a kind of conflict, in so far as the same cause that produces a certain passion in the soul often also produces certain movements in the body, to which the soul makes no contribution and which the soul stops or tries to stop as soon as it perceives them. We experience this when an object that excites fear also causes the spirits to enter the muscles

which serve to move our legs in flight, while the will to be bold stops them from moving.

48. *How we recognize the strength or weakness of souls, and what is wrong with the weakest souls*

It is by success in these conflicts that each person can recognize the strength or weakness of his soul. For undoubtedly the strongest souls 367 belong to those in whom the will by nature can most easily conquer the passions and stop the bodily movements which accompany them. But there are some who can never test the strength of their will because they never equip it to fight with its proper weapons, giving it instead only the weapons which some passions provide for resisting other passions. What I call its 'proper' weapons are firm and determinate judgements bearing upon the knowledge of good and evil, which the soul has resolved to follow in guiding its conduct. The weakest souls of all are those whose will is not determined in this way to follow such judgements, but constantly allows itself to be carried away by present passions. The latter, being often opposed to one another, pull the will first to one side and then to the other, thus making it battle against itself and so putting the soul in the most deplorable state possible. Thus, when fear represents death as an extreme evil which can be avoided only by flight, while ambition on the other hand depicts the dishonour of flight as an evil worse than death, these two passions jostle the will in opposite ways; and since the will obeys first the one and then the other, it is continually opposed to itself, and so it renders the soul enslaved and miserable.

49. *The strength of the soul is inadequate without knowledge of the truth*

It is true that very few people are so weak and irresolute that they choose only what their passion dictates. Most have some determinate judge- 368 ments which they follow in regulating some of their actions. Often these judgements are false and based on passions by which the will has previously allowed itself to be conquered or led astray; but because the will continues to follow them when the passion which caused them is absent, they may be considered its proper weapons, and we may judge souls to be stronger or weaker according to their ability to follow these judgements more or less closely and resist the present passions which are opposed to them. There is, however, a great difference between the resolutions which proceed from some false opinion and those which are based solely on knowledge of the truth. For, anyone who follows the latter is assured of never regretting or repenting, whereas we always regret having followed the former when we discover our error.

50. There is no soul so weak that it cannot, if well-directed, acquire an absolute power over its passions

It is useful to note here, as already mentioned above,[1] that although nature seems to have joined every movement of the gland to certain of our thoughts from the beginning of our life, yet we may join them to others through habit. Experience shows this in the case of language. Words produce in the gland movements which are ordained by nature to represent to the soul only their sounds when they are spoken or the shape of their letters when they are written; but nevertheless, through the habit we have acquired of thinking of what they mean when we hear the sounds or see the letters, these movements usually make us conceive this meaning rather than the shape of the letters or the sound of the syllables. It is also useful to note that although the movements (both of the gland and of the spirits and the brain) which represent certain objects to the soul are naturally joined to the movements which produce certain passions in it, yet through habit the former can be separated from the latter and joined to others which are very different. Indeed this habit can be acquired by a single action and does not require long practice. Thus, when we unexpectedly come upon something very foul in a dish we are eating with relish, our surprise may so change the disposition of our brain that we cannot afterwards look upon any such food without repulsion, whereas previously we ate it with pleasure. And the same may be observed in animals. For although they lack reason, and perhaps even thought, all the movements of the spirits and of the gland which produce passions in us are nevertheless present in them too, though in them they serve to maintain and strengthen only the movements of the nerves and the muscles which usually accompany the passions and not, as in us, the passions themselves. So when a dog sees a partridge, it is naturally disposed to run towards it; and when it hears a gun fired, the noise naturally impels it to run away. Nevertheless, setters are commonly trained so that the sight of a partridge makes them stop, and the noise they hear afterwards, when someone fires at the bird, makes them run towards it. These things are worth noting in order to encourage each of us to make a point of controlling our passions. For since we are able, with a little effort, to change the movements of the brain in animals devoid of reason, it is clear that we can do so still more effectively in the case of men. Even those who have the weakest souls could acquire absolute mastery over all their passions if we employed sufficient ingenuity in training and guiding them.

1 Art. 44, p. 234 above.

Index

absolute things (vs relative things), 6f
abstraction, 13
accident(s), 74, 156
  one of the five universals, 180
action(s)
  and passion(s), 218
  as tendency to move, 60
  bodily, joined with thoughts, 234
  of the soul, 225
Adam, Ch. and Tannery, P., xi
affections, as objects of perception, 175
affirmation, as mode of thought/thinking,
  83, 88
algebra, 5, 28, 30
analysis
  geometrical, 28, 30
  in ancient geometry, 4
  method of (vs synthesis), 149, 150–2
ancient philosophy/philosophers, 70
angel, idea of, 92
anger, 176, 202, 227, 235
animal spirits, 43, 64, 201f, 220–38
  passim
animals
  and human beings, 21, 45
  and language, 44
  and reason, 21, 44f, 238
anxiety, 232
appetites, natural, 112, 116f, 176, 183,
  201f, 223, 227, 235
  and volitions, 236
Archimedes, 80
Aristotelians, *see* scholastic
  philosophy/philosophers
Aristotle, 120, 207, 210
arithmetic, 2, 5, 18, 78, 87
Arnauld, Antoine, ix, 75n
artefacts, and natural bodies, 209
arteries, 7
assertion, as mode of willing, 171
assumptions, 12
astrologers, 24
astronomers, assumptions/suppositions of,
  12, 57f
astronomical reasoning, 90, 147, 187

astronomy, 5, 78
atheists, and knowledge, 139f
atomism, 202f
atoms, impossibility of, 197f, 208
attentiveness, and the will, 234
attribute(s),
  and knowledge of things/substances,
    163, 177
  meaning of 'attribute', 178f
  opposition between, 213
  principal, 177f
automatons, 44, 85, 172, 219f
aversion, as mode of willing, 171
axioms,
  see also common notions 155f, 176

Baillet, Adrien, xiin, 25
basket of apples (compared with beliefs), 123
beasts, *see* animals
being, degrees of, 156
beliefs, rejection of, 76, 123
benefit and harm, and sensory
  awareness, 116f, 118, 121, 186, 190
blind, man born, 130, 131
blind man's stick, and transmission of
  light, 58, 63, 66f
blood
  and animal spirits, 221f, 224, 231
  and emotions/passions, 202, 232, 235
  circulation of, 220
  expansion/rarefaction of, 232
body, the (human)
  acts upon the soul, 218
  and the self, 82f
  and sensations, 205
  compared with machine, 44, 81, 119,
    219f, 225
  compared with ship, 46, 116
  distinct from the mind/soul, 36, 46,
    73f, 86, 102, 114f, 119f, 126f,
    143–50, 153, 158f, 162, 163f, 180,
    214f
  divisibility of, 74, 120
  existence of, 115f
  functions of, 219–25 *passim*